Testing Times

Testing Times

GRAHAM
GOOCH

Robson Books

First published in Great Britain in 1991 by Robson Books Ltd, Bolsover House, 5–6 Clipstone Street, London W1P 7EB

A version of some of the material in part one of this book appeared under the title *Test of Fire*.

All photographs by courtesy of Graham Morris

British Library Cataloguing in Publication Data
Gooch, Graham, *1953–*
Testing times: the West Indies, New Zealand, India, Australia – the dramatic inside story by England's captain.
I. Title II. [Test of fire]
796.35865

ISBN 0 86051 743 8

Typeset in Ehrhardt and printed and bound in Great Britain by Butler & Tanner Ltd, Frome and London

Contents

Introduction

'It was the best of times. It was the worst of times'. My apologies to Charles Dickens for borrowing his opening to *A Tale of Two Cities*, but it fits perfectly. Two years, two tours, good times, bad times, as England captain. I've experienced new highs as a Test batsman and leader, highs I never expected to attain in my late 30s. But there have been bad days – one in particular, the worst in all my time as a cricketer – and painful hand injuries to balance up the books.

England have played 21 Tests since the start of 1990 – winning six, losing seven and drawing eight. Abroad, we lost bravely in the Caribbean in 1990 and badly in Australia last winter. At home, England have beaten New Zealand, India and Sri Lanka, and drawn an exciting series against the West Indies in the past two summers.

I've been fortunate that my two years as captain have coincided with the richest run-vein of my 18-year first-class career. After my problems against Terry Alderman and Australia in the 1989 home Ashes series, I had a slight worry about taking over the captaincy. There had been a lot of publicity when I gave up the Essex leadership after the 1987 season, most of it concluding that the captaincy interfered with my batting and there was no way the two could be reconciled. That wasn't true. I had been trying to do all that was required as captain without altering the routine I'd used throughout my career to prepare myself to bat. But there wasn't enough time, and I was walking out to the wicket not ready physically or mentally; and that left me feeling vulnerable and uncomfortable. Once I had worked out the problems and rearranged my schedule, I arrived at the ground earlier and got my own practice out of the way. After that I felt much happier about taking on that responsibility of captain again.

I was delighted to be given a second chance as England skipper. My earlier two-Test reign had been cut short when the 1988/89 tour to India was cancelled because of the South Africa connections of half our party, including me; and then Ted Dexter replaced Peter May as chairman of selectors and I lost the captaincy to David Gower. I felt disappointed because I hadn't really had a chance to prove myself one way or the other. I was convinced the opportunity would never come my way again. But our 1989 Ashes attempt was a disaster. I've never been in an England team that's played so badly; there was no spirit.

I was determined that whatever happened in the Caribbean in 1990, my side were not going to be accused of not fighting, of not competing. The West Indies might be the world champions, but I knew if England played near their potential, we would give them a game. And we did. I'm not an 'ifs' and 'buts' man, but had the rain not come so unexpectedly in Trinidad, England would have gone 2–0 up, and I'm convinced the West Indies would not have recovered with two Tests to play. But Viv Richards' side took their chance and the series. Still, England came home with a lot of credit, and we maintained steady progress through the summer, winning our first series at home for five years.

But then our Ashes challenge collapsed as disastrously as it had done in 1989. I encountered problems I hadn't experienced before or expected; my ideas of what was required weren't shared by the whole party. We never got our act together. We might have taken three steps forward since the start of the year, but England were back to square one after four months in Australia. The annoying thing was that with tougher mental application, there might have been a different result. England had struggled to put together one decent day in 1989, but we had chances in all five Tests last winter. The defeat hurt because the Ashes is still *the* series. If you have to pick one to do well in, Australia is the one: there's always that extra edge. Although I never consider quitting, I did begin to wonder if I was the right man for the job. If players fail to respond to the captain, there are two choices – change the players ... or the skipper!

The 1991 summer went better than I expected or hoped, especially after our winter of discontent. It was going to be difficult to regain ground, but that's what we've done. England's players can compete and beat the best in the world. We've overcome the West Indies in three Tests since the start of 1990. But collectively our players don't have the same competitive edge as the Australians. Some players need motivating. Often, they accept their fate too easily. It's not just on the field; it's about the way you prepare and look after yourself. You can't turn on the tap and expect there to be hot water every time. There's nothing magical about the way I captain England; you get out what you put in. A large part of my job is making sure the team takes the field in the right, positive frame of mind. The captain must set the right example, so the younger players will take his lead. Captaincy is about making decisions and taking the consequences; about backing your experience, judgement and instinct. And you make mistakes. That's part of the job. You're praised when it goes right – and damned when it goes wrong. The secret is to take even less notice of the pats on the back than the kicks in the teeth.

England's most important performance in the past two years was that Test win in Jamaica. There had been a lot of people who could see no further than a 5–0 hiding. Jamaica not only gave us respect, but proved that when we get it right, we can beat anyone. The 1991 Oval victory over the West Indies was also significant because England had to come from behind. You've got to believe in yourself. It doesn't surprise me if we win, but it does others. If you play well, you always have a chance. But you have to be at your best to compete with Australia and the West Indies. Losing at Melbourne was ridiculous because we had played the better cricket for three and half days and threw away the Test in less than a session. We nearly won in Sydney, but our bowling and fielding on the Saturday provided the worst day I've ever spent on a cricket ground. I never thought a side of mine would show such a lack of basic cricket understanding and ability. I was trying my best and hardest, but it wasn't enough on that trip.

I felt pretty low in the Perth dressing-room as the sensation of failure sank in. Amazingly, the next time England played a Test match, we beat the West Indies at Headingley – our first win at home against them for 22 years! That seemed an incredible turnaround to many people, but again there was no secret. We had gone back to basics, worked hard and given it our all.

My 154 at Leeds was certainly the best knock I've played since regaining the captaincy. I'll always be associated with that 333 against India at Lord's, but the Headingley hundred was more important. Conditions favoured the bowlers and we were in trouble. If I'd failed, England would have lost the Test; it was as clear-cut as that. I've scored over 2,000 Test runs since going to the Caribbean last year and have broken all sorts of batting records. What pleases me most is that I think my Test record is now a fairer reflection of my ability. I went to the West Indies with a batting average below 37, with just eight hundreds in 73 Tests; it should have been much better. Now I feel I've set the record straight. I'm not amazed that I'm playing the best cricket of my career in my late 30s, but I'm surprised that I've managed to maintain this level of performance for so long.

Yes, the best of times have certainly outweighed the worst of times since I set out for the West Indies. I've received tremendous support from the players. There have been arguments, that's inevitable. But I get tremendous satisfaction from England taking on and beating the best in the world. Leading the Test team has been a great honour, all the more special because I got a second chance that I never thought possible. Having lost it once, I was and am determined to give it my best shot – in every way – and that's what I expect from those cricketers who play with me.

England in the West Indies, 1990

There wasn't a single current England cricketer who knew what it was like to beat the West Indies when we set out for the Caribbean in January 1990. And, according to popular opinion, there weren't likely to be any on our return. England's last win there had been in 1974 on Mike Denness's tour. My England side hadn't a chance, apparently – an opinion admittedly supported by the statistics. We had just lost the Ashes 4–0. We'd been lucky to get nil: I've never played in an England side that performed so badly. Many leading Test players had decided to go to South Africa under Mike Gatting. I was made England captain at the end of that summer and it was my task to take my 'sacrificial lambs' away for the toughest assignment in cricket. That's not how I saw it: I had dreams, ideas, hopes and plans – but the next three months would test them to the full.

The England team gathered at the Copthorne Hotel on the outskirts of Gatwick Airport the night before we flew off. I'd already said goodbye to my wife Brenda, daughters Hannah and twins Megan and Sally at home, before heading off around the M25 for the team get-together at the hotel. There's always a rather uneasy sense of anticipation just before setting off on tour: everyone has their own particular expectations and worries, and nobody knows quite what the next months will bring.

On previous tours, this get-together had been the first chance for the squad to start developing that all-important team spirit. But the 1990 trip to the West Indies was different. The party, apart from Devon Malcolm, Keith Medlycott, Robert Bailey and Ricky Ellcock, had been together in India for the Nehru Cup.

Then we had spent six weeks in England working on fitness and practising, culminating in a week at Lilleshall.

That preparation eased our fears about entering the Lion's den that, as far as cricket goes is what the Caribbean represents. The Windies were, and still are, undisputed world champions (though the Pakistanis have been pushing them hard lately). Under Clive Lloyd and then Viv Richards, they haven't lost a single Test series since 1980 and suffered only eight defeats in 79 Test matches in that decade. That's a record unparalleled in cricket history. The composition of their fast-bowling quartet – currently Malcolm Marshall, Courtney Walsh, Curtly Ambrose and Ian Bishop – may have changed gradually through the decade. But they were just as lethal, effective and frightening as ever.

Still, no England touring side had prepared so thoroughly before setting off. 'If you fail to prepare, you prepare to fail' was our motto through the cold of December and January. That might sound a bit trite, but England's recovery after that heavy Ashes defeat at home had to start sometime and somewhere. As far as I was concerned, the Caribbean was the perfect place.

Flying to the West Indies is one of the shorter journeys for today's jet-setting cricketer. We travel in the comfort of Club class now; the extra space makes all the difference when you have to practise after a long flight. Big blokes like Angus Fraser, who's 6 foot 5 inches tall, can do themselves real damage if they're cramped in Economy for any length of time. It's a false saving if one of your bowlers gets a strain or pulls a muscle at the start of a tour because he's been sitting in an awkward position for 10 hours.

We travelled to Barbados via Antigua and were met at Grantley Adams International Airport by the usual welcoming committees – official and unofficial. The West Indian cricket press was there, too. Apart from myself and Allan Lamb, our party contained many faces unfamiliar to them. Quite a few 'permanent' fixtures in England Test sides of the past few years were missing. Ian Botham and David Gower, who had captained England during the previous summer, weren't picked. And, because of the unofficial tour to South Africa, Mike Gatting, Chris Broad, John Emburey and Neil Foster were about to start a five-year Test ban.

How were the unsung and untried Englishmen going to combat

the mighty West Indies? We weren't, was the local conviction. The journalists' questions were fairly routine. Maybe they'd decided we didn't have the firepower to cause any surprises. They seemed sure the forthcoming series was going to be a one-horse race. That didn't bother me. There's always a certain advantage in being written-off beforehand. The opposition might subconsciously relax; also, it's a useful weapon to stir the lads up. I've never met a sportsman yet who didn't relish proving the experts wrong!

Most attention centred on our own quartet of West Indian-born fast bowlers – especially Ricardo Ellcock, who was something of a surprise selection for the tour. Ricky was born in Bridgetown, Barbados, and had played for the island in the Shell Shield competitions of 1983 and 1984 when a teenager. He was with Worcestershire at the time; but it was only when he moved to Middlesex in 1989 that he began fulfilling his promise on the English scene. The photographers were out in force for shots of Ricky with the many members of his family who'd turned up at the airport. Unfortunately for him, their cheers were to turn to tears a fortnight later when Ricky broke down in St Lucia with a recurrence of his back trouble and had to return home without bowling a single ball in anger.

Gladstone Small, Phillip DeFreitas and Devon Malcolm made up our West Indian-born bowling attack. The first two had a fair amount of Test experience. Gladstone, also from Barbados, made his England debut against New Zealand at Trent Bridge in 1986, while Daffy, from Dominica, had been in and out of the team since a promising debut on Mike Gatting's Ashes tour three winters earlier.

Devon had played just one Test and the Australians had made it a rather unpleasant experience for him. His figures were 1 for 161. Devon was from Jamaica, but he hadn't been back for 10 years. We'd taken a gamble on Ricky and Devon; you could call them our 'wild cards'. At the original press conference when the squad was selected, Ted Dexter, chairman of the England Committee, explained it as our way of fighting 'fire with fire.'

This was my third England tour of the West Indies in a decade, and I had got to know many of the Caribbean cricket personalities fairly well. At the airport I met up with Tony Cozier, the well-known cricket commentator and writer. Tony, a white Bajan whose father Jimmie covered the famous Ramadhin and Valentine Test at Lord's in 1950, is one of the great authorities on West Indies cricket. He was able to fill me in on the local news as well as giving a West Indian view of our chances in the forthcoming series. He reckoned most people had written us off already. One way of reviving interest, he thought, would be for us to do well in the two opening one-day internationals in Trinidad. If we failed to do so, that would be it. He thought the Caribbean public would dismiss the Test series as a non-event.

The first week of tour was spent at the Rockley Resort in Barbados. It's not a hotel but a complex of apartments with kitchens. Each group has its own swimming pool. It's basically a self-catering place. There are restaurants, but when we stayed there later in the tour, we found it was a pleasant change to do our own cooking. The Rockley is not on the beach but in the middle of a nine-hole golf course five minutes from the shore.

Practising and getting used to the different playing and weather conditions were our priorities on arrival. But, typically, just as we were reaching for the Number 15 sun block, the heavens opened. Nets were washed out on the first day. Day two gave us an even bigger problem: our first injury. Allan Lamb, Robin Smith and I decided to jog back the four miles to the Rockley after net practice and a training session at the Kensington Oval in Bridgetown. It was no race and we were taking it gently when Lambie stepped awkwardly onto a kerb and tore a calf muscle. Micky Stewart was unhappy not only with the injury, but also with the fact that we'd run back in the first place. I don't believe we'd behaved irresponsibly. We'd had a tough work-out at the Oval, but we were well loosened-up and were taking it easy on the way back. It was just a bad break, one of those unfortunate accidents that happen from time to time.

Towards the end of the first week in Barbados we had a couple of practice matches. After spending so much time training and working in the nets, it was a great relief just to get out in the middle again. But cricket is never easy in the Caribbean and a young Barbados side gave us a real fright. Still, no experience is wasted; it helped me hammer home the message that there would be no walk-overs in the West Indies. We'd been reasonably confident when we set them 238 to win, but they got off to a flyer; then lost half a dozen wickets quickly and just when we thought we were cruising to victory, their number 10 (their opening bowler who'd caught-and-bowled me for 3) started smashing the ball all over the place. We won with two overs to spare. It wasn't convincing, but it had been a valuable lesson in demonstrating just how explosive West Indies cricketers can be, whatever number they come in to bat.

But there were promising signs. Daffy picked up four wickets in the first game and Gladstone Small found his rhythm immediately in the second. But Devon Malcolm was causing concern. Nobody doubted his ability to generate real pace, but he was having problems with his control, and setting a field for him was proving almost impossible. To put it bluntly, Devon was bowling far too many bad balls. I knew from bitter experience how murderous West Indies batsmen are to bowling that's not up to scratch. All bowlers have a lot of work to do at the start of a tour to get them into shape. But I was beginning to feel that if Devon's form didn't improve dramatically and rapidly, he wasn't going to make the grade and we would be saddled with a passenger for the next three months.

That apart, our first week had gone well. The squad was gelling off the field as well as on it. I also had a chance down on the beach to polish up my boogie boarding skills. This is the art of lying on a small surf-board with one arm held by a thong and using the other arm to propel yourself wherever the currents, and some can be very strong, take you.

The sea is not the only area of the island where you have to be careful. The beach can also be rather hazardous. During that first week a group of local lads came up to me on the beach and offered me drugs – quite openly. They were doing the same to any likely-looking tourist. They said they could get me anything I wanted. It didn't take me long to convince them that I wasn't interested, but I was shocked at just how open the whole operation was. It's a sign of the times, I suppose, but it's not something I can even begin to understand.

We left Barbados and headed for St Kitts for the four-day game against the Leeward Islands. The Leewards include the island of Antigua and that means Vivian Richards. But Master Blaster was recovering from a broken finger, so Richie Richardson was leading the side. St Kitts is beautiful and we stayed at the Fort Thomas Hotel, high on a cliff overlooking the blue Caribbean, with the island of Nevis in the background. It's easy to forget that you're not here for your health. The ground is only about a mile from the hotel. The groundstaff are not your usual sort – they're inmates from the local prison!

The Leewards had won all their games in the Shell Shield competition and were generally rated the top side in the Caribbean, even without Viv. It was important to make a good start, and I was well satisfied with our first-innings score of 444–6. Waync Larkins and Alec Stewart hit centuries and most of us chipped in with a few runs. Rob Bailey was the only one to miss out. I moved him up to No 3 for the second innings and this time he added just 10. Tour schedules are so packed these days, with the emphasis on international matches – Tests and one-dayers – that a couple of early failures can relegate a player to a waiting role for the rest of the tour. It's not unusual for a batsman to go a month between knocks once the Test series starts. That's not ideal, but there's no way around it. I've been out of the Test team when touring abroad and know it's no fun. But the alternative – being back at home – is even less attractive. You can't regain an England place that way. Anyway, because of the West Indies firepower, touring cricketers are never entirely out of the frame in the Caribbean. Those in possession can easily lose form or get injured; you never know when a late Test call might come.

Richie Richardson showed his best form on the second evening, blasting an unbeaten 83, mostly in boundaries. He was especially severe on our left-arm spinner Keith Medlycott, who was naturally rather nervous in his first bowl for his country. But Richardson's assault was further evidence, if any were needed, that we had to bowl tightly. It's not just that West Indies batsmen are extremely savage on anything wayward; bowl accurately and you increase your chances of getting them out because they don't like being tied down. They want to play their shots, they *need* to play their shots. If you can frustrate them by putting them on the defensive, they will inevitably take risks and give chances. Often, it's bowlers who aren't particularly quick who have caused the West Indies problems by keeping up a naggingly accurate attack.

Richardson and his team – notably Keith Arthurton in the second innings – had shown our bowlers the name of the game in the Caribbean. Their best form of defence is attack and they will have a go whenever they can. The only answer is to bowl on or just outside the off-stump and never give them a chance to drive. Richardson, in particular, also showed how they love to cut. This seemed as good a time as any for Allan Lamb and me to have a meeting with the bowlers and explain all this. We told them that the key to good bowling in the Caribbean was discipline and consistently bowling line-and-length.

Lambie's experience is invaluable in these situations. It's one of the reasons he was made vice-captain. His record against the West Indies is outstanding. But while 'Lamb's Tours' has shown off his many entrepreneurial skills on England's recent visits abroad ('Lamb's Tours' – suppliers of boat, plane, helicopter excursions, all at inflationary rates), the man himself occasionally needs a road manager. It was typical that he left his passport behind in Barbados; it was just as typical that he managed to talk his way past the immigration people to get into St Kitts without it. Nothing surprises me about Allan Joseph Lamb's powers of recovery.

Before the Leewards match was over, England's players were to learn another valuable lesson – this time about where I stood concerning displays of dissent! In our second innings Nasser Hussain was given out lbw. He made it more than obvious that, in his opinion, he'd hit the ball with his bat before it hit his pads. That sort of behaviour is unacceptable in any circumstances. What made it worse was that a couple of overs earlier Nasser had been given out caught at silly mid-off. Nasser was sure the ball had bounced first, a view shared by the Leewards captain Richie Richardson. Nasser wasn't keen on departing, and eventually Richardson asked the umpire to reverse his decision, which he did. That gesture of sportsmanship defused the situation. Nasser was probably still upset by his first 'dismissal' when he reacted badly to the second. It reflects the pressure players, especially the newcomers, are under early on in tours to make an immediate impact.

Whatever the reason, there was no excuse for Nasser's outburst. Later that afternoon, I took him for a walk around the boundary and made it perfectly clear that I wasn't going to stand for any repetition. He'd been at Essex long enough to know my views. That evening I called the team together and told them that, as long as I was captain, they would respect and abide by the empire's decision, however unfair they thought it was. I wouldn't tolerate playing the game any other way.

The Leewards game fizzled out into a draw, although at one stage the islanders made a fair stab at the 402 runs needed for victory. The match was called off when they were 301 for 5, and needing 102 off 12 overs. If we'd been batting, I would certainly have carried on. But we needed the batting practice more; they were well into their season.

We made our second stop at Antigua, this time on the way from St Kitts to St Lucia for the game against the Windward Islands. It wasn't Lambie who nearly didn't make it this time; it was me. The wait at Antigua dragged on, so I sat down in the airport lounge and got stuck into my book. I suddenly looked up to detect a lack of England cricketers; they were all aboard, waiting for take-off. I raced across the tarmac and up the steps of the Dash 8, only to find that the plane was full. My seat had been re-allocated to a lady who had joined the plane there. Instead of her being ushered off, the stewardess pointed at another plane on the runway and suggested I wait for that one; it was also heading for St Lucia, although she wasn't sure when.

The rest of the lads thought that was a great idea and there were taunts from my faithful colleagues about how unkind and unreasonable I was being to the lady in my seat. There was great merriment and disloyal jeering when it was pointed out that the England cricket captain ought to travel with his team. I was beginning to think I might have to make that embarrassing walk to the other plane when the stewardess hit upon the perfect solution. If the captain was that important, why didn't either Mr Larkins or Mr Smith, who were in the same row, give up his seat? Fortunately, the lady solved the problem by volunteering to travel on the other flight. You really find out who your friends are in situations like that!

Sadly, that flight to St Lucia proved the end of the line for Ricky Ellcock. After his first net there, it was obvious that his back problem was serious and he would have to go home. The complaint was nothing new and the selectors had known they were taking a risk in picking him. But at the end of the 1989 season he'd been fighting fit and had put in some exciting and very pacy bowling performances for Middlesex in the championship. Unfortunately, our worst fears were realized when the trouble flared up again and it became obvious that it was best for the lad himself, as well as England and Middlesex, if he returned home for treatment. Even if an operation was necessary and an English summer was missed while he recuperated, he was still young enough at 24 to rebuild his county career and make the Test side.

Still, it's never easy to call a halt, even temporarily, to a youngster's England career, before it's even begun. There's no guarantee the international call-up will ever come again. There's not much you can say in those circumstances, although I explained that Neil Foster had come through an operation for a similar problem and resumed his cricket career as effectively as before. I'm not sure Ricky took much in or if anything I could have said would have consoled him. He had known that the net session in St Lucia was make or break, and he left the nets in tears when he realized his tour was over.

Now we had to decide on a replacement. Micky and I conferred with Keith Fletcher, who was team manager of the England A tour in Zimbabwe and Kenya. The alternatives were Leicestershire's Chris Lewis and Glamorgan's Steve Watkin. Keith, in Nairobi at the time, went for Lewis, who is a talented all-rounder and lively bowler. Lewis, born in Georgetown, Guyana, kept our West Indian-born contingent up to four. He and DeFreitas had played in the same XI at Willesden High School; the pair had also been together at Leicestershire before Daffy made his move to Lancashire.

Our performance against the Windwards wasn't as impressive as the tour opener. Our lack of batting practice, especially, was exposed. We were bowled out in our first innings by a left-arm spinner called Mervyn Durand, who was making his first-class debut at the age of 29 and took 7 for 15. After collapsing to 126 all out, we were asked to follow on by one of the weakest sides in the Caribbean. Victoria Park had also been the scene of disaster on David Gower's tour four years earlier, when we were bowled out for 94 in our second innings and lost by seven wickets.

Durand had been playing league cricket in Middlesex the previous summer. Here he was destroying the supposed cream of English batting. I didn't think he bowled as well as his figures suggested; we batted badly and the Windward fielders held on to some good catches. But Durand's performance is in the record books and I'm sure he'll never forget the day he had England's batsmen struggling.

The match wasn't without some merit as we fought back in the second innings. Lambie hit 83 on his return from that calf injury. But, even with another good knock from Alec Stewart, the Windwards only needed 136 to win in 52 overs. They reached 82–2 when our spinners, Eddie Hemmings and Keith Medlycott, had them tottering and panicking. They took four wickets apiece before the home side crept home by a single wicket. Defeat is never pleasant, but we had made an impressive fightback from a seemingly hopeless position. After all our pre-tour planning about the fast-bowlers, it seemed strange to be involved in a match dominated by spinners, not that I expected them to play a significant part when the real stuff began.

The wet weather early in this match gave our newcomers the chance to see a form of pitch drying that's not used in England. It's set on fire! It's very spectacular and very effective. The Saturday in St Lucia also allowed us to meet up with some old friends from HMS *Invincible*. About 20 of the crew flew in by Sea King helicopter from Barbados, where they were based. They'd given us one of the best parties of the tour in 1986 when we stayed in Antigua, so we were more than happy to line up with them for a group photograph at lunch-time.

Our first serious confrontations – the two one-day internationals at Port of Spain – weren't too far away now. As a diversion we were grateful when the Windward Islands Cricket Association gave us a warm send-off with a reception at the Club St Lucia. A group of holidaymakers from Essex were there, and they make a bee-line for Nasser Hussain and myself at the reception. It's refreshing to get a flavour of home when you're abroad for such a long time.

Back at our hotel that evening, the England lads were introduced to the local sport of hermit-crab racing. It's really just an excuse for betting. To the surprise of most of the England touring cricketers, though not me, and the annoyance of the entire contingent involved, Allan Lamb cleaned up. I've already mentioned that his talents are manifold! Hermit-crab racing is a rather simple affair. About 10 crabs are placed in the middle of a circle which has been drawn on the ground. In the opening race, bets are placed on which crab will be the first to crawl outside the circle once the starter has given the 'off'. The crabs are then returned to the middle and this time the betting is on which crab will be the *last* to leave the circle. Before the start, the crabs are paraded around the circle, rather like racehorses, so the punters can determine which seem lively and which look torpid. Lambie won the first race, but some lads thought he would blow the lot when he bet his entire haul of Eastern Caribbean dollars on the second round. But Lambie had no doubts about who was going to be the winner – or rather the 'loser'. The lads thought Lambie must have second sight because his crab hadn't even ventured out of its shell by the time the other contestants had left the circle.

England's vice-captain had made a killing. There were ugly mutterings of 'Fix!' and even rumours that Lamb's crab had been 'got at'. Unfortunately, no race stewards could be found, so he escaped an official enquiry. Several reliable witnesses testified that they saw Lambie poke his crab several times with his finger during the parade. Every time it threatened to come out of its shell, Lambie would prod it again. By the time the starter gave the off for the second race, the crab was completely shell-shocked and had decided that there was no place like home.

More entertainment followed when we reached Trinidad. Newcomers on tour have to perform a party-piece, a sort of initiation ceremony that's basically an entertainment for the old lags. The Nehru Cup timetable had been so hectic that Angus Fraser, Nasser Hussain, Robin Smith and Alec Stewart had escaped in India. We caught up with them at the Trinidad Hilton. Nasser, Robin and Alec each did a send-up of one of their touring colleagues, with Gus providing a running commentary. These performances are always fun, but there's a productive side to the ordeal. It helps the newcomers feel part of the squad. The captain and other senior players try to make them feel welcome, but it's really up to the individual to find his own way. Nasser was first up and there was no need to guess his target when he appeared wearing three pairs of glasses. He proceeded to take the mickey out of Devon Malcolm's fielding, which was more in the Tony Randall than the Derek Randall class at the time. Robin chose Lambie as his victim, probably because the South African accent wasn't going to be too much of a problem. Robin gave a vivid impression of Lambie's hyper-active, all-action lifestyle. Lambie never sits still for a moment; he always wants to be doing something – shopping, bargain-hunting, sight-seeing. If nothing's happening, Lambie will organize something. He seems to have contacts everywhere in the world. Alec was last and did a great skit on Wayne Larkins, who was spending every waking hour on the phone to his lady back home and running up enormous bills. We had a great laugh and it was an ideal way of easing the tension before the one-day internationals.

Unfortunately, although we played some good cricket, both games were ruined by the weather. That was a great disappointment because we'd all been looking forward to taking on the West Indies. We only managed 13 overs of much-needed batting instead of the scheduled 100.

We held our first serious meeting of the tour before that opening clash with West Indies. I tried to emphasize the importance of being organized, of going into every match with a positive attitude and belief in one's own ability. I've tried to instil that confidence in all the teams I've been associated with. I believe that looking confident has an effect on the opposition. If you think you're second-rate, especially against sides like the West Indies, you're guaranteed the runners-up spot.

We discussed the composition of the West Indies side. Only Malcolm Marshall and Courtney Walsh of their usual squad of fast bowlers were included. Ezra Moseley was back in the fold after the West Indies Board had lifted life bans on the rebels who had toured South Africa in the early 1980s. But I didn't dwell on their side too much. It's not healthy to focus your attention on the opposition in these pre-match talks. I'm a great believer in concentrating on what you do well yourself and bringing out your own individual and collective strengths.

England had proved over the previous few years that we could compete on equal terms with anyone else in the world at the one-day game. We picked roughly the same team that had performed well in the Nehru Cup. We did have one setback just before the start. Phillip DeFreitas, one of our best limited-overs cricketers, twisted his right knee in the pre-match warm-up and had to pull out. But one former pupil of Willesden HS's bad luck was another's good fortune. Chris Lewis, newly arrived, was about to celebrate his twenty-second birthday in style.

It was damp, even at the start. I put the West Indies in because I felt the outfield was not wet enough to hinder our fielders and the wicket would assist our bowlers. We bowled and fielded exactly the way we planned, keeping the pressure on the West Indies and restricting them to 208 for 8 in their 50 overs. Chris Lewis made a confident start, collecting the wicket of Desmond Haynes and taking a cool catch at long-on to dismiss Ezra Moseley.

That total would take some getting, but we were in the game. Wayne and I started slowly against a good opening spell from Ian Bishop and Malcolm Marshall and we were 25 for 1 after 13 overs when the rains came. Although we hoped to resume our chase, the number of available overs was reduced to a point that would have made it farcical to carry on. Viv Richards wasn't keen on continuing; he felt the conditions underfoot weren't good enough for his fielders. Eventually, the umpires abandoned the match late in the afternoon.

It felt pretty unsatisfactory all round, not least for cricket fans back home who were looking for some warm Caribbean relief in the middle of the English winter. Sky television were beaming live cricket action from the West Indies for the first time. But it's not only in England that you can't guarantee the weather. They say at Trinidad that if you can't see the hills behind the ground, it's raining; and if you can, it's about to! My day of disappointment was made complete when I heard that West Ham had been thrashed 6–0 by Oldham in the FA Cup.

Most of the English fans who visit the Caribbean follow the

Barbados and Antigua Tests. They assume we spend most of the three months on the beach; that's not exactly true. In Trinidad and Jamaica we were advised not to wander around alone or even in groups too far from the hotel. In effect we were confined to our hotels and the cricket grounds and the various taxis and coaches needed to take us from one to the other. Just to emphasize the danger, Peter Deeley, the *Daily Telegraph* cricket writer, was mugged when crossing the Savannah just outside the Hilton. Deeley didn't argue and wisely gave his assailant some money.

We were back at Queen's Park three days later for the second international, and weatherwise it was more of the same. We kept the same side and, again, I decided to put the West Indies in after winning the toss. This time I was more worried about my fielders and bowlers because the outfield conditions were worse. My fears were justified. On one occasion I bent down to pick up the ball in the slips; next thing I knew I was on my backside. It felt as if a carpet had been pulled from under me.

I was surprised the match had started at all. There was a heavy downpour half an hour before the start, and when Viv and I inspected the outfield and bowlers' run-ups, the ground condition was three times worse than it had been when the first match was abandoned on Wednesday. Yet the umpires insisted on a scheduled start at 10 o'clock. They needn't have bothered. After 35 deliveries, the downpour returned and the day's cricket was washed out.

I went off with Lambie to play squash against Jeff Dujon and Carl Hooper. That was the West Indies' one success of the day. England's victory came at Twickenham. We've a lot of rugby fans in our squad and there was great delight at news of their massive win over Wales. Even our physio Laurie Brown was happy: Scotland had trounced France at Murrayfield.

Despite our limited opportunities, we had begun to confound those who had labelled us 'no-hopers'. Certainly our bowlers had done their job; but, through no fault of our own, the English batting had yet to be put to the test. Still, the one-day series was 0–0, and we headed off confidently to Jamaica and the first Test.

First Test, Jamaica

Our journey to Jamaica was almost as much of an ordeal as we expected the Test to be. We asked to be woken at 4 am and grabbed a quick breakfast just after 5 o'clock to catch the 7 am flight. It was the only Sunday flight, but at least it was direct – or so we were told. The airline's idea of 'direct' was to allow us the pleasure of seeing Barbados, Antigua (yet again) and Puerto Rico before Jamaica. Direct simply means not changing planes; a flight that goes straight from one island to another without intermediate stops is described as non-stop. If a flight isn't direct or non-stop, you're really in trouble. Airlines like LIAT (Leeward Islands Air Travel, or Leaves Island Any Time, as it's also been called) take a fair amount of stick. But they do exist to provide a service for the needs of the Caribbean majority. Unfortunately, that rarely fitted in with our requirements. Door to door it took six hours, and we arrived in Kingston absolutely shattered. Trips like that do nothing for players trying to maintain peak physical condition. It's not just a one-off trip. Each tour comprises dozens of internal flights – and that doesn't include all the direct ones we undertake!

This was my fourth time in Jamaica. I had not only toured with England but had been there with the Young Cricketers. And, for the fourth time, I was staying at the Pegasus, a pleasant hotel with a big swimming pool, jogging track and tennis court. The British High Commission put on a party for us when we arrived, but many of us were too tired to do it justice. I sat down to eat at a table in the garden and nearly fell asleep. It was no reflection on our hosts or their hospitality, but we left fairly early. A good night's sleep was the only remedy. Today I'm as fit as I've ever been, fitter than I was 10 years ago. But it's vital I get my rest. One late night and that's me wiped out. The only way I can give my best each day on the cricket field is to make sure I'm getting my regulation eight hours' sleep.

Fitness wasn't a preoccupation only of the 1990 England cricket team. The large press corps was to be seen most mornings and evenings on the jogging track and in the field opposite the hotel. They probably saw as much of Kingston as we did. Because of the warnings against venturing out of the hotel, even in groups, today all I know of Jamaica after four visits, apart from a few restaurants, is the Pegasus Hotel and the Sabina Park cricket ground.

Sabina Park didn't hold too many happy memories. Our Test match there in 1986 was played on the fastest wicket I've ever come across. Patrick Patterson was almost unplayable on his Test debut as we lost by 10 wickets after being bowled out for 159 and 132. As in 1990, Jamaica hosted the first Test on that tour. Hopefully, history wasn't going to repeat itself: we never recovered from the onslaught in 1986 and were whitewashed 5–0 in the series. Sabina Park had as much to do with our defeat then as any West Indies bowler. Even before the Test, the 'Terror Track', as it became known, had cost us Mike Gatting, whose nose had been demolished by a Malcolm Marshall bouncer in the one-day international. During that Test, the ball was flying up from just short of a length. It's one of the few times in my cricket life when I thought I could be seriously injured. I wasn't frightened or intimidated, but I felt there was a good chance of getting hit. Facing the world's fastest bowlers on any wicket always causes some apprehension, but that Test in 1986 was the first time I'd ever got a whiff of real danger in the nostrils. The West Indies had the firepower and experience to exploit that wicket. We knew it, they knew it – and they did a thoroughly effective job. The defeat had a demoralizing effect on our team. I was determined to do everything I could to prevent a repeat not only of the defeat, but – even if we did lose – of the tour taking a nose-dive as a result.

'Reading' the probable nature and behaviour of a pitch is as important as winning the toss, especially at the start of a series. The opening exchanges usually dictate the mood for the rest of the Tests. In England you get to know the various county pitches and how they usually behave. And if any wicket is showing uncharacteristic tendencies, the jungle telegraph works pretty efficiently on the domestic circuit. On the other hand we tour the West Indies only every four years. True, that 1986 Sabina Park wicket will always live in my memory, but generally you forget the precise nature of foreign wickets. And you never know how they are going to be prepared.

The Sabina wicket had been dug up twice since our 1986 visit and the locals insisted it was now as gentle as a lamb. I'd heard that one before! The Indians had been bowled out for 152 on it the year before, when opener Navjot Sidhu's hand was badly damaged by Marshall and touring skipper Dilip Vengsarkar accused his batsman of cowardice. (The crowd had rioted when Viv Richards was given out, caught behind, and the police moved in with tear-gas.)

Our meeting with Jamaica would at least allow us a close inspection of the Test wicket. If I hadn't been told, I wouldn't have known it had been relaid by looking at it; its appearance was very similar. The surface was shiny, glass-like, rock-hard and almost grassless, with small cracks that would open as the match progressed. You could never be certain in advance, but it looked a good flat batting wicket to me. And that's how it turned out to be, although the odd delivery kept low from the middle of the second day. I put this down to the relaying, with parts of the under-surface not as hard as others. But no amount of pitch-studying would have told you that before the start.

It was just as important for us to get to know the new Sabina Park wicket as it was to forget the old one. It would help if the Test wicket behaved in the same way as the one used in the match against Jamaica. The new Sabina Park track did prove a good batting wicket, despite the occasional low bounce. We batted well against Jamaica, even allowing for the fact that both Patterson and Courtney Walsh were 'rested' from their attack as they were certain to play in the Test. That wasn't a problem. I was more interested in seeing how the wicket performed than in their bowlers.

Our side was the probable Test line-up. It was decision time. Nasser Hussain came in as the extra batsman, while Rob Bailey, Phillip DeFreitas, Keith Medlycott and Chris Lewis missed out. They knew that missing the Jamaica game was a reliable indicator that they weren't going to make the Test side. It's about this time that those on the sidelines begin to wonder where their next game is coming from. Touring can become even tougher in those circumstances. Already, Bailey and Medlycott knew their opportunities to impress could be extremely limited. But they still practised hard and gave encouragement and help to those in the side.

With one eye on the Test, the match against Jamaica eventually drifted towards a tame draw. I reached my first century of the tour; a double one, too – 239! I had to retire at 222 with bouts of cramp caused by the heat and humidity. My knock included five sixes and 31 fours and some said it was more like the old, destructive Gooch of the early 1980s. But many of my runs came off the Jamaica spinners; I wasn't going to get many chances to attack like that on the tour. My opening partner Wayne Larkins was continuing his good start, hitting his second hundred of the tour in the second innings. Our batting looked in reasonable shape. It was also pleasing to realize that, although the ball was keeping low, this Sabina wicket was not going to be used as a lethal weapon this time.

Test cricket has a habit of undoing the best of intentions. So far we'd given a good account of ourselves, but the weather had made our two one-day meetings with the West Indies inconclusive. As yet, we were untested. And my memories of that 1986 Jamaican Test were still fresh enough for me not to be entirely confident that this good-looking pitch wouldn't turn out to be a monster in disguise.

The West Indies side wasn't much different from the 1986 model. Viv Richards, Desmond Haynes, Gordon Greenidge and Richie Richardson still formed the hard core of the batting; Jeff Dujon remained behind the stumps and Patrick Patterson, Malcolm Marshall and Courtney Walsh again led the bowling attack. Ian Bishop was a newish face, although he'd been on the 1988 tour of England, as had Carl Hooper. Carlisle Best made the side because of Gus Logie's injury; this was Best's first Test appearance since making his debut against us four years earlier. Curtly Ambrose was also sidelined with pile trouble; that was a relief. Curtly was no mere imitation of Joel 'Big Bird' Garner. He was the genuine article and used his height just as effectively.

We stuck with the policy of six batsmen – two (Alec Stewart and Nasser Hussain) were making their Test debuts – and four seamers. All-rounder David Capel was one of those bowlers, so our batting was further strengthened. And with Jack Russell, who'd hit a century off the Australians the previous summer, coming in at number 8, we looked to have strength in depth. But there's not always been safety in numbers for England against the West Indies.

Viv won the toss and batted. I would have done the same, although he took his time making the decision. Eddie Hemmings was made 12th man; the Windies left out Ezra Moseley and Keith Arthurton. We took the field and gathered in our rugby-type huddle, as we'd done all tour. There was nothing sinister about it. Many dressing-rooms have only flimsy partitions, so the only way of being sure about having a private team-talk is on the field. That's how it started. Also, there are no distractions and it's the perfect place to concentrate everyone's mind on the job in hand.

The old firm of Gordon Greenidge and Desmond Haynes got down to business as usual. Just before lunch the Windies were 62 without loss. Enter Devon Malcolm. Not Malcolm the bowler, but Malcolm the fielder. Greenidge turned the ball from Gus Fraser down to long leg and Devon, in his haste to get down to it, felt it smash into his knee. The ball bounced off a fair distance and Greenidge saw the chance of a second run. There's an old maxim about not running on a misfield, but these West Indies openers have shown themselves pretty good judges of a run over the years.

While Devon's hands may be suspect, his arm is not. The throw came in low, fast and over the stumps. Greenidge was stranded by a yard. All the hard work and encouragement Micky and I had put in with Devon were repaid in those few crucial seconds. Suddenly, Devon Malcolm's fielding was no longer a laughing matter – certainly not to the West Indies. A few years ago, he fell over while stopping a boundary for Derbyshire and lost his glasses. The batsmen ran five while Devon stumbled about on his hands and knees trying to find them. He wears contact lenses now. Even that doesn't always help. During a fielding practice in Trinidad, he kept losing sight of the ball because he was looking directly into the sun. Micky Stewart thought the solution was obvious and told him to get the other side of the sun. We collapsed as Devon replied; 'How can I do that? It's 93 million miles away!'

Devon had the last laugh in Jamaica. It was a moment of inspiration from an unexpected source that transformed that first day. After lunch, the wickets started to fall and we ran through them in the last session. England's Test novices had dismissed the best cricket XI in the world for 164, the 10 wickets falling for a mere 102 runs. It was the Windies' lowest total in the Caribbean for 22 years.

It was no more than our bowlers deserved. They'd learnt the lesson of bowling tight and Gus Fraser found the luck and the edges that sometimes evade him. Gus mopped up the tail in an astonishing 5 for 6 spell in five overs after tea. The Windies are past masters at digging themselves out of trouble, but Gus ended all resistance. It was all the more remarkable because he'd looked totally out of sorts against Jamaica. He wasn't happy either and felt the ball wasn't coming out of his hand the way it should. That was the reason we bowled 14 overs at the end of the Jamaica game when there was no chance of a result. It certainly paid dividends. Devon and Gus needed the work. Gus is a very determined character. He wants to win; you can see that the determination of Mike Gatting and John Emburey has rubbed off on him at Middlesex. It was a world-class performance to produce the best bowling figures – 5 for 28 – of your career against the West Indies on a flat wicket like this one.

But this was a team effort. All the bowlers chipped in; Devon was especially delighted to trap Viv Richards lbw. So were we. One confident lbw shout off Gladstone and another caught behind off Gus had both been turned down. 'Capes' removed Richardson and Best, while Gladstone caught and bowled Haynes when he was beginning to look dangerous.

But the day wasn't over and there were still a couple of hours for Wayne Larkins and me to negotiate our reply. We had to be very careful and not undo all the good work of the bowlers. It was vital to stay on top and not immediately hand back the initiative. That had been an England failing in recent times. We'd reached 40 before I was caught down the leg-side by Dujon off Patterson. I felt a trifle unlucky because I'd applied a fair amount of wood to the leg-glance, but Dujon was standing a fair way back and made up a lot of ground as he dived to his left for a brilliant catch. Alec Stewart hit a couple of crisp fours to launch his Test career, but was caught at slip when Ian Bishop got one delivery to rear up viciously to remind us of possible reprisals.

There were no further mishaps and we ended the first day

nearly half-way towards the West Indies total with eight wickets remaining. It was the perfect start. If we were still batting at close of play on day two, we had a chance of causing one of the biggest upsets in Test Cricket for a long time.

This was my fifth series against the West Indies, but only once before – in my first encounter at Trent Bridge in 1980 – had I been in a side that even looked like having a chance of winning, and in the event we had lost by two wickets.

The second day in Jamaica belonged to Allan Lamb, with vital support from Wayne Larkins and Robin Smith, as we batted the West Indies out of the game. Lambie was magnificent. Not surprisingly, his 132 (his fifth century against the Windies and 10th in all Tests) won him the Man of the Match award. He's a great fighter and there's nobody you would rather have on your side when the chips are down. He keeps up a constant banter with the fielding side, especially the bowlers. The biggest surprise was that this was Lambie's first Test hundred outside England. Robin Smith hit a half century in his fourth-wicket stand of 172 with Lambie.

We finished the day as I'd hoped – still batting and 178 ahead. It was an ideal position. The opposition had nothing to play for other than saving the Test. That gives you a great advantage when you bowl for a second time; the batting side are inhibited while the bowlers and fielders go after victory for all they are worth. England had enjoyed odd good days against the Windies in the 1980s, but it had been almost impossible to string them together. Now we'd been on top for two days; one more similar day would almost certainly give us the Test.

Our tail caused the Windies minor irritation on the third morning as Jack Russell found a stubborn partner in Gus Fraser. Their ninth-wicket partnership gave us a lead of precisely 200 runs. This time I was expecting a more professional display from the home batsmen, who had been below par in the first innings. Although they appeared much more determined, once again our own fast-bowling quartet kept them under pressure. And again it was Devon who made the vital breakthrough when he bowled Haynes for 14. The best of the West Indies batting came from Best (64) and Richards (37), who staged a minor recovery with a fifth wicket stand of 80. But when Devon dismissed the Windies skipper for the second time in the match, the wickets started tumbling again.

By the end of the third day, the home side had edged ahead. But it wasn't serious. The Windies' lead was only 29 runs and Marshall and Walsh were at the crease with only Patterson to come. At last we had them. Now it was merely a question of administering the last rites. The first three days hadn't only gone beyond my expectations, but my wildest dreams. Nothing is certain in this life, but surely the Windies weren't going to escape this time and at the 20th time of trying?

I wasn't the only one enjoying himself. What a homecoming Devon Malcolm was having. On the rest day he took his wife Jennifer to visit his gran, who had brought him up after his father left for England. Devon joined his dad in Sheffield when he was 16 and this was his first trip back since then. The local lad had made good and they gave him a hero's welcome. After only three days of the series, he'd taken five wickets – Haynes, Greenidge, Dujon and the great Vivian Richards (twice!). And don't forget that run out. When we arrived, Devon kept getting being called Donovan and was constantly being approached by relatives he didn't know he had. Certainly, the Malcolm family tree was being stretched to its limits. We thought Donovan must be a colloquialism for Devon until it was discovered that a Jamaican spinner called Donovan Malcolm had left for English league cricket a few years earlier. It suddenly all fell into place: that's where all those distant cousins came from! And no wonder the Windies dismissed him as a fast-bowling threat when they heard he was returning! But no one was making that mistake now, especially the best of the Caribbean batting.

Strangely, the rest day brought the first signs of danger – rain! It poured for most of the day and we just hung around the Pegasus, praying that it would clear up by morning. Rain isn't the same threat in the Caribbean as it is in England. The heavens can open, but you can be playing again an hour later. That's the good news. The bad news is that more rain can fall in a few minutes than you'd see in Manchester in a month, and it can appear from nowhere.

I got down to Sabina Park early the next morning. The prospects weren't promising; the ground was under water. The chances of play, even after tea, looked slim. Surely, we couldn't be denied now? The groundstaff mopped up for most of the day. I wouldn't say they were busy. Life moves at its own pace in the Caribbean. Nothing seemed to happen very quickly, although they were there all day and there were plenty of them. They'd work for half an hour – well, some of them – then they'd have a break. Maybe it's the normal working practice, but it drove us mad. I'd never been in such a commanding position against the West Indies, yet it looked like the weather might snatch it away. There was hardly any rain on the fourth day, yet the ground was still very wet. I hung around, for even half an hour's play would have been a bonus for us. But at five o'clock the umpires decided there was no chance and play was called off for the day.

Our day of depression was made complete with the news that Colin Milburn had collapsed and died at the age of 42. Les Ames, the great Kent and England wicket-keeper, had passed away the day before, but he was twice 'Ollie' Milburn's age. I suppose it wasn't a complete surprise because 'Ollie' had lived a very full life, but it was still a great shock. He was recognized, liked and looked after wherever he went. The Aussies and West Indians loved him for his larger-than-life figure, larger-than-life batting and larger-than-life attitude to living. They still talk of the time he bludgeoned 196 runs between lunch and tea for Western Australia at Brisbane in the Sheffield Shield. His weight had become a topic of national concern in the sixties and had cost him his Test place at one time. He is one of a rare band that scored a century in his last Test innings. His career was virtually ended when he lost an eye in a car accident, although he enjoyed a brief comeback as a bowler and once claimed the wicket of Geoff Boycott. But he never found anything to replace the game he loved and played so uncomplicatedly. He'd been dealt some rotten cards, but was always jovial. And he was one of the few commentators who didn't seem envious of or grudging towards today's players.

Our wonderful match-winning position had lost some of its certainty to become more than a little precarious because of the weather. If we got a full day's play, then no problems. But if the start was delayed and only a couple of hours were possible, then the West Indies' two remaining wickets and that 29-run advantage might prove a major stumbling block. The weather forecast was good, but there was still the smell of rain in the air, and I went to bed with more than just a feeling of trepidation. I don't think I've ever pulled the curtains back so early in the morning or so tentatively. Thankfully, the forecasters were right for once, the sun was shining. Surely our day had dawned!

Micky was down at the ground by seven to keep an eye on the drying-up process. When we arrived the umpires told us that, although the conditions were still very slightly damp, we would be starting on time. My worry was a patch to one side of the square which had taken much more water than anywhere else. It looked as if a big puddle of water had run off the tarpaulin cover when they removed it. That happens more often than it should. I would have gone out in waders just to get the game going again.

Still, there was an overall feeling of relief that we could get back to worrying about the cricket, not the weather. The final West Indies wickets didn't hold us up for long and we only needed 40 runs for an historic victory. After all the trials and tribulations of so many West Indies defeats over the past decade, it was a wonderful feeling to know that the win was a formality. I'd been on the receiving end so many times. But nothing could spoil this day, even getting out six runs short of our target. I'd have loved to have been there at the finish. But it wasn't to be, and I was just as happy for Wayne Larkins who had come out of his 10-year Test exile to beat the West Indies in Jamaica. Lambie described it as the greatest cricket day of his life.

There were 15 others in the dressing-room who agreed, as well as all the other Englishmen who were at Sabina Park that day. It had been 30 Tests and 16 years since England's last triumph over the West Indies. But this day was significant to us for more recent events. England had been humiliated in the summer and nobody had given us a prayer, home or abroad, on this tour. Now England had turned the cricket world upside down, and I must say it was a most exhilarating feeling. 'I told you so' never entered my head: everybody was my friend this day.

The Windies must have been disappointed. Losing is not a

common occurrence in their own backyard; it was only the second time it had happened in a decade. But Viv, having experienced his first Test loss at home as captain, and Clive Lloyd, the West Indies manager, were generous in defeat. That was something that Clive and I had discussed at lunch given by the sponsors, Cable & Wireless, at Lord's before we left.

Clive had approached me and we talked about how we could make sure the series was played in a friendly and sporting manner. Test cricketers do fall out in the heat of battle, but there's usually a healthy respect. Clive suggested that at the close of play each day the batting side should visit the other dressing-room for a drink. That's what happened throughout the Jamaica Test. Our West Indies opponents are hardly strangers, anyway. Many have been regulars on the English county circuit and, as I've stressed before, the composition of their side is more constant than probably any other Test team. This was Richards' and Greenidge's seventh series against England. In any case, we saw a lot of our opponents off the field – we stayed in the same hotels for most of the Test series.

The impact of winning a Test like this takes time to sink in. It starts as a very private affair for the touring party. It had been our sole purpose for quite a time and success brought a sense of relief as much as anything else. But it was not long before it became a public celebration; it started with the press, who kindly gave us a case of champagne, and the fans who'd travelled to support us. The mood spread quickly and soon it appeared as if the whole world had joined in. There was a flood of phone calls and telegrams. I've stuck the one from Margaret Thatcher on my study wall at home.

There was quite a party in the Hotel Pegasus that afternoon/night/early morning, I can tell you. At least, I think there was – my memory of the occasion is rather vague. But the pile of empty bottles outside room 175 and the state of the carpet next day told its own story. When the bath full of iced water no longer had any champagne to chill, it was used to cool down certain members of the England cricket party. I don't think anyone escaped! David Gower, who had not been selected, was covering the Test for the London *Times*. It was good to have him join in because he'd been captain during the Caribbean traumas of 1986. He knew how much the victory meant to us; I'm sure it meant a lot to him. He might not have been with the official England party, but he was still a Test player of undoubted class and his absence from the line-up was only temporary.

The ground had been a strange sight on the last day. The locals had lost their appetite for the contest and nearly all the spectators had been English fans. They included Bill Sykes, a friend of mine who lived in Portugal at the time. Bill's a businessman who settled in the Algarve and I'd taken the family to spend holidays there. Bill had watched a lot of cricket but had never seen a Test match outside England, and he had always promised himself a trip. So he travelled all the way from Portugal to Jamaica; I should have paid for him to follow us around – he was obviously a lucky charm! There were also quite a few of England's old cricket favourites around like Godfrey Evans, Alec Bedser and Sir Len Hutton. They'd been invited over by the Jamaican Cricket Association to celebrate the 40th anniversary of the West Indies' famous victory at Lord's. There had been a special benefit dinner for Sonny Ramadhin and Alf Valentine, those 'Terrible Twins', before the Test. It lasted an age and there must have been a speech for every one of the forty years, but Sir Len stole the evening with an absolutely brilliant speech. Sir Len had captained England to their only other win at Sabina Park in 1954 and Godfrey had also been in the side. This was the first of two occasions in 1990 when Sir Len and I were linked. The other was when I hit 333 at Lord's against the Indians. Another guest was Reg Hayter, who'd covered the 1954 game as a journalist. Still going strong at 76, Reg had the advantage over the rest of the English press gang, including his son Peter, the cricket correspondent of the *Mail on Sunday*: he was the only one of them to have seen both England Test victories at Sabina Park!

The impossible had happened; we were one-up now. But our victory meant the hard work was just beginning. It hadn't been a fluke. The West Indies hadn't played well, and we didn't give them an inch. Unusually for a Test, we dominated the entire match, session by session. But they didn't become world champions by tamely accepting any defeat. They fight, with everything they've got. They would be after us now, starting in Saturday's third one-day international at Sabina Park, and the real test of this England squad would come in the next month.

Second Test, Guyana

The Windies wasted no time. Two days later, on 3 March, they came back with a vengeance in Saturday's one-day international. But we weren't overpowered and lost a fantastic game of cricket only off the last ball when Ian Bishop belted Gus Fraser for four. The local fans were delighted after that Test shock and invaded the pitch to congratulate Bishop and 'Man of the Match' Richie Richardson, who was undefeated on 108.

Gus was despondent, but it happens to the best of bowlers. The frantic slog at the end of limited-over games pays little regard to the quality of ball or bowler. I've seen Richard Hadlee's last four deliveries get thumped to the boundary. My own thoughts went back to the previous summer when Eddie Hemmings hit John Lever for four to lift the Benson & Hedges trophy for Notts off the last ball at Lord's. As Essex captain I spent the next three days wondering if I could have handled the situation any differently. It's hard, and probably unfair, on the bowler. I can't think of anyone better than John Lever to have bowl the final delivery in a tight one-day match. He has given great service to England and Essex, but the casual cricket follower remembers him as the man who lost a cup final. I don't see it that way, but Joe Public can be quite harsh.

At Sabina Park, we made 214 for 8 off the 50 overs. Eddie Hemmings and Phillip DeFreitas, who had both played in the 1987 World Cup final in Calcutta, came in for Nasser Hussain and Devon Malcolm. Six specialist batsmen aren't necessary for a 50-over match; and Devon was being saved to cause shock waves in the Tests. Lambie carried on his good work with 66, while Bishop was the pick of their bowlers with 4 for 28 in his 10 overs. That wasn't a total to make us feel safe, but it gave us a fighting chance. The Windies needed a big innings to win and Richie Richardson provided it.

The last over began with them needing six runs to win with four wickets left. You had to back the batting side at that stage. Richie took a single off the first ball before Ezra Moseley gave me a catch to extra cover. The odds were now about even. Two dot balls swung the match in our favour and, despite two runs off the penultimate ball, we still had the edge. Actually, two more runs would have been enough to give the Windies victory because they had lost fewer wickets. (At the time I thought level scores might mean a tie as it does in the Texaco matches in England, where a result is required only to decide the series.) But Bishop settled all arguments and ended all doubts. Gus didn't quite put the ball where he wanted to; it was on off-stump but slightly over-pitched and Bishop hit it through extra cover for four.

We'd lost, but hadn't been outplayed – and that was important. The Windies had simply nipped in at the death for victory in one of the best matches on the tour. But the victory cost them the services of Malcolm Marshall; he broke the index finger of his left hand attempting a caught-and-bowled off Allan Lamb. But he's a tough character. I remember him batting one-handed against England at Headingley in 1984 with his left hand in plaster after he had broken his thumb in two places. Then he took 7 for 53 in England's second innings to wrap up the series! But now the West Indies injury list was lengthening. Gordon Greenidge was also struggling; he'd missed this match with a recurrence of a back problem.

These one-day matches can be as tiring, mentally and physically, as a five-day Test match. But neither would be a patch on the ordeal we faced the next day. The journey from Jamaica to Guyana was the worst of the tour. A direct flight would take about four hours. The problem, though, is that there were no direct or non-stop flights from Jamaica to Guyana. We had to fly to Trinidad and stay overnight, before heading for Guyana the next morning. Unfortunately, the first leg was a stopping-all-stations affair and we hopped from Puerto Rico, Barbados and Antigua (my third 1990 visit and I'd yet to get out of the airport) before landing at Trinidad. Hotel to hotel, it took nearly 11 hours. That, on top of the one-day international, left me shattered and we still weren't near our destination. It wasn't even a ploy to try and tire out the visiting opposition because the West Indies cricketers were going through exactly the same torture. The two teams made up a total of about 40 passengers; the travelling press, radio and TV personnel outnumbered us by two to one. So I couldn't understand why, with that sort of number, the two Boards didn't charter an aircraft. We could have gone directly to Guyana without all the hassle.

We left Trinidad on Monday morning for Guyana. Half the press corps came with us, the rest were flying out that night. It became a real trek for some of them when the night flight was overbooked and four of them had to spend a second night in Trinidad. By the time that quartet reached the Pegasus in Guyana, 50 hours had elapsed since they had left the Pegasus in Jamaica. One of the four was Tony Lewis, the former England captain, who now works for the BBC and the *Sunday Telegraph*. His absence from Guyana on the Monday night led to a rather amusing incident. His wife Joan, looking at his itinerary, assumed he had settled in at the Georgetown Pegasus. She rang up and asked to be put through to Mr Lewis, but was taken rather aback when he asked who it was.

'Your lover,' was her reply.

The immediate response, 'Which one?' left her rather stunned.

'You've only one, I hope,' gasped Mrs Lewis, before realizing she was speaking to Chris Lewis, not Tony, and was told that her husband was still stranded in Port of Spain. Chris was back in his hometown and had thought some old friends were trying something on.

All the participants had finally reached Georgetown – when it was discovered that some of their luggage was missing. Some 21 bags, including those belonging to Viv Richards and Clive Lloyd, had failed to arrive. It was while we were aboard the plane in Jamaica that it was discovered that the plane was overweight. Horrified passengers saw their bags being unloaded, and they were still on the tarmac as we taxied off. The Guyana leg was going to be tough enough without our being deprived of essentials for a few days. It wasn't the best of starts in a venue that's not regarded as the highspot of the trip. But, gradually, Guyana didn't appear as bad as we'd been led to believe. Rumours of food shortages had been rife and we heard that everyday commodities like bread and toilet rolls were hard to come by. Most of us arrived from Jamaica with emergency supplies in our suitcases, along with biscuits and cheese. The Pegasus had been our hotel on the 1981 tour; that visit had been cut short when Robin Jackman was deported because of his South African connections and the Test was cancelled. My South African connections meant Guyana was not on the itinerary for our 1986 visit. Little did we know that a third England tour was going to pass without a ball being bowled in the Guyana Test.

Guyana is not a Caribbean island but part of the South American mainland. It's a poor country and there's a great shortage of foreign currency – without which they struggle to buy imports. Most foreign firms have departed and currency exchanges are conducted by taxi drivers or street dealers, who operate openly in America Street (or Wall Street, as it's known locally).

But there are compensations. You'll struggle to find friendlier people, and they couldn't do enough for us. We had no problems with the food and our precautions proved totally unnecessary. We had only one complaint about Guyana in 1990: the weather. When we arrived at the airport, one of the officials asked why we'd bothered to come. When I asked him to explain, he said that the full moon was due in a few days, and that would bring rain for about a week. He was quite serious; apparently it happens every year. Another problem was that Georgetown is five feet below sea-level; once a place becomes flooded, there's nowhere for the water to go. Georgetown itself is protected by a sea wall that was built by the Dutch during their occupation. There's a lot of truth in the local joke that the way to guarantee rain is simply to place two sets of stumps in the ground. It certainly proved to be the case in March 1990.

After that one-day international defeat in Jamaica we needed to get our winning momentum back. We'd proved ourselves a match for the West Indies, but that would count for nothing if we became complacent. Winning the series wouldn't happen by magic. That's what I said at the team meeting, but it seemed to have little effect because we were trounced by six wickets the following day at the Bourda. The West Indies didn't need to play particularly well: we played badly. I realized that this poor performance was one of the setbacks that any young and inexperienced side must expect from time to time. That didn't excuse it, but it's important to keep things in perspective. Beating the world champions didn't make us world-beaters overnight or turn our raw recruits into a battle-hardened unit. We batted poorly in Georgetown. The pitch was good enough for a total over 230, but we managed only 188 after an opening stand of 71. Five wickets then fell for 41 runs and only Jack Russell helped make the total semi-respectable. Our bowlers kept it tight and the Windies didn't get home until two overs from the end, but they were always in control. Carlisle Best, opening in place of Greenidge, hit a brilliant century to win the Man of the Match award. That gave the Windies a 2–0 winning-lead in the one-day series – a perfect way for them to celebrate Viv Richards' 38th birthday.

Unfortunately, that was just about the start and finish of our serious cricket in Guyana. The airport official had been right: the rains came with the full moon and ruined the Test match. I was amused to see that the postcards on sale in the hotel shop were the same as those I had bought in 1981. The message on my card home announced that it had rained only twice in Georgetown that week – once for three days, once for four! Actually, some of the days were quite bright, though humid; but every night and morning the rain just hosed down. I've never seen a cricket ground as wet as the Bourda was that week. The ditches which are supposed to carry the water away were already overflowing and the outfield was under several inches of water. It was suggested that this state of affairs suited us, but that's nonsense. Although we were 1–0 up in the series, we had no wish to hide behind the rain and use it to keep our lead going into the third Test. We wanted to press home our advantage from Jamaica.

The rains did not prevent us from picking a Test squad – not surprisingly, the same 12 as in Jamaica. The only injury worry was me. I had two boils on my left thigh, a hangover from the Nehru Cup when I developed a similar one on my face. Laurie Brown, our physio, was relieved when the rain delayed the start of the Test as the boils were causing some discomfort, especially if my leg became hot and sweaty under a thigh pad. Laurie had been with England since he took over the physio's job from Bernie Thomas on the previous tour of the West Indies. That was a tough baptism, especially for someone who had been more used to dealing with the 90-minute soccer stars of Wolves and Manchester United. Laurie reckons he spent nearly as much time in the field as the players in 1986 as we took a fearful battering from their fast bowlers. His worst moment came when Denis Waight, the West Indies' Aussie-born physio, collapsed in the Kensington Oval dressing-room with kidney trouble. Laurie went with the ambulance and gave him oxygen as he was rushed to hospital. Fortunately, no one needed attention at the ground while the two physios were absent.

Laurie is one of the cheeriest characters I know, but even his powers of fortitude were stretched to breaking-point as he tried to relieve the monotony and boredom of doing nothing. We would hardly venture outside the hotel some days because of the rain. We tried to find practice facilities, even concrete ones, but it seemed as if everything was under water in Georgetown. We ran along the sea wall, sprinted in a nearby park and played indoor football. Anything, in fact, to keep busy. The hotel had a gym and I was able to do some weight training. I carry a set of bar bells with me and often Jack Russell and Robin Smith would join in.

The Pegasus had a tennis court which we also used as a makeshift practice area. It was the scene of our one mishap, although it gave Laurie, at least, something to do. Nasser Hussain fell and jarred his wrist while playing tennis. Initially, it healed well, but he wasn't fit for the third Test in Trinidad and went to Barbados without having played any cricket for a month. (Nasser did play in the final two Tests, but it later emerged that his wrist was broken. He needed an operation on his return to England, and missed the first half of the 1990 summer.)

England and the West Indies did do battle in Georgetown – on the tennis court. Viv Richards, who's played in the Antigua Tennis Championship, and Richie Richardson took on Robert Bailey and Phillip DeFreitas. Our pair proved to be much like the rest of British tennis and went down 6–4, 6–1. The Richards/Richardson combination was very skilful and especially strong at the net; Richie also has a really vicious, swerving serve. Daffy showed some nice touches, but Rob's main shot was an overhead smash that unerringly found the net.

The following day the All-England Cricket Diving Competition was held at the Pegasus pool. Eddie Hemmings, Gladstone Small and I were the judges. The best moment came when Devon Malcolm's poor eye-sight nearly resulted in his landing back on the diving board. Devon got the bronze medal, Angus Fraser the silver and Robin Smith the gold. It was Robin's technical marks that gave him the title, not least the ability to dive without seemingly getting his hair wet. Lambie might have been in the medals, but for a spot of mooning. Other mentions should go to Jack Russell and tour manager Peter Lush, minus knee-caps, who caused a great splash. We were certainly seeing a fair amount of water in Guyana.

But nobody was getting any cricket. We were all in the same boat, so to speak. By the official rest day it was clear there was no chance of a meaningful Test match. We'd suggested to the West Indies Board that perhaps it might be an idea to go early to Trinidad and play a couple of one-day games there. Apparently, moving us early wasn't that easy and the news about the local weather was more promising. Most of us went sightseeing to keep busy; some flew to the Kaiteur Falls in the interior, reckoned to be one of the highest waterfalls in the world. Allan Lamb, Gladstone Small and I were taken by the hotel manager for a trip up the Demerara River, which flows into the sea at Georgetown. We went a mile up river before turning off into a narrow creek which carved its way deep into the dark, green jungle. It was like a scene out of one of David Attenborough's nature programmes as we chugged through the black water, with vines and creepers dangling into the boat and shutting out almost all the light overhead. Three miles upstream we came to an Amerindian village, where all the children were paddling back from school in their little dugout canoes. The hotel manager, Paul Stephenson from Ireland, was building a weekend cottage in the village; it would obviously make an exciting holiday spot for someone with a sense of adventure.

England trained on the rest morning, so David Gower was put in charge of 'Lamb's Tours' for the day. A breath-taking flight to the interior was planned, but all Gower's party did was get fairly merry on the tarmac for three hours, waiting vainly for better weather reports. As ever with a Lamb's Tour, the small print should be read carefully: organizational expenses are invariably deducted before any refund!

At the end of the rest day, the Test was officially called off. It was the first time this had happened in the West Indies, and only the fifth time anywhere. It was decided to play a couple of one-dayers on the final two days. But, although the weather was improving, it was too wet for the first match. So, on the last day of the second Test, we played a one-day international instead. That set something of a precedent, but I didn't feel it would be very meaningful to play just one day of a Test. It was better for the fans and for all concerned if we played a complete match, which we did. Unfortunately, the wait hadn't improved our cricket and we lost heavily again. We played on the wicket that had been prepared for the Test; it had been covered for the past several days and was very lively early on. It was a good toss for Jeff Dujon, skipper in the absence of Viv Richards, Desmond Haynes, Gus Logie and Malcolm Marshall, to win. We faced Curtly Ambrose for the first time on tour; he showed what a threat he'd be for the rest of the series, taking 4 for 19 as we stumbled to 166 for 9 in 49 overs. The one plus mark was Rob Bailey, in the side for Nasser Hussain, who hit 42 in his first knock for six weeks. The Windies emphasized their superiority in the one-day game with a seven-wicket win, Greenidge making 77. The abandonment of the second Test had done us no favours at all. We'd lost all the impetus gained from that first Test win and needed to regain it quickly with the Trinidad Test fast approaching.

Third Test, Trinidad

Getting out of Guyana proved a lot easier than getting in. For once the whole party – the players (West Indies and England) and the press – had their own DC-9 to take them to Trinidad. Immigration was no problem at either end, no bags were lost, and we arrived at the Hilton Hotel in reasonable nick. It made a nonsense of our exhausting journey to Guyana.

Our warm-up match was against the West Indies Board President's XI at Guaracara Park in Pointe-à-Pierre, a small town 40 miles south of Port of Spain. After the inactivity of Guyana, we were in desperate need of cricket, but it did mean a very early start and two hours sitting on a coach each day. Guaracara Park was one of the strangest cricket settings I've come across – right in the middle of the third largest oil refinery in the world! The oil generates much of Trinidad's wealth. Unfortunately, we had to put up with the acrid smell; to most of us it was just unpleasant, for Eddie Hemmings, who suffers from asthma, it made breathing difficult at times.

Our cricket was certainly rusty and the President's XI – composed largely of players on the fringe of the West Indies Test team – took a first-innings lead. Rob Bailey, though, grabbed one of his rare opportunities with 52; he'd gone 40 days without a first-class knock, but that half century put him in the frame for the third Test. He had handled his period of inactivity well. Life can be pretty tiresome when you are practising and not playing, but Rob had done a wonderful job, especially during the Jamaica Test, in helping look after the needs of the other lads. Now his tour was beginning to have Test possibilities that he must have feared might never come.

We batted more convincingly in our second knock, setting them 237 for victory, although the situation looked precarious on the final morning, when we led by 92 and had only four wickets left. Robin Smith was another who used Guaracara Park to shake off the Guyana cobwebs. The pitch was showing signs of deterioration on the final morning. But Robin hit a marvellous undefeated 99 before he ran out of partners. Devon Malcolm had promised to hang around long enough for him to get his century, but Robin was left stranded when Devon could contain himself no longer and went for a wild hit. Robin is an extremely talented player, with all the courage and determination characteristic of South African cricketers. He likes to dominate bowling, but that's not always possible on tricky pitches; Robin was advised by several old wise-heads on the trip to show a bit more discretion and curb shots that could cost him his wicket as well as bring a boundary.

I was reasonably happy with my form, hitting 60-odd in each innings, although I was disappointed not to go on to reach three figures at least once. I made just two mistakes in the match, and each time it cost me my wicket to Robert Haynes, the tall leg-spinner from Jamaica. The match's top scorer was left-hander Brian Lara, whose 134 confirmed the good reports we had heard about him. He's a wristy player who strokes the ball around, a technique more reminiscent of some of the more accomplished Pakistan batsmen than a typical West Indies player. Devon Malcolm's batting may be a joke, but he soon wiped the smiles off the faces of the Board XI as he and Phillip DeFreitas ran through them, with the ball keeping increasingly low. The Board XI were bowled out for 123, to give us a 113-run victory and the perfect boost for the Test.

Back at the Hilton Hotel, English fans had begun to reappear. Only a brave handful had ventured to Guyana. I was glad to see that Colin Tomlin and his wife Carol had arrived in Trinidad. Colin had been brought in to help co-ordinate our fitness programme before we left for the West Indies. He's an athletics coach, but he's mad keen on cricket. He's a fine coach, and I enlisted him to work with Essex for the 1990 season. He's a quiet chap and confessed to being rather nervous on his first day about the prospect of shouting at people like me and Allan Lamb. He soon got over that, though, and he taught us a lot about fitness. A couple of times he told me to ease off while training. I always try to run and train as hard as I can, but Colin pointed out the benefits of taking it easy from time to time.

Nasser Hussain's wrist was still troubling him, while Lambie had missed the Board game with a bruised thigh. The vice-captain's absence was just a precaution, so Rob Bailey's entry for Nasser was the only change from the squad that had won the first Test. The Windies had more serious problems, with both Viv Richards and Malcolm Marshall out of action. Viv had a recurrence of his haemorrhoid problem. This was going to be the first time I'd ever faced a West Indies line-up that didn't include the great man. They were going to miss his leadership and, of course, his batting. No matter how settled a side is or how well it's playing, a change of captain has a disruptive effect. Marshall was another major blow; he's taken more Test wickets than any other West Indies bowler. But at least they were able to welcome back Curtly Ambrose and Gus Logie. Logie had skippered the Board XI and had impressed me with the way he handled his bowling changes and field placings. But it was Desmond Haynes who was given the job of leading the West Indies in their attempt to level the series. Lara, after his timely century, was added to their squad, although no one expected him to appear in the final line-up.

The Windies were certainly far more determined now than they had been in Jamaica – and much nearer their best form. But we kept our nerve and proved that our first Test victory was no fluke. And yet what was so nearly the greatest triumph for English cricket in many a year was, in the end, transformed into one of the biggest disappointments of our careers – and it would cost us the series. How that happened after England had resisted the West Indies retaliation was all part of one of the toughest, most enthralling and most controversial Tests it's been my good fortune to play in. Certainly, for me personally it was the most painful: my hand was broken badly enough to put me out of the final two Tests and make me a passenger for the rest of the tour.

Let's start at the beginning: the toss. This was a good one to win because the wicket looked green and, I was sure, would favour the seam bowlers. I expected it to improve on the second and third days before gradually becoming more uneven. So I was grateful the coin showed 'heads' in answer to my call, and I put the West Indies in. I'm often asked if that decision was a committee one. The answer to that is No. Of course, I talked things over with Micky and Lambie and we discussed the pitch's possibilities and how each of us thought it would behave. But finally it was the captain's decision about whether to bat or bowl. Some wickets make choosing obvious, others are pure guesswork. On those latter occasions it's usually better to bat. On a few occasions I'm happy to call wrong and let the other captain scratch his head and make the choice.

After I had put the West Indies in, Alan Lee, *The Times* cricket correspondent, asked if my choice was based on not wanting the West Indies to bowl at us first. No way! That's a defensive ploy and my decisions, whether right or wrong, are based on what is best for Essex or England in a positive way. I consider my team's strengths, not the opposition's or even my side's weaknesses. I make my choice simply on whether the pitch is better for batting or bowling. Obviously, in England a captain has to take regard of what the weather is like as well. If there's rain about, I like to bowl, particularly in a one-day match, because you are more in control of the game.

I guessed right about the Trinidad wicket. I'm not claiming any bonus points: it wasn't difficult. It played as predicted and only an unusual set of circumstances contrived to prevent us going 2–0 up in the series. My decision to insert brought immediate results and the West Indies had crashed to 29 for 5 after 80 minutes' play; the pace of the wicket was as varied as the bounce. We bowled accurately, but the Windies contributed to their own downfall. I couldn't believe our luck that we were in such a commanding position on the first morning. Carl Hooper and Gus Logie took them to 92 without further loss, but we had reduced them to 103 for 8 before Logie's gutsy knock of 98 enabled them to reach 199. I was disappointed with that after the trouble they had been in. At the start of the day I would gladly have accepted a West Indies total of under 200; and yet I couldn't shake off the feeling that we had let them off the hook somewhat. And as things turned out we would have won the Test and the series if we had skittled them for 150, as we should have done.

Gus Logie has proved a stumbling block to most Test attacks. He's not a conventional batsman; he improvises and hits the ball late, normally to unfamiliar (and untenanted) parts of the ground. He doesn't use a lot of power, relying more on subtlety, stealth and placement. You think he's struggling to score, then notice that he's already got 20-odd on the board. Once in, too, he's very difficult to dig out. His Test average in England on the 1988 tour had been 72.80, and here he was, once again proving a major stumbling block. Gus saved the Windies from annihilation that day, providing almost half their runs.

Our batting objective was now exactly the same as it had been in Jamaica – to still be there at the end of the second day. Our progress was slow, slower than in Jamaica, but this track was far more treacherous and it was important not to lose wickets. Both Wayne and I like to attack – that's how we established our reputations – but discretion was the order of the day in Trinidad. Another crucial factor was that the Windies attack wasn't bowling many loose deliveries. But, by the end of the day two, despite losing a couple of hours through rain, we were almost level with just two wickets down. Ned and I put on 112 for the first wicket. I was pleased to still be there on 83 because my previous eight Test innings had brought just 68 runs and I was being troubled with a stye in my right eye. That couple of hours under the covers certainly livened the wicket up and the ball started moving all over the place when play resumed after the rain stopped. That didn't make for quick scoring; nor did the Windies over rate of just over 11 an hour. (Not that we had bowled our overs much quicker. That had disappointed me as I wanted to bowl them at the 15-an-hour rate.) Yet the drinks breaks, including two in the second and third sessions, added to a few wickets falling, can mean the loss of nearly half an hour in the day. Two drinks breaks aren't necessary. And the blame doesn't lie solely with the fielding side; batsmen can mess around during the overs and often aren't ready when a bowler turns to start his run. Ninety overs in a day was supposed to be the minimum in the series, but that was never going to happen in the allotted time. Often we carried on for nearly an extra hour, but when we eventually came off because it had got too dark or the shadows were distracting the batsmen, there could be anything up to a dozen overs remaining. Ted Dexter had arrived to see us in action in the West Indies for the first time. Our Chairman admitted that when, at the airport, he heard the score was 103 for 8 on the first day, he had to check to make sure it was the West Indies who were batting.

The West Indies got themselves back into the game on the third day when they bowled us out for 288. We'd been 214 for 3, then lost three wickets without adding any runs and were 244 for 8 before David Capel and Gus Fraser (again) added 40 for the ninth wicket. I was disappointed to add only a single to my overnight total as I'd hope to build up a lead similar to the 200 advantage we had in Jamaica, but the Queen's Park wicket was more difficult. The Windies batsmen were left with eight overs to face at the end of the day. For an opener it's a horrible time to bat; you've everything to lose (your wicket) and little to gain (a few runs). One thing was certain; we had to make sure we didn't give the umpires an excuse to offer the batsmen the opportunity to come off for bad light. But that's exactly what we did, and that was my fault: I shouldn't have given Devon Malcolm the new ball. The Windies had already discovered how quick he was – as quick as anyone they had. In this match, he'd appeared the quickest. So when Devon bowled Gordon Greenidge a bouncer, the umpires conferred, offered the batsmen an early night and off we went.

In hindsight I should have let Angus Fraser share the new ball with Gladstone Small. That way we might have guaranteed our eight overs and picked up a very valuable wicket. I had instructed Devon to keep the ball up, but, although he was improving, his line and length could still be rather wayward. Greenidge belted a couple of half volleys past mid-off in his first over, but Devon over-compensated and bowled a bouncer that hit the Windies opener on the helmet and went for four leg byes.

So Greenidge and Haynes survived to fight another day – and were still together at lunch on the fourth day, having wiped out our lead. The rest day in between had offered us a chance to relax and get away. Quite a few of us took a boat and went to former West Indies captain Jeff Stollmeyer's old beach house. There we watched a home-made video of the West Indies 1951–2 tour of Australia, when Jeff had been vice-captain. It certainly looked a much more relaxed affair than today's helter-skelter. Jeff had died in a Florida hospital six months before our tour after being shot five times and beaten about thc head by intruders in his Port of Spain home. Just before the attack he had been named as Australia's first Honorary Consul in Trinidad and Tobago.

We had been glad to get away from the ground and hotel. That morning Robert Bailey had been approached by an England fan and asked if he'd enjoyed his knock the day before. Considering that the score-card read 'R.J. Bailey c Logie b Moseley O,' Rob did well to remain polite. Later the fan reappeared and apologized: he'd mistaken Rob for Gus Fraser!

By lunch on day four, then, you could say we were back to all square. But not for long. Angus Fraser turned the Test our way again by trapping Greenidge leg before early in the second session. The Windies' healthy 96 without loss became 100 for 4 when Devon removed Haynes, Carlisle Best and Jeff Dujon in four balls. As with his run-out throw in Jamaica, a few moments of Devon had turned the Test again. It's remarkable how often, even in Test matches, the fall of one wicket leads to a collapse and a relatively safe position becomes a struggle for survival. Now the Windies were effectively 12–4 in their second innings, and we moved in for the kill. We had some trouble with the tail, but the home side finished the day at 234 for 9, leaving them 145 ahead and us still in command.

The last morning was the brightest and sunniest of the whole tour: not a cloud in the sky. We headed for Queen's Park Oval with a great sense of anticipation. The result was no formality, but if we kept our nerve I knew we would win. Devon quickly removed Courtney Walsh to finish with 6 wickets, giving him the splendid match figures of 10 for 137. We needed 151 for victory and an unbeatable 2–0 lead in the series.

That wasn't going to be easy because the wicket was playing tricks. But, for once, the West Indies bowlers performed as other mortals do when they're under pressure. Instead of dropping it on the spot and keeping us pegged down, they bowled short and by lunch we were 70 for 1. That score doesn't tell the complete story because by then both England openers were back in the pavilion. Wayne Larkins had been caught behind off Ezra Moseley, and the same bowler did for me. I was smashed twice on the hand and forced to leave the field. Laurie had come to my aid and half the world seems to have seen that picture of me wincing with pain as he started prodding it about. At the time I wasn't too worried about the injury; I was just glad we were winning the Test. Lambie and Alex Stewart were playing positively and England needed only another 81 more runs after lunch to rock the cricket world. The way the Windies were bowling reflected our view that the Test was going England's way.

After being hit, I went off to a nearby hospital for an X-ray; while I was being treated I heard a noise that sounded like machine-gun fire. I thought they were joking when they told me it was rain: conditions had been perfect when I left the ground. The locals tried to reassure me, saying it was a passing shower. No such luck! The rain-bearing cloud dropped anchor over Queen's Park and was still there three hours later, long after I'd returned to the ground. Living with rain is part of every cricketer's life, but this was the cruellest of showers. The weather had been perfect; now, as though specially ordered by the West Indies, the rain was going to drown our hopes of making history.

Just when the door had seemed to slam on us, it opened briefly to offer a final glimmer of hope. The rain relented and the umpires, after a major mopping exercise, announced a resumption. Officially, there were 30 overs left, but we knew that target would never be approached in the fading light. As it was, the West Indies bowled 16 overs in nearly two hours and we gave up the chase at six o'clock with five wickets down and 30 runs needed for victory. I saw no point in continuing. It would have taken us at least another 20 minutes to get those runs at the rate they were bowling; and by then Queen's Park would have been in darkness. Anyway, I was next in with my broken hand and, despite our frustration at not winning, it would have been irresponsible to risk defeat. The umpires had already offered us the light and we might not have the choice again if we got into trouble. If we'd been three wickets down, we might have stayed on.

It was a bitterly unsatisfactory end to what had been a tremendous Test match. The weather robbed us. I will never look at a clear blue sky again and feel safe. Lambie and Alec Stewart, in particular, had batted well and we had the Windies on the run. Alec had begun to play his shots after looking rather inhibited in his earlier Test innings; he was unlucky to be on out when we resumed, caught on the widish third-man boundary from one that flew off the middle of the bat. A few yards either way and it would have been six. It was a brave knock from him as he'd been short of runs going into this Test.

Alec was in a potentially tricky position because his father was the team manager. Actually the relationship seemed more of a problem to those outside the party than inside. Micky treated Alec like any other England cricketer. Alec confessed that his one big worry about having Micky as a father was that his hair might start disappearing in his early thirties, as his dad's had done. During our St Kitts stop, Alec had taken the hotel portable phone and pretended to be his brother Neil back in England. When Micky passed the front desk, the receptionist told him there was a call for him. Alec, from the safety of the restaurant, kept up the pretence for five minutes until he told his dad to stand up straight and not lean on the reception counter, much to the amusement of the rest of the England party.

Alec's run-in with Desmond Haynes during the final day of the Trinidad Test was less friendly. Haynes was fielding at short square leg and several times wandered up to Alec; it was obvious that a fair amount of chat and eye-balling went on before Haynes returned to his position. Haynes was obviously under a lot of pressure in his first game as skipper, but if he thought he was going to intimidate Alec he had picked the wrong man. Alec was a veteran of grade cricket in Perth, Western Australia, where 'sledging' is part and parcel of the scene. Both players were to blame on this occasion and I didn't regard it as anything serious, though in general I find it a pretty unattractive spectacle.

David Capel also made an important contribution in this match. His batting showed a lot of determination, with scores of 40 and 17 not out. 'Capes' had a good record at county level, but he was taking his time finding his feet in the England side. His bowling had improved on the tour; too often he'd bowled the perfect length for batsmen to drive; in the Caribbean, the opposition weren't finding him so easy to hit.

Yet, despite the fact we'd done nothing wrong, the Trinidad Test was snatched away from us and we were left with a great sense of disappointment. Our depression must have matched the Windies' elation at saving a game that looked lost. It was a double blow for me – the day that cost England the series also ended my tour. Some papers reported that I was the victim of a bumper attack, but that wasn't true. The two deliveries from Ezra Moseley, who was the quickest of their bowlers in this match, were good-length deliveries that simply flew off one of the cracks in the pitch. I'm certain they both hit the same spot: they certainly hit the same part of my hand. The first struck the top of my left hand as I moved back defensively; it trickled away to the bat-pad fielding position and I took the single, even though the hand was hurting. I could still hold the bat and decided to carry on. But the very next time I faced Moseley I played back and the ball reared up to smash me on the hand again. That finished me off.

Getting hit on the hand is all part of batting, but I'd never broken a finger before and wasn't sure what had happened. I couldn't grip the bat. At first I thought it was a dislocation as the small knuckle on the left hand was depressed. Those photographs of me in agony show Laurie trying to put back a dislocation that wasn't there. I went for an X-ray at St Clare's Medical Centre during the lunch interval and it was confirmed that the finger was broken in two places. After 17 years without missing a game for Essex and England through injury, these fractures couldn't have come at a worse time. Because of the tight situation in the Test, I asked the doctors to keep it to themselves and say it was just badly bruised. That was what the media were also told. If I had to bat again, I didn't want the West Indies to know about the break. It might have given them a lift just when they needed it most. During the downpour, Jeff Dujon came into our dressing-room to ask how I was. I thought maybe he was on a spying mission. I told him about the bruising and said I would bat later, but doubted that I would be needed as we were going to win by nine wickets. You've got to be positive at all times!

After the Test I returned to the Medical Centre, though not in the same spirits as I'd arrived a few hours earlier. The operation lasted an hour. My hand was numbed by a local anaesthetic and two wires were put through the broken bone and into the joint in the adjoining finger to lock it like a splint. The wires would be in place for at least two weeks, so that definitely put me out of the Barbados Test. And with the final Test in Antigua following on straight away, I was sure even then that my tour was at an end.

Fourth Test, Barbados

The England captain wasn't the only casualty as we headed to Barbados. Our increasing injury list was becoming a growing problem. We had a three-day game against Barbados, then the final one-day international to sort ourselves out before the fourth Test. Nasser Hussain's wrist was still a problem, although it wasn't until we reached Antigua that we discovered it was broken, not sprained. Task number one was to find my replacement. Wayne Larkins and I were the only regular openers. Alec Stewart was our reserve in the tour party and he stepped in for the Barbados match. It was a temporary measure that, as it turned out, lasted until the end of the tour. With our batting so thinly spread, specialist cover was required and we sent for Sussex's David Smith, who had toured the Caribbean with England in 1986.

Sending for Smith was only one of several options we considered. He'd been on official stand-by during the winter and had been practising indoors in England. Two England players on the A Tour of Zimbabwe were also seriously discussed: Mike Atherton and Graham Thorpe. Atherton had played in the final two Ashes Tests of 1989 and had narrowly missed selection for the senior tour. He'd regained his best form with the A team and might well have been our choice had he not been suffering from a groin strain at the time. We just could not afford to take any fitness risks at this stage. Thorpe was also one of the successes of the A tour, but we felt it would be unfair – and another unnecessary risk – to pitch someone so inexperienced into two crunch Test matches against the might of the world champions. 'Smudge' Smith had faced the Windies firepower before, was one of the best players of quick bowling in England and wasn't the type to be intimidated.

Alec opened against Barbados and with Smith on his way, we called upon our emergency 'wild card' – none other than David Gower. The fact that he had been left out of the original party wasn't a problem. All along I felt that his was merely a temporary absence; present circumstances just meant his recall came slightly earlier than planned. We were in a spot and the man who could help us out was right there in the press box. We didn't even feel it necessary to check with Lord's. I had no doubt that David would jump at the chance. Only a week earlier I had told him, more as a joke than anything else, that we might need to call on his services. His reaction indicated he wasn't averse to the idea. More than anything, we used him against Barbados to give us a breather, a chance to sort out our injuries. David Smith wasn't arriving until the second day of the Barbados match, so he would have a couple of days to shrug off his jet-lag and get some practice in the sun before the one-day match. We also wanted to give wicket-keeper Jack Russell a match off. He'd been in action almost throughout the tour and would be needed for the last two Tests as the tour reached its climax. Alec Stewart, our official reserve opener, was also our number two keeper, but he'd been carrying a damaged finger for most of the tour. While it was okay for him to bat and field, putting him behind the stumps at this stage was another unnecessary risk. So Robert Bailey, who had occasionally worn the gloves for Northants, agreed to fill in. After a quiet start to his first England tour, Rob was getting plenty to do in the final month. Unfortunately, after a couple of hours, his hands were battered and bruised because he wasn't used to the constant punishment. Luckily, the unmistakable figure of David 'Bluey' Bairstow had been spotted on the island. 'Bluey' had toured the Caribbean with England in 1981 and was on a pre-season trip with Yorkshire. Desmond Haynes, the Barbados captain, and the umpires raised no objections when we sought the necessary permission.

David Gower was understandably nervous about venturing into the firing line again after all that had happened to him recently. He had lost the England captaincy, then his England place – and he hadn't batted in match conditions for nearly six months. David got just one chance, coming in at number 6, and was just starting to find his touch when he was caught at square leg. The game itself petered out into a tame draw when Barbados batted on in the second innings, giving us no chance of getting the runs or them any hope of bowling us out.

But we needed the practice, although it was a couple of the West Indies Test team who seized the best chances of getting in the batting groove. Gordon Greenidge hit 183 and Carlisle Best scored 95 and 71. In their first innings Barbados had been 340 for 4 overnight before our spinners claimed the last six wickets for 27 runs on the second morning. Eddie Hemmings finished with 5 for 77 and Keith Medlycott 4 for 115. Our batsmen weren't half as effective and were dismissed for 158, only Nasser Hussain, despite his wrist problems, looking impressive with an undefeated 70. Desmond Haynes didn't enforce the follow-on and batted well into the final day before declaring, leaving us an impossible 435 for victory with less than two sessions left. That decision ended David Gower's hopes of a second innings on his 33rd birthday, although David Capel managed an undefeated 50 as we batted out time.

This had been Lambie's first outing as England captain. I'd played in every game on tour so far and had planned to stay ever-present. But this annoying injury ended that idea. It's pretty frustrating hanging around the dressing-room as a non-player. I was still tour captain, but I strongly believe that the man in charge on the field should call the shots. Lambie, Micky and I were a close-knit unit, but Lambie was the man leading the team now; he gave the team talks and was in full control. That made my job even harder; a captain who wasn't captain. I knew it wouldn't be right to interfere, but I still wanted to retain an overall influence. Lambie made the decision to put the opposition in against both Barbados and the West Indies in the fourth Test match. We had discussed it and felt that, if there was ever going to be anything in the Bridgetown pitch to help the bowlers, it would be there on the first day. It wasn't a defensive ploy; it simply suited our resources better. But as things turned out the wicket in the Test never gave us the help we had hoped for, despite the perfect start of seeing Desmond Haynes return to the pavilion without a run to his name.

The final one-day international took place two days before the Test. If David Gower had hit a confident 60 or 70 against Barbados he more than likely would have played. But it was decided he'd be better off practising with his new county colleagues from Hampshire who were also in Barbados for a pre-season tour. The proviso was that David could be called upon again if there were any further injury mishaps. David sportingly agreed to remain on stand-by.

Hampshire's captain, Mark Nicholas, had just returned from leading England A in Zimbabwe. That tour, like ours, had gone well. Unfortunately, Mark's Barbados visit was less of a success and his address soon became the Queen Elizabeth Hospital after he went down with an attack of malaria, presumably caught in Africa. Mark was forced to spend a week in hospital, the first two days in a public ward, and the whole experience was far from pleasant. He looked in a dreadful state when I first visited him, and he suffered the after-effects of his illness well into the English summer.

England suffered a further setback, and one we could ill afford, when David Smith was in the nets. Angus Fraser injured his side bowling to 'Smudge' and, although we didn't realize it at the time, his tour, like mine, was at an end. That was a real catastrophe. Gus was by far our most consistent bowler. None of the West Indies batsmen looked happy when tied down by his nagging accuracy and we had relied on him more than any other bowler. 'Smudge' eventually got a game for Wanderers against Hampshire and looked in good nick with a half century. We had tried to fix him up with a match for Yorkshire, but their coach, Steve Oldham, said that wouldn't be possible as they had come to Barbados to give their own players as much practice as possible.

Ironically, our efforts were to prove futile anyway. 'Smudge's' left thumb was broken in the one-day international. Ezra Moseley was again the bowler and Smith's hopes of rejuvenating his Test career were dashed at the very outset. Like Gus, Nasser and me, 'Smudge' was to carry the effect of his injury through the months ahead. This crop of bad luck with injuries was threatening to undermine all the confidence and spirit we had worked so hard to develop.

Rain and the slow over rate reduced the final one-day international to 38 overs, so I was reasonably happy with our total of 214 for 3. Wayne Larkins and Lambie batted well, but the outstanding knock came from Robin Smith, who displayed awesome power in making 69. You could hear the sound of bat on ball and then, almost immediately, the crack as it walloped into the boundary boards. For once, Malcolm Marshall, Courtney Walsh and Mosley weren't very economical: Marshall's eight overs cost 50 runs. Unfortunately, our bowlers, apart from Gladstone Small, followed their wayward example. Line and length disappeared – as did the ball when Richie Richardson (80) and Carlisle Best (51) got going. It was Best's lowest score in a fortnight which brought him 398 runs before he broke a finger in the Test. Phillip DeFreitas conceded 63 runs in eight overs, David Capel went for 53 in six and the West Indies won with three balls to spare, although it was never really that close. That concluded our one-day programme. It hadn't been very successful: two games had been washed out and we'd lost the other four, including the unofficial match in Guyana. After our good limited-over record against the West Indies in recent years, our form here reflected a pretty serious decline in that department.

The tightness of the series was beginning to put a strain on relations between the sides. Gladstone Small, the best of our bowlers, had a nasty run-in with Gordon Greenidge early in their innings in the one-day international. Gladstone wasn't alone in thinking he had trapped the West Indies opener lbw, but the umpire rejected the appeal. Shortly after, 'Stoney' had Greenidge caught behind and told him that was the second time he'd been out that day. Greenidge must have thought he'd been sworn at because he waded into a group of players before walking off. The matter wasn't forgotten and, at the after-match presentation, Greenidge grabbed 'Stoney' by the shirt and threatened to continue the argument. They were quickly pulled apart, but our manager Peter Lush, who had seen the incident, felt obliged to report it to the West Indies Board. Greenidge was handed a severe reprimand, and he apologized. It all served to show the pressures that build up in a Test series as it nears its climax.

That flare-up was of minor importance compared to our worries about whether we had 11 fit players for the fourth Test. In any case there was no animosity between the teams at the West Indies Board dinner, held that night at the Hilton Hotel. I was one of two definite non-starters; the other was David Smith, who looked unlikely to recover for the final Test. And Angus Fraser was also struggling. My injury was improving. In Barbados I made several visits to Winston Searle, an orthopaedic surgeon. As far as he could tell, the two pins were doing their job. I was also being treated by an occupational therapist, Suzie Marsden, from England. As well as protecting the injury with a sling and little straps, she gave me some orthopaedic putty to squeeze and strengthen my finger. Fractures like mine can be healed in one of two ways. One way is to encase the fracture in plaster. Obviously, this completely immobilizes the injured part. The problem comes when the plaster is removed and the pins are taken out. By now the hand will have become stiff, and regaining normal movement and flexibility takes time. The second method, and the one preferred by me, is to use a light strap to 'tie' the two end fingers together. This allows you to work them about during the healing period. It's fairly painful, and after 10 minutes' work, you apply ice. The finger will then stiffen up and become sore; but it pays dividends in the long run because when the injury has healed, it takes much less time and effort to get full movement back. That was important for me. I might not play again on tour, but we were going straight into the English season on our return. I'd sent home for my jogging shoes and they arrived during the Barbados game.

Our injuries meant a fair amount of rejigging. Alec Stewart was picked as Wayne Larkins' opening partner; that allowed Rob Bailey to move up to his county spot of number 3 and Nasser Hussain came back to the sixth batting place after missing the Trinidad Test. Nasser's wrist wasn't right, but he gave it a go against Barbados and scored 70. This wasn't the time for waiting for players to be 100 per cent fit – anything over 85 per cent had to be good enough in our present predicament. Phillip DeFreitas got his chance because of Angus's injury. Because of his importance to the side, we gave Gus until the very last minute; but this was more in hope than expectation, and it was no real surprise when his bid to play ended in disappointment.

Allan Lamb was getting his first taste of Test captaincy. This was never going to be the easiest of baptisms. Although England were ahead in the series, we had lost one of our best batsmen, who was also the skipper, and our best bowler. And the Windies, by a stroke of irony, were boosted by exactly the opposite – the return of skipper Viv Richards and fast bowler Malcolm Marshall. Moreover, the Kensington Oval had become the West Indies' favourite Test ground: they'd had eight successive victories there.

Lambie won the toss and, for reasons explained earlier, decided to field. When Desmond Haynes went for a duck, I thought we might have them rolling again. But things didn't really work out for us after that early success. Devon Malcolm failed to fire for the first time in this Test series. That was hardly surprising; he's a rare commodity, a genuinely fast bowler; but he's still a raw one. In this match Devon bowled far too short and, as was always going to happen, was pulled and cut to the boundary and went for a lot of runs. No one was more disappointed than Devon himself, but had to put it down to the learning process. For the first time Viv Richards got the better of Devon, taking 18 off one of his overs – although the risks inherent in the West Indies captain's onslaught were themselves a tribute to Devon's success in previous matches on this tour.

The Windies finished the day at 311 for 5 with Carlisle Best hitting his maiden Test century. We were pleased with the five wickets – but not with the 300-plus runs. More discipline in our out-cricket would have restricted the Windies to around 250. The wicket had not behaved as helpfully as we had hoped – but that's one of the risks you have to take when you win the toss.

The Windies were eventually bowled out for 446, with Best finishing on 164. He'd taken his time in making his mark. He had made his Test debut against us four years earlier in the Caribbean, but he failed to make the tour to England in 1988. Despite his 'newcomer' tag, Best was 28 and really had reached the make-or-break stage in his Test career. He certainly had the ability and all the shots, with a tendency to hit square rather than straight. Best is also one of the greatest slips fielders in the game. He took some great catches in the series, and it was a cruel irony that a rare missed chance broke his finger in this Test. Best is, or at least was, one of cricket's great eccentrics: at one time he was in the habit of delivering a running commentary as he was actually playing his shots. He would name the bowler as he came running in, describe the delivery and then add exactly how Best had dealt with it, how the fielder had been unable to stop it, and how the crowd had applauded the shot. Obviously, he'd spent a lot of time with the radio glued to his ear when he was a kid!

But the batsman I studied most carefully from the balcony was one Viv Richards. The old determination to play a long innings was back; it had been missing in Jamaica, when he seemed to be trying to smash everything for four. In his 70 at the Kensington Oval he was much more like the Richards of old. He still hit his fair share of boundaries, but he was more watchful, solid and cautious – and that was ominous news for England. He was bitterly disappointed when he was caught behind off David Capel. He wanted that century, and when he came in he sat by himself on the steps leading to the dressing-room for almost half an hour afterwards and didn't talk to anybody. There were those who'd been writing Viv off and he was keen to prove there was still a lot of good cricket in him. I could see that for myself, but Viv, as usual, wanted to show the world.

Jack Russell, behind the stumps, took the catch that dismissed Viv; and he took four others edged by the Windies' top six batsmen. Jack had a cracking game. Those five catches were just a start. He didn't concede a single bye in their first innings: an immaculate performance. But Jack's never satisfied. He's always working to improve and there's no more determined fighter in the England set-up. I wasn't the only one who held the opinion that in Jack Russell we had the best wicket-keeper in the world.

We suffered the same fate as the West Indies and lost one of our openers for a duck. But England recovered to reach 358; not quite as good as them, but not a bad effort considering all our injury problems and the fact we were on the back foot for the first time in the series. The loss of Wayne Larkins to the second ball of the innings, his first, was the worst possible start because he was now the senior opener. At 75 for 3, England were tottering, despite Alec Stewart's lively 45. But, as has often happened in the past, our South Africa-born batsmen Allan Lamb and Robin Smith came to the rescue. They added 193 for the fourth wicket and we look very handily placed at 268 for 3. Lambie's century was his sixth against the West Indies, an England record he now shared with Colin Cowdrey. Incidentally, Lambie was the first England captain to mark his debut in charge with a century since A.C. McLaren way back in 1898.

We needed to be batting at the end of the third day. Time was as vital as runs if we were to thwart the West Indies' bid to level the series. With Jack Russell and Nasser Hussain going well in the last session, it had looked likely until both of them were given out leg before. It was a bit discouraging to see the Windies begin their second innings before the end of the day. Yet, although for the first time in the series the home side had the upper hand, England were still in with a fighting chance of a draw. Lambie made them work as hard as possible for runs in that second innings, but the Windies, especially Desmond Haynes with a forceful century, batted positively and declared at 267 for 8, leaving us to make 356 for victory.

We had 50 minutes on the fourth evening, plus the whole of the fifth day, to get the runs. It was in those 50 minutes that we lost the match. Three wickets fell in that final session, including that of nightwatchman Gladstone Small, and now England would have a desperate struggle to survive on the final day. Winning was now out of the question for us. If we had started well and threatened the target, the West Indies would have slowed the over rate down. That's not a criticism of them: we had done exactly the same when they began to accelerate in their second innings. The earlier they declared, the longer we were going to have to bat to save the game. Runs were important, but wickets were crucial and we couldn't afford to lose three of them on the fourth evening. And, amid a furore of controversy, it was shown that we didn't really deserve to. Wayne Larkins had already gone, lasting just one ball longer than in the first innings and collecting a Test pair. But then Rob Bailey was given out, caught down the leg side off Curtly Ambrose's bowling. My initial impression was that the ball had come off Bailey's thigh pad on the way through to Jeff Dujon. The row erupted because umpire Lloyd Barker seemed initially not to be going to give the decision, but then the excited appeal by the West Indies, led by their skipper, appeared to play a part in Barker eventually raising his finger. Cricketers do get very excited on big occasions and I don't doubt that the Windies players were convinced Rob had hit the ball. You must accept the umpire's decision. Without them, you can't play the game. Rob did so without a fuss. But it's disappointing when you think a decision is not right, especially when it looks like having a vital effect on a match and series.

The incident was 'meat and drink' to the vast press corps. The row was further complicated when the BBC's Cricket Correspondent Christopher Martin-Jenkins claimed that umpire Barker had been intimidated by the West Indies captain. His remarks were widely publicized and his invitation to broadcast on the 'Voice of Barbados' was withdrawn. There was even talk of umpire Barker suing him for slander. Just to make our day complete, Gladstone Small's stay as nightwatchman was a brief one and we finished at 15 for 3.

The final day was going to be our hardest of the tour so far. We were grateful for the rest day. The side gave everything on that last day and displayed all the character and fight that had formed the basis of our success in the Caribbean. Alec Stewart went in the first session and Lambie in the second; but Jack Russell, our second nightwatchman, and Robin Smith fought a tremendous rearguard action. Just when it seemed as if the impossible might happen and we might save the day, Jack got a pig of a delivery from Curtly Ambrose that shot along the ground. Jack had batted five hours for his 55 and it was only that cruel delivery with the new ball an hour after tea that finally cracked his defence. Our final four wickets were all lbw in an impressive spell from Ambrose with that second new ball. He finished with 8 for 45 and we had lost by 164 runs. Robin Smith remained defiant with an unbeaten 40; he'd shown a tremendous amount of application because his natural instinct is to crash the ball about. But, because of the match circumstanccs, Robin had taken eleven hours to compile his two-innings total of 102 runs and had proved himself a batsman for all occasions. When Devon Malcolm was last man out, there was less than an hour and 11.2 overs left. So near and yet so far. With the Windies back to near their best, we'd taken them to the wire. But the Caribbean cricket kings were now back on level terms and we had a great fear that all our hard work and success could be undone in the final fortnight of the tour.

Fifth Test, Antigua

Antigua, our final stop, is one of the favourite Caribbean island holiday spots, but it was not going to offer us a relaxing time. With only one day between our defeat in Barbados and the start of the final Test, we were really up against it. There was no time for injuries to heal; even for those physically fit, the cumulative mental and emotional strain had become a problem. After such an arduous tour, it was unfair to impose this frantic finale on us when it was bound to play such a significant part in the result of our three-month expedition. During the time I've been playing Test cricket, overseas tours have steadily become more work and less leisure. Tours today have three priorities: playing cricket, preparing to play cricket and travelling to play cricket. Days off are few and far between; there's little chance to establish any sort of a rapport with the locals or locality. Lambie and I did manage one day's fishing during the rest day in Barbados, when Professor Edwards, a former island cricketer, took us out on his boat. We left at six in the morning and cruised around the area off Sam Lord's Castle. We caught four biggish fish, including a dorado or dolphin fish; it's not a genuine dolphin, and it regularly appears on the menus of local restaurants. Our largest catch was a kingfish, known in those parts as a wahoo. This one weighed in at 28 pounds and took quite a bit of landing, especially with my broken hand. But we parked the rods in cleats on the side of the boat and just reeled it in.

Barbados had seen a massive influx of English support: something like 5,000 had flown out to enjoy the sunshine and cricket. They hadn't been happy with our performance there in 1986, when we lost by an innings and 30 runs in just over three days. This time, although we lost, they got their money's worth as we took the Windies all the way. Many of the fans then travelled on to Antigua for the finale. The West Indies Cricket Board have cunningly coupled together the two best Test venues, holiday-wise, to attract visitors from abroad. Their support is certainly welcome. The West Indian fans are a noisy lot, with live reggae music and ghetto-blasters blaring away, and it helped morale to hear some shouting on our behalf.

Some of the players' wives and girlfriends had turned up in Barbados, but I had to wait until Antigua to see Brenda and the three girls. They're a handful at the best of times, so Brenda brought Karen Kaye (then the girlfriend, now the wife, of Essex batsman Alan Lilley) to give her a hand.

We had to draw this final Test to tie the series with cricket's world championship – something few believed possible when we had left Gatwick three months earlier. Just a draw! But our list of walking wounded was getting longer all the time. During the final Test, Nasser Hussain went for another X-ray on his troublesome wrist. The break, which hadn't shown up in the Guyana X-rays, was now clearly apparent. I wished we'd known that a month earlier, because we would have sent him home and asked for a replacement. It wasn't a faulty diagnosis; it was an injury in which the break opened up in the weeks following the accident. Now he was going to need an operation on his return to England and would miss most of Essex's 1990 season.

We kept quiet about Nasser's break, as we had in Trinidad about mine, because we still wanted Nasser to play. But it underlined the need for an adequate replacement to be standing by. Including Nasser, we had only seven batsmen available – the minimum, in my view – and no cover. A balanced side should include seven batsmen, one of whom is an all-rounder. That role was filled by David Capel in the Caribbean. The question of whether to play four fast bowlers or include a spinner doesn't come into it. The key factor is to make enough runs to allow you to dictate the course of the game. A decent first-innings total means you're always in the game; you're forcing opponents to think more about saving the game than winning it. That's why 'Capes' played in all the Tests. If you replace your all-rounder with a specialist bowler, the batting line-up starts to look thin. Moreover, with me injured, our batting line-up was fairly inexperienced at Test level. Apart from Lamb, none of our batsmen had played 15 Tests.

The loss of Angus Fraser had upset the balance of our bowling attack. He and Gladstone Small were our two bankers, the guys we relied on to plug away with testing line and length for over after over, keeping the Windies pinned down as much as anyone can. I'm not making excuses because things went against us at the end of the tour. It's part of the game. The Windies at various times on our tour were without the services of Viv Richards, Desmond Haynes, Gordon Greenidge, Gus Logie, Carlisle Best, Ezra Moseley, Courtney Walsh, Malcolm Marshall and Curtly Ambrose – all world-class cricketers. In fact Moseley, Marshall and Best were ruled out of the Antigua Test. But it's always easier for the home team, especially with the bowling talent the Windies have, to plug the loss of key players. Angus Fraser was crucially important to us and we gave him every chance to make it for the final match. He had a work-out the day before the game and, although he was still sore, his injury wasn't any worse. We gave him another try-out on the morning of the match. There was a great temptation to include him, but he wasn't right and it would have been inexcusably risky to have included him, even if we had known we were going to win the toss and bat. One day's further rest would not have made much difference at this stage. So Gus was left on the sidelines.

David Smith was another problem. It was obvious in the nets that he was struggling. Lambie noticed he was in pain every time he played the ball. We were down to the bare bones, so once again we asked David Gower to stand by. He was never led to believe that he would definitely play, so press suggestions that he was badly treated when we left him out were wide of the mark. We were grateful that he'd given us this option in time of trouble, but he was released when everybody in our selected 12 reported fit, and he flew back to England on the rest day, during the Antigua Test.

Although by now I was a confirmed passenger, the question of my flying home never arose. When the injury in Trinidad happened, we were in a winning position and there was a slight chance the hand might recover in time for the final Test. I would have stayed, anyway. I was, after all, the tour captain and I wanted to retain a sense of continuity in our party and give moral support to the lads. Lambie was responsible for motivating the side in the dressing-room and on the field once the game started. But I wanted my say and continued to help pick the side. And it was still my job to talk to those who had been left out. It was less of a problem now than it had been at the start of the tour. By this stage, if you were fit, you were virtually guaranteed a game! It's never easy telling players they've been dropped. Often they know which way the wind's blowing; but at other times it comes as a shock. As a captain, you've got to be absolutely straight with your players.

Try as we might, we were forced to admit defeat as far as Angus Fraser and David Smith were concerned, so went into the final Test with the side that had lost in Barbados. Lambie won the toss and batted because there was no reason to field and it looked the best wicket of the series. We thought it might deteriorate, but actually it stayed more or less the same throughout the match. The ball didn't seam around much but the wicket favoured the tall bowlers who could bang the ball in and get some bounce. That's not surprising because Andy Roberts, the former West Indies fast bowler, had helped to prepare the wicket. His view was that if you were prepared to put something into your bowling, the wicket would give you something back.

Still, this was a tremendous batting track and we paid the penalty for scoring only 260 in our first innings. That's where we lost the match. No excuses. If you bat badly on a good track, then you are always under pressure. We started well enough and were 143 for 2 at one stage; but although eight of the top nine batsmen got to double figures, nobody really settled in and Rob Bailey finished top scorer with 42. The West Indies gave another impressive bowling performance. Ian Bishop, only 22, looked a terrific prospect with his 5 for 84 in 28 overs and Courtney Walsh, coming on first change, took 3 for 51 in 21 overs. Robin Smith, especially, was given a good working-over by Walsh and ended the Test with his right forefinger broken. Lambie, too, ended up on the injured list with a chipped bone in his elbow. But, even allowing for their top-class bowling, we had been looking for a minimum of 350 and would have felt comfortable only with 400 or more. We paid dearly, but deservedly, for indiscreet shots from several of the top-order batsmen when they seemed to be well set.

The rest day – Good Friday – came next. The papers had got hold of a story that Viv Richards had sent Lamb on his way with a V-sign after he'd caught him off Curtly Ambrose's bowling. Viv's gesture was actually aimed not at Lambie's departure but towards a lone local fan who had been heckling the West Indies captain every time he bent down to field the ball. Viv wasn't too happy at the insinuation that he'd insulted Lambie and took exception to journalistic enquiries on his day off. His angry reaction was also reported and the second morning of the Test found Viv making an unscheduled visit to the press box instead of leading the team out onto the field. Viv had a few words with the journalists before returning to the fray. When the West Indies Board found out the reason for his absence, team manager Clive Lloyd was ordered to investigate and Viv was eventually given a reprimand and a warning as to his future behaviour as West Indies captain.

England were eventually dismissed after lunch. We were up against it now and needed to make the Windies work hard for their runs. But it was not to be. Our bowlers started throwing loose deliveries around like confetti. That Saturday was our worst day of the whole series: we performed like second-raters. Our bowlers looked absolutely exhausted. Gladstone Small, one of the great tour successes, seemed to be absolutely spent, as did David Capel.

Suddenly, all the efforts of the previous three months had caught up with them. And with the old firm of Gordon Greenidge and Desmond Haynes, the West Indies had the perfect pair to take advantage of our weakening attack. Our worst fears became a reality when they passed our total without being separated, and their opening partnership of 298 equalled their own Test record, providing the West Indies with their victory platform. Greenidge celebrated his hundredth Test with his eighteenth century, making 149.

Oddly enough, he finished the series as he had started it, by being run out unnecessarily. That run-out sparked a revival, and we skittled their last nine wickets for only 148. Haynes made 167, but no one else reached 35. Devon Malcolm picked up four wickets, including Viv Richards again, and was more economical than either Gladstone Small or David Capel. We were rather surprised when 'Capes', who is brisk rather than quick, was cautioned for two successive bouncers at Ambrose after the onslaught that Robin Smith had faced in our first innings. Both teams were rushed between these last two Tests, but the West Indies had the benefit of two fresh bowlers, Walsh and Eldine Baptiste, who hadn't played in Barbados. I'm not criticizing my bowlers. It was a flat wicket and it needed a special effort to get something out of it, as Andy Roberts had predicted. It was just that our bowlers had nothing left to give.

Now 186 behind, we needed to bat for about two days to save the Test and the series. Again, it was crucial not to lose any wickets in the short time left on the third evening. Once again, a wicket went down in controversial circumstances. Wayne Larkins was the victim this time. He'd been complaining about confusing shadows across the wicket caused by the trees around the western boundary. To nobody's surprise, he misjudged the length of an Ambrose delivery and was bowled. Wayne's despair was increased when the umpires then decided that conditions were now unfit for batting after all and the players came off. I knew how he felt; it had happened to me in 1981 during the famous Headingley Test. There's nothing worse than returning to the dressing-room and turning round to see the rest of the players coming off for bad light. John Emburey was bowled by a full toss from Colin Croft during the 1981 Antigua Test, the first ever held there. He'd backed away because he could not see the ball – for all he knew it might have been travelling straight at his head. Wayne was bowled at the same end. There the ball can come down in line with the edge of the screen and out of the faces of the members in the pavilion. Not the easiest of backgrounds – especially in the gloom.

The Windies rolled us over on the fourth day and wrapped up the series. We lost the match by an innings and 32 runs and the series 2–1. Three wickets went down in the first hour to end any thought of a late rally. Robin Smith retired hurt and both Lambie and Nasser Hussain counter-attacked. But the result was predictable after our poor batting on the first day and sloppy bowling on the second. It was a sad and cruel final act to a brave campaign. For the first time on the whole tour, we didn't compete, we were outplayed. We had worked so hard and come so close. England had dominated the first Test; the second had been washed-out; we had controlled the third; and, despite losing the fourth, had battled bravely throughout. But this Antigua defeat was reminiscent of the bad old days of 1984, 1986 and 1988 when we were twice whitewashed by the West Indies.

Our main objective when we left England had been to make sure the Windies knew they'd been in a fight, whatever the result. We had achieved that. I'm sure they were confident of winning the series at the start, but we rocked them with our performances in the opening Tests. But, in true world-champion style, they did their homework, got down to business and came back to maintain their position in the game.

To return home as just another side that had failed in the Caribbean with nothing tangible after dominating for so long was very deflating. I tried to stress to the lads that the trip had not been a failure, that a lot had been achieved. What had gone wrong? It's easy to blame our dreadful run of injuries or the weather. I was disappointed that we didn't share the series at least – we deserved that – but we ran out of luck in Barbados and out of steam in Antigua. On the other hand, we'd won a Test match – and the last time England had done that, other than against Sri Lanka, had been on Mike Gatting's tour of Australia in 1986–7! England were back on some sort of winning trail and I was determined we would stay there.

New Zealand, 1990

Whether our Caribbean adventure was adjudged a success or failure didn't matter now. It was over and the English season had already begun. The opportunity of a few weeks off with my feet up would have been nice after such an arduous trip, but it was back to work. Originally, I had intended to take the family to Florida for a holiday, but the schedule was so tight that an extra few days in Antigua was all we could fit in. That did allow me to have the pins removed from my fingers before I returned. The hand was still sore, but the bones had healed well and mobility wasn't a problem because of the special hand exercises.

We arrived back in London on a Saturday morning and I was hopeful of being fit enough to face Nottinghamshire on the following Tuesday in the Benson & Hedges zonal match. But after a net at Chelmsford before the Sunday League game, I decided to play against Kent that afternoon. The hand was sore but not really painful and, after a word with Keith Fletcher and some catching practice, I was relieved to be back in action after the most frustrating month of my cricket career.

Nasser Hussain wasn't so lucky. The operation to pin his wrist would keep him out for six weeks at least. Angus Fraser was the other Caribbean casualty who was going to spend the opening weeks of the English season on the side-lines. Not surprisingly, our plan was to use the West Indies squad as the nucleus of England's upcoming Test series and to strengthen the side in certain areas. Ian Botham and David Gower had missed the tour. Out of sight did not mean out of mind. Both were keen to win back their Test places and there was no reason why they should not. Their replacements in the Caribbean had done an admirable job, but players like Ian and David are rare and you don't expect to replace them overnight. Ian signalled his intentions with a typical knock of 138 against Gloucestershire in the Benson & Hedges. Because of his back and other injury problems, you had to go back to July 1987 for his last three-figure innings.

The England Committee reappointed me as skipper for the New Zealand series a week after I got back. Allan Lamb was named vice-captain. Picking a deputy at home was a break with tradition, but the committee obviously wanted to keep the West Indies unit together. Micky Stewart had said publicly in Antigua that he wanted me to carry on, and the early announcement was intended to remove all doubts. It's nice to have that sort of backing, although nobody was surprised by the news. I could have got the job for the whole summer at the time, but I asked to be appointed for the New Zealand series only. I don't think it's right to name a captain for the whole summer if there's a natural break half-way through because two sides are touring. That break allows scope for change if necessary. Why not take advantage of it? But if there's a five-Test series, it's obviously better not to have a change of leadership in the middle. England had had four captains during the 1988 campaign against the West Indies and had suffered accordingly.

While it was comforting to know the selectors still had faith in me, England were also going to have to make moves towards unearthing someone to take over. Lambie and I are at the veteran stage of our careers. Very few others of the Test side had captaincy experience, while very few county captains had Test experience. The Australians pick their Test side, then find a captain; England have usually picked their captain first. Test cricket is a tough environment these days and it's difficult to imagine a player's leadership qualities alone justifying a Test place.

This was my first real experience of leading England at home. My other chance had come at the end of the 1988 series against the West Indies after Chris Cowdrey had been injured. The Test against Sri Lanka followed; unfortunately, the proposed winter tour to India was cancelled, so my first spell as a test captain was over almost before it had begun. When Peter May quit as chairman of selectors, Ted Dexter was brought in to pick a captain for the

1989 Ashes series. I came a poor third in that particular race with Mike Gatting getting the nod over David Gower. That result was overturned by Ossie Wheatley's veto of Mike Gatting – and the rest is history. England lost 4–0, Mike went to South Africa and David was sacked. I found being England captain a harder job at home. Abroad there are fewer distractions: you have a group of players and work with them. But at home, everyone has a variety of commitments, and not just to cricket. There's county and country; there's home and business; and there's a ridiculous amount of time spent on motorways.

That's why Micky and I requested extra time together before Test matches. We asked for that while in the West Indies. The whole structure of playing Test cricket was changing. The itinerary for the forthcoming Ashes tour included four Tests that would be played without a rest day. That had been the practice with other countries, but England had usually insisted on their rest day. The Ashes trip was only the start. The 1991 summer in England was going to include Sunday Test play. England had experimented with Sunday play in the early 1980s, but it had only been partly successful. I was less concerned with that than with ensuring that the team spent more time together before Tests.

Getting to Test matches has always been a rushed job. You finished a county match on Tuesday, went home, and the following morning drove anything up to 200 miles to ensure you got to the Test venue by three o'clock in the afternoon. Then it was out of the car and straight into the tracksuit. I've never been very impressed by this way of going about things. It's much better to arrive at the venue the night before and to have a bit of a lie-in before getting to practice by 11 o'clock. Then you can work for the same time as before, but with a bit more purpose. This would also allow the side to have a team-meeting early in the evening after their arrival, before relaxing at the team dinner, when cricket shouldn't be on the menu.

Unfortunately, England's first international of the summer was even more hurried than usual. Because proposed changes to the county programme hadn't taken place, there was some re-scheduling around the time of our two Texaco one-day matches. Normally, these are played over the Whitsun weekend, but this year they were played on the preceding Wednesday and Friday. County matches did not finish until the Tuesday, so we had no time at all for practice. Players arrived at the Post House at Bramhope, just outside Leeds, as soon as they could. Jack Russell had to come from Bristol, while Devon Malcolm's journey from Taunton, where Derbyshire had been playing Somerset, meant it was after midnight before he checked in.

Devon hadn't been in our original Texaco squad: he was never considered the tightest of bowlers. But then Angus Fraser was declared unfit, so we drafted in Devon. Gus wasn't the only one suffering from injury. Ian Botham's comeback was cut short by an exploratory operation on his left knee, while David Capel was out with a double-cracked kneecap. Wayne Larkins had been in the original squad, but a smashed finger was going to ruin his season.

The first month of the season had seen an avalanche of runs. Fortunately, my return to fitness allowed me to join in. My best score was 215 against Leicestershire when I shared in an Essex record second-wicket partnership of 403 with Paul Prichard, who hit 245. There were all sorts of monster scores around; the biggest being Neil Fairbrother's 366 against Surrey at the Oval. Mike Atherton chipped in with a modest 191 in reply to Surrey skipper Ian Greig's 291. Lancs replied to Surrey's 707 for 9 with 863. The match aggregate at the Oval reached 1,650, a new record for the championship and the second-highest for a match in England.

Our game against Leicestershire was no different. They scored 520 at Chelmsford with Chris Lewis hitting his maiden first-class century; we responded with 761, including a Neil Foster ton off just 79 balls. Fossie was especially delighted to smack his old adversary Jonathan Agnew all over the place. Agnew's bowling figures were 35.5–4–170–0 and a note of these statistics arrived through Agnew's letter-box at regular intervals for the rest of the summer from various parts of the country. Neil Foster, I can reveal, was the sender!

With the change in the ball, the brilliant weather and the placid pitches, it was becoming increasingly difficult to decide the true source of the amazing glut of runs. I'm not trying to take anything away from anyone's performance, but the scores that were being posted indicated that the pitches were batsmen-friendly, to say the least. The massive scores and the new specification for the ball stitching meant bowlers were struggling. After nine matches, Essex were averaging just a single bowling point a game. And with the threat of a 25-point penalty for a bad pitch, wickets were devoid of grass and pace, to the delight of every batsman. Essex had suffered that 25-point penalty in 1989, and when we finished only six points behind champions Worcestershire, we could be forgiven for feeling that the punishment had cost us the title.

Neil Fairbrother was the outstanding batsman in May and earned a recall to the England side for the Texaco matches. As well as that massive 366, he smashed 145 off Hampshire's attack in the B&H – only to have it wiped off the record books because the weather intervened and the match was restarted. (The weather in fact failed to relent and the tie was eventually declared 'no result'. Sad, because Lancs' original 352 for 6 would have been a competition record as well. That happened to me once in my benefit year when we played Derbyshire in the B&H quarter-final. In a rain-affected game I was bowled by Michael Holding for a single. We didn't play the next day and the match was restarted on the Friday. I took my second chance and won the game with 70 not out.) It was easy to understand Neil's disappointment, but two scores can't stand from the same one-day game.

Our Texaco 13-man squad included 11 of the West Indies party (twelve if you count David Gower, who had been there as a journalist). Derek Pringle was the odd-man out; he claimed the all-rounder's spot as both Ian Botham and David Capel were injured. Like Devon Malcolm, Neil Fairbrother had not been in the original party, but was drafted in after Wayne Larkins lost the fight to get fit in time.

We were not going to play two spinners, so the only player really discarded from the West Indies tour was Robert Bailey. Rob, as we've seen, was thrust into the fray towards the end of that tour. After starting with a 'pair' at Trinidad, he had been involved in that controversial dismissal in Barbados, and then he had top-scored in our first innings of the final Test in Antigua. Our injury problems had allowed us a much closer examination of his ability than had looked likely in the early weeks of the tour. My judgement then was that I was not convinced he was good enough for Test cricket. Like it or not, this work of critical assessment is part of my job as captain, and I have to back up my judgements with decisions. Of course, I can make a mistake – and nothing delights a skipper more than being proved wrong in a positive way by a member of his team. Rob's a good player with a very good county record; he's also a nice bloke who won't let you down. We took him to the Caribbean because he did well when he came into the side against the West Indies at the Oval in 1988. He's a good team man who stands up to pressure well. But, performance-wise, after getting his chance, he did not come up to scratch on the tour. Doing better than other players isn't always the criterion; you expect more from some players. Selectors are always searching for the right combination and not everyone you pick is a success.

Ian Botham's knee operation was untimely. 'Beefy' had shown good early season form when I faced him on his return a few days after the Texaco squad had been named. I scored my fifth hundred of the summer, and we won by 10 wickets. As we felt Worcestershire had 'stolen' our 1989 county championship title after that 25-point fine, it was a satisfying victory. Ian scored 53 in the first innings and took 4 for 25 in the Sunday League game. He looked impressive; he bowled well and with a lot more zip than he had managed in the previous summer, when he was obviously getting over his back operation.

Texaco Trophy

Our victory at Worcester meant that I was able to head off early to Leeds for the first Texaco match and I reached the hotel in mid-afternoon. Others, as I've said, weren't so lucky and we really got together only on the morning of the match. Fortunately, it was little over a month since the end of the West Indies tour, so the lack of preparation wasn't as serious a problem as it might have been.

During the course of my career, New Zealand had become a Test team to reckon with. When I started, anything other than a win against them was a disappointment. But Glenn Turner, Richard Hadlee and Martin Crowe, three world-class players, transformed them into a formidable unit. They received a lot of support from their team-mates, but without their special talents it would not have been possible. In my time, they've beaten England in a Test at home for the first time and in this country for the first time. And again for the first time, the Kiwis have defeated England in a series, both at home and away. And don't forget that, going into 1992, they were the last country to overcome the West Indies in a series. Yet, while all professional cricketers are aware of their improvement, the public still regards them as one of the weaker Test sides, and losing to New Zealand is much less acceptable then going down to Australia or the West Indies.

The Kiwis arrived in England having just beaten Australia, who had inflicted that 4–0 humiliation on us the previous summer. Hadlee was obviously their key player and New Zealand were going to miss him when he retired. He'd already announced that this England tour would be his Test finale. New Zealand's bowling might look suspect without Hadlee, but their batting was strong. Crowe is one of the top batsmen in the world, while Mark Greatbatch and Andrew Jones had shown themselves to be two of the best young prospects. John Wright, the skipper, was having the best run of his Test career, while wicket-keeper Ian Smith was a gutsy competitor and off-spinner John Bracewell a useful all-rounder.

New Zealand's bowling weaknesses were emphasized when Martin Snedden was troubled with a stomach strain and Chris Pringle was called up for the Texaco opener from the Pudsey St Lawrence club in the Bradford League. Pringle apparently had just missed out on the original tour selection. He impressed me – and not only because he got me out! – as better than some of those they had brought. John Wright put us in; but, despite the early loss of David Gower, Robin Smith and I passed the hundred mark without further mishap. I reached 50, but Robin played the key innings; his 128 was his first one-day century for England. Even when he was out, we kept up the momentum. Alec Stewart scored 33 off 25 balls, Jack Russell 13 off 5 and Derek Pringle 30 off 17, including smashing Hadlee's final four deliveries to the boundary.

A total of 295 for 6 from 55 overs was more than respectable and certainly a target that we ought to be able to protect. But we didn't – and we didn't because we bowled poorly. Much of our one-day success in the late 1980s had been due to our out-cricket: accurate bowling to well-set fields. Sides had found it difficult to score heavily against us. Our opening attack generally kept it tight, which forced the batsmen to take liberties later on and give chances. By then Eddie Hemmings and John Emburey would be operating, often in tandem. Another key to our success had been to leave several options for the closing overs, depending on the situation. Often that's where I came into the act to bowl a few overs.

This wicket at Headingley wasn't really my scene. It was very flat and my bowling becomes a lot less valuable in unhelpful conditions. I need the ball to swing or the pitch to do something. This flat wicket demanded five specialist bowlers. Using bowlers like me helps because it gives the captain 'spare' overs and bowlers, allowing him to be flexible in case of injury. Over the years my bowling has had an adverse affect on my knees; it's more of a wear-and-tear problem than anything else. Strangely, the knees are sore only when I bowl, not when I go running. But I enjoy bowling because it keeps you involved in the game. Essex are lucky because we have Mark Waugh and John Stephenson as well as myself to fill the role of one-day all-rounders. In Test matches I probably under-use myself. Basically, I'm there to bowl 5 or 10 overs to give the front-lint bowlers a rest and, maybe, pick up a wicket. A wicket is a bonus, but it does happen and so far I've taken 17 in Test matches. The majority have been batsmen, not tail-enders, and most have gone to false shots. The sight of bowlers like me appearing has a funny effect on batsmen – some relax, others make not getting out to this part-time bowler their main objective. When Geoff Boycott put the ball in his hand, you could see batsmen dreading the worst and starting to concentrate like mad. I bowl a bit quicker than Boycs did and have a career best of 7 for 14 against Worcestershire at Ilford in 1982. But I remember Keith Fletcher warning me not to tire myself out bowling when it might affect my batting. That's the job I'm paid to do, not bowling. Ian Chappell was my first Test victim and Malcolm Marshall is my 'rabbit' – I've dismissed him three times.

At Headingley our less-than-tight attack brought me into action a lot earlier than I had planned. The Kiwis hit 87 off the first 20 overs and Chris Lewis went for 28 in his first four. I doubled my tally of wickets for the season by removing both openers, but Martin Crowe and Mark Greatbatch kept the New Zealand reply on course with 118 runs in the next 20 overs. They didn't miss a run and Greatbatch soon demonstrated what a powerful hitter he is – I particularly remember a punched drive off Derek Pringle that soared over the mid-wicket boundary for six. The Kiwis stuttered a bit, going from 224 for 2 to 259 for 6 after they needed 72 runs off the final 12 overs with eight wickets in hand. But Ian Smith joined Greatbatch and the keeper won the game with a boundary off the penultimate ball.

Greatbatch's maiden one-day hundred was the backbone of New Zealand's victory charge – their 298 for 6 was the highest total by a side batting second in any one-day international. It was a great effort, but we had helped them on the way with bowling that wasn't up to standard. Phil DeFreitas, who's often conceded less than three-an-over, went for 70 runs in 10.5, while Derek Pringle had 45 hit off his seven overs. Chris Lewis recovered well after his bad start, his final seven overs costing 26 runs as he dismissed Crowe, Ken Rutherford and Richard Hadlee.

I was disappointed, but not distraught. Sides are so much better equipped at chasing totals now. When I first started, 160 to 190 used to win games. Now you are never safe. With the four-men-in-the circle rule, there are always gaps. You have to bowl to your field. We didn't at Headingley, and we paid the penalty.

We made one change for the Oval clash with Devon Malcolm coming in for Derek Pringle. And Devon confounded all of us who thought he was too erratic for the limited-overs game by starting with four maidens and finishing with figures of 11–5-19–2. I was pleasantly surprised – his bowling was as good as any I had seen in a one-day game. But Chris Lewis was the bowler who inflicted most damage after I won the toss and put New Zealand in. The wicket had pace and bounce and Chris looked very sharp indeed. After Devon and Chris reduced the Kiwis to 54 for 3, the tourists lost Rutherford and Hadlee through injury. Rutherford, without a helmet, went to hook, but was only half-way through his shot when the ball hit him above the left eye with a fearsome crack. No bowler likes causing injury and I had to have a few words with

Chris as Rutherford lay on the ground (he was in no state to continue and was taken off to hospital). I understand the incident converted him to wearing a helmet again.

Hadlee's injury, potentially more serious, happened in much more mundane circumstances. A lifting ball from Chris hit him on the gloves shortly before lunch, but he carried on without any delay. We weren't aware there was any great problem, but after further inspection during the break, he too went off to King's College Hospital for an X-ray. That revealed a broken bone just below the knuckle, rather similar to my injury in Trinidad, and put his participation in the Cornhill Test series in doubt, although he returned to bowl his quota of overs that afternoon. Rutherford was less fortunate and was detained overnight.

Greatbatch completed his second century in three days, but with less support than at Leeds, and the Kiwis managed only 212 for 6 in their 55 overs. Greatbatch had been involved in a lengthy debate with umpire David Constant about whether some of our shorter deliveries should be called 'wides'. In New Zealand the regulations stipulate that any ball above shoulder height is a 'wide', whereas in England it's above head height. I think we have it right, but I certainly believe that, whatever the ruling, it should be the same throughout the cricket world.

Greatbatch had been at the other end when Rutherford was injured and this obviously added to his concern. But his dialogue with Constant went on far too long. At one stage Constant went across to his fellow umpire, John Hampshire, to inform him of Greatbatch's complaints. When Greatbatch was out, he had further discussions with Constant on his way back to the pavilion. Constant asked for an apology, but received none, although Greatbatch was subsequently fined by the New Zealand management. We discovered later that this confrontation was the reason Constant withdrew from the Test panel. He had just returned to the list after a season off and had been due to officiate in the first Test at Trent Bridge. But he admitted he was close to walking off at the Oval, and he wanted no further part in Test cricket.

Players today have a lot more to say to umpires – and are a lot less willing to accept decisions. It's a matter of discipline, or rather a lack of it. I don't see why umpires should be abused. Verbal dissent has been creeping into the game for a while now and it's time it was stamped out. Umpires should be given more teeth, the power to stop the trouble on the field before it spreads. Reporting the player at the end of the day's play is useless – the damage has been done by then. Rugby's always impressed me in that area. The minute there's any backchat about a referee's award of a penalty, the offending side is penalized 10 yards. It's a short, sharp punishment, but, most importantly, it's effective since it often puts the other side within scoring range for a penalty. That's not possible in cricket and I don't believe in penalizing sides runs or wickets – that would upset the whole balance of the game. But I'm in favour of players being sent off. Not for the whole match, perhaps, but for an hour or a session. A captain would soon put a stop to unruly behaviour if it lost him a front-line batsman or bowler at a vital time.

With a target of 213 for victory and Hadlee injured, we were pretty hopeful of success. But after six overs, England were 29 for 3 with David Gower, Robin Smith and Allan Lamb gone. A broken hand appeared to be no handicap to Hadlee, who took the first two wickets. And even when I began to look settled, he came back and bowled a couple of brilliant overs. You're never safe when Hadlee's about; batting can suddenly become a very hazardous occupation. But, with good support from Alec Stewart and Jack Russell, we won by six wickets with 5.3 overs to spare. My undefeated 112 earned me the Man of the Match award. More importantly, this victory gave us the Texaco Trophy on the basis of a better run-rate.

New Zealand worries about Hadlee and Rutherford eased. Rutherford, who had suffered a hairline fracture of the skull, determined that after two years without a helmet, he would wear one in future. He claimed that, had Devon been bowling, he would have called for one, but that he hadn't realized that Chris Lewis was so quick. Hadlee, too, was optimistic of being fit for the Tests. Although it was a similar injury to mine, he would benefit from being a bowler. If he needed to protect the hand, he could always bat at number 11. It was obvious that he was desperate not to miss his Trent Bridge farewell after his many successful years there with Nottinghamshire.

First Test, Trent Bridge

Chris Lewis's form earned him a place in the England 12 for the first Test, David Gower being the only casualty from the Texaco squad. David hadn't performed well after filling in as opener. When Wayne Larkins had withdrawn, we needed someone to do that job and asked David. He had performed creditably there when skipper against the Australians the previous summer. I phoned David with the bad news. It was the third time in two months sincc losing his England place that he had come close to regaining it. The role of a Test opener is somewhat different from that in a limited-over game and Michael Atherton was picked after his successful winter tour with England A. Mike had been batting three for Lancashire, unable to break up the Graeme Fowler–Gehan Mendis partnership. But I felt the opening spot was his best position – and the fact that he was flexible enough to bat in the middle order was an advantage for him and England. Mike was going to be my sixth opening partner in my last nine Tests. People wonder whether that's a problem. I find it doesn't affect the way I play, though obviously it's helpful if you know your partner's game and vice versa. The only regular partner I had had in all the years I'd opened for England, was Geoff Boycott. I remember that during a 'Question of Sport' television show I was asked what half-a-dozen or so England batsmen had in common. All I could think of was that they had all opened in Tests. The correct answer was that they'd all opened with me!

If you are the senior partner, it's part of your job to settle the other player. But it works both ways. Even the most experienced players need their confidence and egos boosting; it's important that you and your partner keep talking. Boycs was a great talker, encouraging me and telling me to think positively. And, despite all that's been said about him, he ran me out only once – against the West Indies in 1980. In one-day cricket, the openers have to be good judges of quick runs and take them unfailingly to keep the score moving. I remember being involved in three run-outs in a week with John Stephenson at Essex. In the one-day game you have to rely on the call of your partner. The more you play together, the more you get to know each other's running habits, and the less likely you are to run your partner out.

Neil ('Harvey') Fairbrother was the one player who had not toured the previous winter to make the squad. But he was accumulating runs at an astonishing rate and gave credence to our insistence that entry to the England side wasn't a closed shop. Anyone scoring runs and taking wickets had a chance to make the Test team. Neil had been the outstanding batsman in May and had worked hard for the chance to revive his Test career; he's also a first-rate fielder. Alec Stewart reverted to number 3 after playing in the last two Tests in the West Indies as opener, so 'Harvey' was going to have to bat at number 6.

This was an important series for England, and not only to prove that the winter success wasn't a flash in the pan. Since reclaiming the Ashes in 1985 we had struggled badly at home. Both India and New Zealand had won their 1986 series; Pakistan had triumphed in 1987; and the West Indies had blown us away 4–0 in 1988. The following summer had brought a similar scoreline against the Australians. Worse still, in the course of those series – a total of 22 Tests – we had failed to win a single match. The long-suffering English public had been very supportive and patient. It was time to give them something to cheer about.

Essex's win over Worcestershire in the championship had completed the first half of a revenge double for the county's 1989 disappointments. Unfortunately, our plans to make Notts pay for their last-ball victory in the Benson & Hedges final went astray. We had the advantage of a home draw in the quarter-final of the 1990 competition but struggled after being put in. At lunch, we'd only scored 137 for 5 off 37 overs. I was still in and needed to be there at the end, but I went for 87 and we could do no better than 216 for 8 in the 55 overs. Notts skipper Tim Robinson and Paul Johnson saw them home with overs to spare, and our interest in the B&H was over for another season.

Before the Cornhill Test series got underway, Essex's game with Middlesex reunited me with one of my adversaries from the winter, Desmond Haynes. And it was an all-too familiar scene as he spent the entire first day at the crease, running up a double hundred. Gordon Greenidge might not have been around, but Desmond found a more than adequate substitute in Middlesex's Mike Roseberry, who hit 135 in an opening stand of 306. Essex had to follow-on, as John Emburey claimed five wickets and Paul Downton took five catches. But, after a duck in the first innings, I got my act together with a century in the second and we saved the game comfortably. I was playing as well as I'd done for years. The next stage was to transform that into runs for England.

The 1990 summer will be remembered for the glorious weather and the record number of runs scored. But rain interrupted all three Tests against New Zealand, especially the opening encounter. Two hours were lost on the first day, only 23 minutes were possible the next, and on the third day, Saturday, play was possible only until noon. Nobody wants rain. Players accept it as part of the job. I feel more disappointed for the crowd. Cricket fans look forward to seeing Test cricket. They pay good money but, if there's a single ball bowled, there's no refund. It's the most frustrating part of the game for me. Players don't pray for rain; you can't get points while you're stuck in the dressing-room – and even a couple of bonus points may make a crucial difference at the end of a season. The dressing-room certainly becomes a hive of activity on rainy days. It used to be cards and not much else; nowadays, it's the personal stereo and the portable phone.

John Wright had won the toss and decided to bat. Chris Lewis had failed a fitness test, so our four bowlers were Devon Malcolm, Phillip DeFreitas, Gladstone Small and Eddie Hemmings. They had the best of the first day as the tourists struggled to 171 for 5. Repeated interruptions tend to unsettle batsmen more than bowlers. It gives the latter a rest, while the batsmen are always having to play themselves in again. No matter how well you are playing, you're never settled. The ground staff had struggled to get the covers on quickly during the first of the four breaks because they had to be manoeuvred from behind the advertising hoardings. John Wright was unhappy and made his feelings known to the Test & County Cricket Board representatives. The innings of the day came from Martin Crowe, whose 59 was in a class apart from the others. It was a great relief when Daffy, the pick of our attack, bowled him near the close. The wicket had been slow and dead at the start, but it quickened up during the day as Daffy began to swing the ball. Crowe was his one success on Thursday; then he had Priest caught behind first ball after the five o'clock start on Friday and finally cleaned up the tail on Saturday morning. He finished with 5 for 53, his best Test return, as the Kiwis were dismissed for 208. Daffy's bowling had changed in character over the years. He'd lost some of his pace, but his bowling was more accurate. He rediscovered that zip over the next 12 months. A cricket curiosity occurred with Martin Snedden's innings of nought. He scored no runs, but batted during the first three days of the match.

Despite the large amount of time lost on Thursday and Friday, we were still in a good position. If we batted for five sessions, we could hope for a lead of around 250 and the last day to press for a win. But the rain ended that scenario at mid-day on Saturday after just 13 balls of our innings. Sadly, that was 12 more deliveries than I lasted: for the first time in my Test career I was out first ball. I'd been around long enough to know it was going to happen some time, but it still dented my pride. And, after the form I'd been showing, it was a disappointing start to my Test summer. What made it worse was that John Hampshire gave me out leg before. That mode of dismissal reminded everyone of my problems with Terry Alderman in 1989. It was a marginal decision, and I was disappointed with the umpire's verdict: I had thought the ball was going to miss leg stump.

The rain started five minutes later and that was the end of our victory chances. It hadn't been a great opening three days for me. My car window had been smashed on Thursday night, although nothing was stolen. My Friday evening meal didn't agree with me and I was up most of the night being sick. They say bad luck comes in threes and the golden duck was my final pay-off.

Although our chance of victory had gone, New Zealand could conceivably still win if Hadlee ripped into us early on Monday morning. Once we had weathered that storm, this Test headed towards its inevitable end. But the great thing about Test cricket is that a lot can be salvaged and learnt even in these circumstances. Our players had the chance to bat for two days, at their own pace and in their own way. A responsible knock here would almost certainly guarantee a test place for the summer duration. It was a prospect that Geoff Boycott used to relish and one which Mike Atherton accepted with similar enthusiasm.

Mike's Test baptism had been less pleasant the previous summer when he came into a side that had already lost the Ashes. He'd just missed out on the West Indies tour and was injured when the late call for the Caribbean came his way. Here he showed the temperament and authority of a senior Test player. His knock of 151 established his role for the summer. Mike's a solid player, not easy to get out; he copes with the short ball and has a good armoury of shots. He's not a flamboyant type; he has developed the method that works best for him. He enjoyed the challenge of meeting one of the great all-time bowlers in Hadlee and was soon displaying his excellent defensive technique. Lots of good young batsmen have flair and can attack, but they haven't learnt how and when to defend. That's not being negative; a good defence is necessary if you want to survive at Test level.

Mike was 78 overnight and had provided early stability after Hadlee had threatened briefly when we were reduced to 45 for 3. Even the manner of Mike's century showed maturity, as he cut Snedden for four. He'd been on 98 for 22 balls and that would have tested the nerve of the most experienced Test batsman. But the young Lancastrian, only 22 and in his third Test, appeared the calmest person at Trent Bridge, where his Test career had started with a duck 10 months earlier. Even more impressively, Mike went on to pass 150 in an innings which lasted for over eight hours. He was the youngest England century-maker since David Gower against India in 1978, and it seemed likely that an illustrious career lay ahead of him. Of course, he was billed by the tabloids as the 'Boy Wonder' and the answer to England's cricket problems, but Micky and I tried to reduce the euphoria to reasonable proportions. Mike, a Manchester Grammar School student and Cambridge University graduate, had all the right credentials and had made a very good start to his Test career. But that was all it was: a start.

Second Test, Lord's

England picked the same 12 for the Lord's Test after Chris Lewis confirmed his fitness with a 50 in Leicestershire's four-wicket victory over the tourists. Despite the problems with the weather, we had batted and bowled reasonably well and certainly held the upper hand in the first Test. But there was nothing to get complacent about, especially as New Zealand could now call upon the services of a sporting knight: Richard Hadlee had been honoured in the Queen's Birthday Honours list. Some said it was the first time a bowler had been knighted since Sir Francis Drake. What was certain was that he was the first cricketer to be honoured in this way while still playing on the Test circuit. The Lord's match score-card became a collector's item and the electronic scoreboard displayed 'Sir R Hadlee'. John Wright, New Zealand's captain, acknowledged Hadlee's contribution to his country's cricket: 'We've been calling him "Sir Richard" for years.'

Hadlee's attitude to the game had attracted a fair amount of criticism over the years. He was unerringly single-minded in what he regarded was the best for him and his Test career. But the bottom line came out in his favour. At 39 he was still at the top of his profession – and he went out at the top. He might not have had quite the zip of the old days, but could still turn a Test batting line-up upside down. Hadlee's way of looking after himself had a bearing on his being able to continue into his 40th year. Most bowlers of his era hadn't made it past the mid-thirties; Hadlee had outlasted them all. His feat of taking five wickets in an innings more than 100 times is one of the most remarkable achievements in sport.

I first played against him in 1978. He had nearly joined Essex the previous season. Keith Boyce was injured and Hadlee agreed to join us for the final six weeks of the season. Lord's insisted on a three-year contract, but New Zealand were due to tour the following summer and we didn't want to commit ourselves. If we'd seen him for those six weeks, he might well have joined Essex, not Nottinghamshire. I got back into Test cricket in 1978, but the Hadlee I faced then wasn't the finished article we later knew. He later shortened his run and changed his style.

Hadlee was a great one for setting himself targets. That has never been my style, but it worked for him. And life hadn't been easy for him because he has had to carry New Zealand's Test attack for over a decade. If he didn't make his overs count, then

New Zealand struggled. But, consistently and frequently, Hadlee produced the goods. And Hadlee the batsman certainly benefited from the introduction of helmets. They gave him confidence at the crease; he could be a savage hitter, and he scored over 3,000 Test runs. When he arrived at Notts in 1978, they moved him up the batting order from number 11 to 6, and the new responsibility worked wonders. As well as heading the English bowling averages for four of the first five seasons in the 1980s, he achieved the double in 1984, the first player to do so since Fred Titmus in 1967. Notts won the championship in 1981 and 1987, Hadlee's final season with the county. It was amazing that Hadlee's career should coincide with three other great Test all-rounders – Ian Botham, Kapil Dev and Imran Khan – all of whom have scored over 3,000 Test runs and taken 300 Test wickets. Of the four, I would say that Hadlee was the outstanding performer with the ball, although the others were better batsmen.

John Wright put us in at Lord's (where the delay in completion of the new Nursery End stand reduced the capacity all summer) and allowed Hadlee to lead the tourists out. As I walked to the middle, I mentioned to Mike Atherton that I didn't want to be the first batsman to be bowled by a knight in Test cricket. I'd offered my congratulations to Sir Richard during nets the previous day. Mike did go early on, but Danny Morrison was the successful bowler. After Mike's marathon knock at Trent Bridge, he lasted just 11 balls. I just hoped that those who crowned him king after Nottingham weren't going to demand his abdication now. The lad was finding his way in Test cricket and doing so fairly successfully. His was the only wicket to fall on Thursday, not because we batted so well, but thanks to the rain that reduced play to less than an hour. The Lord's Test is always a big occasion and it was a great disappointment when play was finally abandoned for the day at 4.30.

Alec Stewart was the first to have the honour of being dismissed by a cricket knight when he was trapped lbw, but not before scoring his maiden Test 50. I was caught and bowled by John Bracewell for 85; I was annoyed with myself because I've let a few hundreds go begging and it was over two years since my last century for England. Bracewell did me in the flight. It was the right shot – I was trying to hit it over the bowler's head – and I made good contact, but my feet were too close to the ball and he took a good catch. At one stage, England were 216 for 3, but we finished the day at 329 for 8. Robin Smith was the other half-century maker before he miscued the ball to mid-on. The biggest disappointment was another failure by Neil Fairbrother – and even that came after he had been given a life. The difference between Neil Fairbrother the Test player and Neil Fairbrother the county batsman was extraordinary and he was running out of chances to make the transition.

England added only five runs on the Saturday morning before the Kiwis started their reply; but again the rain had the final word, with over two hours lost after tea. New Zealand had made a good start, and Wright and Franklin were still together at the close with an opening stand of 156. It was very frustrating. All eight days of Test cricket in this glorious summer had been shortened by bad weather. The two New Zealand innings I shall remember were of contrasting styles. Trevor Franklin's maiden Test hundred took 309 balls, while Hadlee's swashbuckling 86 lasted only 84 deliveries, with 12 fours and two sixes. Franklin's seven-hour stay produced eight boundaries, none of them sixes. Hadlee had come to New Zealand's rescue as they'd tumbled from 278 for 1 to 285 for 5 and, with support from keeper Ian Smith, a very useful Test number 9, boosted their total to 462, a first-innings lead of 128. Devon Malcolm was our best bowler on a wicket that gave him little help. He finished with 5 for 94 in his 43 overs. Alan Lee in *The Times* commented that Devon might have produced those figures off 15 overs in days gone by – testimony to his rapid progress as a Test bowler.

New Zealand's lead allowed them to attack us on the final day without fear and Mike Atherton was fortunate to escape a pair when the umpire's no-ball overtook the wicket-keeper's appeal for a catch behind. Smith then dropped a simple chance, again off Hadlee, when Mike had made four. With those chances went New Zealand's slim victory hopes and the match headed towards the expected draw, with Allan Lamb hitting an undefeated 84; Robin Smith trod on his stumps before scoring and Neil Fairbrother used the final hour to make his highest Test score of 33. By the finish

Hadlee, with a strained hamstring, and Snedden, with a sore shoulder, were back in the New Zealand dressing-room. After two Tests, we hadn't progressed beyond the third innings and both sides could claim they had dominated one of the Tests. I was searching for some more tangible proof of our improvement and hoped Edgbaston would provide it. My position as England captain was confirmed for the India series during the final day at Lord's; after these two uneventful Tests, it was difficult not to look beyond this New Zealand series.

Essex started their NatWest campaign the day after the Lord's Test finished. Round one is giant-killing time, when the counties meet other qualifiers. Leicestershire and Hampshire were the only two Championship counties facing each other, Hampshire triumphing by one run to earn a trip to Chelmsford to face us in round two. Scotland were our first-round opponents, the second time we had come across them this year – they'd been in our Benson & Hedges zonal group. In that match I'd been run out for two by South African Omar Henry, after colliding with the bowler. This time I was more careful and scored a century to take the Man of the Match award as Essex won by nine wickets.

After the problems of 1988 and 1989, England managed to field an unchanged squad for the entire New Zealand series, although Angus Fraser was included for the squad practice and preparation in Birmingham: Middlesex had no game, and it was a good idea to bring Gus back into the set-up. He's obviously part of England's long-term Test plans for the 1990s. We'd been fighting to get him fit for the fourth Test in Barbados at the start of April and it was now early July, so the seriousness of his injury could be judged. Essex met New Zealand over the weekend prior to the Test; there were plenty of runs about. Wright, Martin Crowe, John Stephenson and myself all hit hundreds. As far as my form was concerned, I hoped it was an omen for Edgbaston.

Third Test, Edgbaston

World Cup fever was all around as we prepared for the Test: Bobby Robson's soccer side had their semi-final against West

Germany on the Wednesday evening. We sent off good luck telegrams, just as they had done to us in the West Indies. Like us, they had been given little or no chance; like us, they got within sight of their goal before faltering. The lads dispensed with the sit-down team dinner in favour of a buffet, so we could watch the semi-final. It was agonizing viewing and England didn't deserve to go out like that. I don't think penalty shoot-outs are unfair; the tie has to be settled somehow. Our experiences in the closing stages of the Caribbean tour left us knowing exactly how gutted our soccer counterparts would be feeling.

The wicket at Edgbaston looked pretty good to me and I was surprised when John Wright, after winning his third toss of the series, asked us to bat. Later he admitted: 'I was wrong to put England in. No two ways about it. It was a bad decision.' I would have batted if given the choice. Chris Lewis came in for his Test debut after Phillip DeFreitas withdrew because of hamstring trouble. New Zealand's wicket-keeper Ian Smith had a similar complaint and his replacement, Adam Parore, who was only 19, was also playing in his first Test.

The rain, as it had done at Trent Bridge and Lord's, soon got into the act and the Test didn't begin until nearly three o'clock on the Thursday. There were also problems with the Brumbrella, Edgbaston's giant motorized wicket cover, which failed to deploy, so conventional covering was used for the rest of the match.

I've always been a bit wary of Edgbaston, despite the fact that it's rapidly becoming England's favourite ground. England have won 15 of their 27 Tests here, losing only twice. Unfortunately, the first time was in my Test debut, when I collected a pair against the 1975 Australians. This 1990 visit proved much more successful: Mike Atherton and I put on 170 for the first wicket and England finished the day at 191 for 1. That was the positive response I'd planned after we'd been put in. I passed 1,000 runs for season, as did Mike; and earlier I'd reached 5,000 Test runs, the eleventh Englishman to do so.

Overnight I was on 95 and thoughts of my ninth Test century were certainly hard to ignore. Since my eighth – 146 against the 1988 West Indies at Trent Bridge – I'd scored 84 against Viv Richards' side at the Kennington Oval that same year and again at the Queen's Park Oval in 1990. I'd also scored 75 against Sri Lanka, 85 against the Kiwis at Lord's and seven 50s in all – but had failed to reach three figures. I was determined not to blow it this time and took 40 minutes accumulating those vital five runs. But I was also determined not to give it away, either, and dug in for a long stay so that we could build up a big total. I made 154 and we finished with 435. It should have been better, but had it not been for the solid batting of the later order, it might have been a lot worse. Our four middle order batsmen totalled 32 runs, and failures by Alec Stewart and Neil Fairbrother certainly put pressure on them to do well in the second innings. Hadlee took the catch to end my six-hour vigil; I was aiming Danny Morrison down the leg-side, but the ball hit the back of the bat and flew to second slip.

We had built the platform and a good Saturday would put us on the victory trail as New Zealand tried to save the follow-on. The Kiwis, despite some early damage by Devon Malcolm and Chris Lewis, whose first Test wicket – Martin Crowe's – was a good 'un, looked reasonably comfortable at 161 for 3 just before tea. Crowe initially didn't look at umpire Barry Meyer when Chris and the supporting cast appealed for leg before. The umpire had to raise his finger a second time before Crowe, who later apologized, went on his way.

Devon had started the rot when he bowled Mark Greatbatch, but then centre stage belonged to the oldest member of our side, whose county career had begun on this ground when another England soccer team had enjoyed World Cup glory – this time in 1966! Eddie Hemmings had never been a regular as his total of 11 matches over eight years before this match amply demonstrated. Nor was that surprising: the former Warwickshire, now Nottinghamshire, off-spinner had taken just 19 Test wickets. In fact, his outstanding Test performance was his 95 as night-watchman in the Sydney Test on the 1982–3 tour.

Eddie had spent a long time waiting for his chance, with John Emburey a permanent fixture in the Test side, although the pair had operated very effectively together during the 1987 Reliance World Cup in India. Embers was now serving a five-year Test ban for the South Africa tour with Mike Gatting's side, so Eddie had very little opposition. But the pressure was on now, and he responded with a spell of 6 for 33 in 90 balls that saw New Zealand collapse to 249 all out.

The tourists had prevented the follow-on – just – but we had a lead of 186 going into the final two days. The pitch and our fielding had helped Eddie, but once he had got his hooks into the Kiwi tail he wouldn't let go. Eddie often complained that he'd rarely been asked to bowl in such an attacking manner for England – but I don't think it's necessarily negative to tell your bowlers to keep it tight. Pressure brings wickets in test cricket because it stops the opposition scoring runs. Part of the stranglehold the West Indies have exerted on the cricket world in the past decade is that opponents have found it impossible to score runs quickly against them, while their own batsmen, with a natural inclination to attack, have the ability to butcher loose bowling.

Eddie had faced a fair amount of flak over his recent Test displays; it was good to see him on top for once. He was supported by some fine close catching – especially Robin Smith's effort at silly point to dismiss Franklin, who again proved a tough obstacle to remove in his four-hour stay, and Mike Atherton's dive at first slip to end Hadlee's innings. I felt that our display that afternoon had recaptured much of our Caribbean spirit.

I wanted quick runs on Monday, so that we would have enough time to bowl out New Zealand in their quest for what I hoped would be the 400-plus they would need for victory. That was the plan – but it went wrong after Mike Atherton and I had added 50 runs in even time. Hadlee and Bracewell seized the chance to exploit our chase for quick runs and took our last seven wickets for 29 runs. Only Mike Atherton kept his nerve, anchoring our total of 158 with a knock of 70.

Our collapse gave New Zealand an hour longer to bat than I'd wanted and 50 fewer runs needed for victory. Our middle order fared only marginally better the second time around and put question-marks against Fairbrother and Stewart's immediate Test prospects. Bracewell took four wickets and became the second New Zealander to achieve the Test double. The first – Sir Richard, of course – went one better and claimed five wickets for a record 36th time in a Test. He signed off his international bowling career with

5 for 17 in a remarkable eight-over spell. Devon Malcolm was really chuffed to be Hadlee's 431st and final Test victim.

We should have made the game safe, but our batting had given New Zealand a chance, albeit a slim one. It was crucial that we hit back on Monday evening. Runs weren't too important – they needed 345 to win – but we had to get amongst the wickets quickly. Our collapse had sheltered me from making a declaration, although I would have preferred to use my judgement. Maybe our failure had opened up our best chance of victory, but it's always better to be in control.

The Kiwis had reduced their target by more than 100 by the close, but both their openers had gone. Wright looked furious with himself when he steered Chris Lewis into Robin Smith's hands in the gully shortly before stumps.

A Test that should have had only two possible results – a win for us or a draw – now had three, owing to our carelessness. And then there was Hadlee. The man had a distinctive way of saying farewell: he'd left Nottinghamshire with the county championship and the NatWest Trophy; his Test finale in New Zealand brought another five-wicket haul and Australia's nine-wicket defeat. Now he was about to enter the fray for one last batting sortie, with the stage perfectly set for his special talents. This and other unpleasant possibilities flashed through my mind on Monday evening. I felt that, if we took our chances, we would win. But give players of the calibre of Crowe, Greatbatch, Jones and Hadlee half a chance, and they would make England pay.

The first chance came from Jones and it went flying above my head at second slip in the third over of the day. I got both hands to it and it stuck. That was just the start we needed, and soon afterwards Crowe was trapped leg before for the second time in the match. The Test was now effectively over. Eddie Hemmings, not for the first time, removed Greatbatch, then Devon returned the compliment and destroyed Hadlee's stump on his final visit to the crease. Devon also wiped up the tail to ensure our win by 124 runs – our first victory at home in a Test series for five years. Devon finished with 5 for 46 and was named Man of the Match. He was one player who was certainly continuing the progress shown in the Caribbean. Hadlee was named their Man of the Series and Mike Atherton was ours. Mike had really established himself, with 357 runs in the series at an average of 71. Just as significant was the mature way he made those runs. Here was a youngster who could look forward to a decade of Test cricket, and this success gave us something to build on for the second half of the summer against the Indians.

India, 1990

The next day, following our series winning Test, I came down to earth with a bang as Essex's interest in the one-day competitions came to a rather cruel end. We scored over 300 runs at Chelmsford, but Hampshire matched our total and made the quarter-finals because they had lost fewer wickets. I felt pretty peeved at scoring 144 – a new NatWest record for Essex – and finishing up on the losing side. Hampshire had needed seven runs for an outright win off the last over. Skipper Mark Nicholas and Jon Ayling brought them level at 307 with a ball to spare. But they'd lost only five wickets to our six, so Nicholas just played the final ball defensively rather than risk losing a wicket in the search for another run. His side had achieved the highest winning score by a side batting second in the NatWest. There's always a sense of disappointment in the club when you realize that the chance of a Lord's cup final has gone for another year. Essex have earned a reputation as a good one-day side in recent years, but that hasn't translated into silverware in the trophy cabinet. Our success in the 1979 Benson & Hedges Cup ended a 103-year wait for a trophy, and our NatWest triumph came six years later, when we beat Nottinghamshire by one run – our only appearance in a 60-over final. Notts gained revenge with a last-ball victory in the 1989 B&H final, the fourth time we'd come back empty-handed from Lord's in that competition.

There's another final now – the Refuge Assurance Cup, for which the top four sides in the Sunday League compete. We won the League three times in five years at the start of the 1980s. The Cup started in 1988, and we beat Notts in the final the following year. We weren't going to make that final this season either after our bad start in the Sunday League. I certainly feel that, with our resources, Essex should have a better one-day record than we do.

Worcestershire are another county which should have done better considering their talent. But their search for a Lord's trophy again ended in failure when they were beaten by Lancashire in the Benson & Hedges final on the second Saturday in July. It was their sixth attempt to beat that duck. The Lancashire skipper David Hughes himself had been involved in no fewer than eight Lord's finals – and he had collected six winner's medals. By the end of the summer, Lancashire had become the first county to win both Lord's finals in the same season and Hughes' cup haul had increased to seven.

The Indian tourists had arrived during our Lord's Test against New Zealand. Like the Kiwis, their strength lay in their batting. Their line-up was formidable – Shastri, Sidhu, Vengsarkar, Manjrekar, the teenage prodigy Tendulkar and Azharuddin, who had taken over as skipper. Their aggressive opener Srikkanth had lost not only the captaincy but his Test place as well. Kapil Dev and Prabhakar are no mean batsmen, either, so the Indians had a pretty short tail. Their bowling, however, was another matter. Kapil had been troubled with back problems recently and certainly wasn't taking Test wickets at the rate he used to. He had been Indian captain on their last tour of England four years earlier, when they won the series 2–0. That was his second spell as leader. In his first India had claimed the 1983 World Cup at Lord's. But it was a semi-final defeat in the 1987 World Cup, when England beat them in Bombay, that cost him the captaincy the second time around.

At 31, Kapil was the youngest of the four great all-rounders of the 1980s and he looked likely to be the first to reach 4,000 runs and 400 wickets in Tests. He had already got the runs and came to England with 364 wickets. The rest of India's bowling was much stronger in the spinning department than pace, but they had seldom played a decisive part in a series in England. That again proved to be the case, and my doubts about their lack of penetrative bowling were amply confirmed. Not an Indian tourist reached double figures in wickets taken during the series. Their batting, however, was still of the highest standard – as we discovered to our cost in the two Texaco matches.

Texaco Trophy

Headingley was again the venue for the opening Texaco game. David Gower returned to the side, with Alec Stewart (suffering from a back injury) and Neil Fairbrother omitted. John Morris, of Derbyshire, was a new face. John had always looked a talented batsman, but had recently become more consistent and had shown a more professional approach after earning a 'playboy' tag in his early days. He had been scoring a lot of runs for Derbyshire on wickets that are generally sporting. Nassar Hussain was still struggling to overcome his Caribbean wrist injury. He had come through his test of fire against the West Indies well and was obviously looking forward to taking on the less intimidating attacks of New Zealand and India. His form in the Caribbean would have earned him that opportunity, but it was not to be. In a run-filled season, Nasser was either recovering from injury or adjusting to his long lay-off. It must have been frustrating, but he was never allowed to put himself in a position to challenge for a Test spot. Still, Morris was the batsman in form, the man with the right credentials, and I'm sure we would have copped it in the press if we hadn't picked him.

The press are always ready to tell you who to select. Often those players are in our minds too but the media will still claim the credit, unless the newcomer does badly! All cricketers, not just Test or county captains, make mental notes about players. You never know when you are going to have to make a judgement about a player. I'm always keen to know how players, especially young ones, are progressing. I believe a shrewd captain talks to everyone. Umpires are good judges and often point out strengths and weaknesses that aren't always apparent. Moreover, umpires have no allegiances – they aren't promoting their own players. I'm not saying county captains try to get players into the Test team who don't deserve it, but they know their own players so well, sometimes too well. That may not always work in the candidate's favour. As the season progresses, you find that if one name keeps cropping up, you've probably got a genuine prospect. I like to take a cross-section of opinion, although I trust certain opinions more than others. Keith Fletcher, Mike Gatting and John Emburey are three whose assessments of players I value highly.

John Morris was omitted from the XI at Headingley, along with Gladstone Small. Angus Fraser was back at last and David Gower was to go in first wicket down. Azharuddin won the toss and put us in. We were bowled out for 229 with three deliveries remaining. That was a disappointment because two of the first four batsmen reached fifty and I hit 45. However, the spin of Shastri and, especially, Anil Kumble kept us pinned down in the middle of the innings.

Leg-spinner Kumble, only 20, looked a tremendous prospect on our first sighting and was nominated Man of the Match. He didn't concede a single boundary in his 11 overs; his prodigious spin brought him David Gower's wicket and then bounce did for Robin Smith. We were 186 for 4 at one stage, but faded badly in the closing stages.

Given India's batting line-up, it was going to be a struggle to defend that total, although Phillip DeFreitas gave us the perfect start when Raman pulled him to Mike Atherton at mid-wicket off the second ball of the innings (Daffy's first delivery having been a no-ball). But with such a modest target the Indians didn't have to take too many risks. Sanjay Manjrekar, son of Vijay who had played over 50 Tests for India, was on his first tour here and looked a batsman of real quality. We also had our first sighting of 17-year-old Sachin Tendulkar. He'd been only 16 years and 201 days old when he made his Test debut against Pakistan. At Headingley Tendulkar hit Eddie Hemmings, almost 24 years his senior, over his head for six, so there was little sign of this precocious youngster being intimidated by his elders and betters. But it was the old heads of Azharuddin and Shastri who saw the Indians home with two overs to spare. That was no surprise. We were 20 or 30 runs short of the total we needed to put any kind of pressure on the Indians. Blame for that lay with David Gower, Lambie and me. We all reached 45, but none of us passed 56. One of us should have made at least 80.

The most distressing aspect of our trip to Headingley was the racial taunting that Devon Malcolm received from one section of the hospitality boxes after the game. Leeds is no stranger to this disgusting behaviour – both Imran Khan and Viv Richards have been targets in the past. Devon went up to confront the heckler, but decided that drink was the real problem and merely warned him as to his future conduct in no uncertain terms. Devon was upset to think this could happen on 'home' territory. He'd started his cricket career in the Yorkshire League and might well have joined the county staff but for their policy of selecting only Yorkshire-born cricketers. Lambie and I had to calm him down before he got in his car, as we headed for the second Texaco clash at Trent Bridge.

Devon was left out at Nottingham, Gladstone Small replacing him after injury. India again won the toss, again put us in, and again won with some ease. I hardly got us off to an auspicious start when I played no shot at a delivery from Prabhakar and it removed my off-stump. No excuses. Just bad judgement. David Gower hit six boundaries in compiling 25, then was run-out when his mind appeared to be elsewhere. Lamb went the same way soon after, when he responded slowly to Mike Atherton's call. England were in some trouble at 62 for 3, but a century stand between Mike and Robin Smith, who went on to his second one-day England hundred of the summer, saved the day. Jack Russell chipped in with an enterprising fifty. Our total of 281 may have looked a good score, but the last six overs had brought us only 35 runs – for the loss of six wickets. With that many wickets in hand at the death, most sides would fancy scoring 10 an over at least.

Still, it was a defendable target provided we bowled well. But Gladstone's opening over went for 12, and thereafter we were never in the hunt. Angus Fraser was the only bowler not to go for more than 50 runs in his 11 overs. Manjrekar was again the anchor as Azharuddin, Vengsarkar and Sidhu all scored quickly; again Tendulkar came in and played some daring shots for a teenager. We might have found some success as a Test team, but England's one-day form had deteriorated badly. This was our 10th defeat in the last 11 completed matches. We had lost three Texaco matches out of four; our only victory had come on the one occasion we batted second. The trio of defeats had occurred as we struggled to protect totals. We weren't bowling as tightly as we should do. With men in the circle, it's imperative that you bowl to your field. At present too many loose deliveries were allowing opponents to belt the ball to unguarded parts of the field.

Daffy was in trouble after the game, when he was interviewed by the police. There were suggestions that he had gestured obscenely to the crowd after some barracking and heckling. He was seen by Inspector Ted Curtis, who had been part of the investigating team after Brian Clough hit two Nottingham Forest fans who ran onto the City Ground pitch. The matter went no further, but Daffy was warned that if he stepped out of line again he could face a hefty fine or worse.

Daffy was in the 12 for the Lord's Test which we picked immediately after the Texaco series. Gladstone Small had looked increasingly out of sorts and was omitted. John Morris, who hadn't got a game in the Texaco, retained his place in the squad and was certain to bat at number six in the Test, with David Gower coming in first wicket down. Morris would have preferred to bat higher, but, like Neil Fairbrother in the New Zealand series, he had to fit in where he could and I didn't see it as a major problem. The overriding concern for John Morris was that he was in the England team at last, and I'm sure he would have batted at number 11 if it had guaranteed that coveted England cap.

Before that Neil Fairbrother, out of favour with the Test selectors, displayed the other side of his batting ability when Lancashire came to Colchester just before the first Test. Claims that he was one of the most exciting and talented young bats in the country had seemed over the top during the New Zealand series. In fact, he'd looked more like a novice, playing some shots better suited to a beer match. My northern friends, however, assured me this was not the real Fairbrother. How right they were! With Lancashire going for a second-innings declaration, Neil thrashed our bowling all over the place. If he'd batted like that for England, he would already have been an established member of the side.

Essex were set 348 to win in 54 overs and we came home with six balls to spare. I was finding the middle of the bat fairly regularly with 177, and Mark Waugh and John Stephenson hit half-centuries for our third successive championship win. That took us from 15th place to seventh in the championship. The side was buzzing now, and although Middlesex were well clear at the top, we genuinely felt we had a chance of overtaking them on the run-in.

First Test, Lord's

I now headed off to Lord's, not knowing that the next five days of cricket were going to be the most significant of my England career and that the figure 333 was about to become my personal call sign for ever. The 1990 Lord's match turned out to be Gooch's Test. I can honestly say that it was the best Test match I've ever played in, not from a selfish point of view – it was a great feeling to pass 300, though I'd got close once before – but in terms of sheer Test match entertainment. Six centuries, including my triple hundred, were scored. I may have grabbed the headlines, but I've rarely seen a better innings than Azharuddin's 121 or more outrageous hitting than Kapil Dev's four successive sixes off Eddie Hemmings to save the follow-on. The test produced over 1,600 runs and a victory for England.

My hour of triumph might never have materialized if Azharuddin had done what I would have done and batted after winning the toss. When he called correctly, I thought we were sure to be fielding, but he surprised me and most of those at Lord's by asking England to bat. To be fair to the Indian captain, the atmosphere was pretty humid that morning; and if his wicket-keeper Keiran More had held on to a simple chance when I'd made 36, England would have been 61 for 2 and his decision might have been judged an inspired one. At that point Mike Atherton had already departed, bowled between bat and pad by Kapil Dev. But the rest of the day belonged to England and we reached 359 for 2 by the close. David Gower and I put on over 100 for the second wicket before umpire Nigel Plews decided David had given a chance to silly point. David, on his record 17th Test appearance at Lord's, was quite sure the ball had bounced off his pads.

Lambie joined me to begin the trickle of record-breaking efforts that became a torrent before the end of the summer. Lambie and

I had taken part in an unbroken third-wicket stand of 218 by the close, a new record against India. We had 104 and 194 respectively, becoming the first players to score four test centuries at Lord's. We couldn't have asked for a better start, but I was absolutely shattered. I was suffering from an ear infection and was almost falling asleep at the dinner table when I went out with Doug Insole and his wife Norma in Primrose Hill. Brenda wasn't with me. You can't plan the big scores: she was coming to watch on the Saturday!

A triple century wasn't on my mind at that stage. I wanted to carry on, but with the strength and depth our batting had, I was more interested in posting a total of around 600. This we achieved on Friday, finishing up with 654 for 3 declared. By then I was the proud possessor of that 333 total, the highest score ever made at Lord's, the highest by an England captain, the third highest by an English man in Tests and the sixth highest in all. And I ended up only 32 behind the all-time record 365 of Sir Gary Sobers. When I was asked what it felt like afterwards, I answered 'OK'. I suppose even by my standards that was fairly low-key, but it hadn't really sunk in. I was emotionally, physically and mentally drained – and I was still captain of a side trying to win a Test match.

I remember going in to tea on 299. In that last over, Robin Smith was looking for an extra run, but I told him to bat normally. There was no panic and I wasn't going to do anything stupid. My previous best was 275 and I remembered how bitterly disappointed I had been not to make three hundred. I promised myself if I ever got close again, I'd make sure next time. You don't get many chances, and not only because you're not batting well enough. A number of factors have to come together, the most important one being time. How often does a match allow you enough time to make that sort of score? I'd been around for over 15 years and had had only one previous opportunity to get close. I fully understand Martin Crowe's anger at ending up on 299 against the Sri Lankans at the start of 1991. He had the final three deliveries of the Test to reach the magic number – and was caught off the last ball!

Once you pass the 250 mark, the 300 target more and more dominates your thoughts. I slowed up as I moved towards it. I wasn't nervous, just determined not to make a mistake. I took no chances at all during the final 10 runs. But it's not all selfishness;

you can't completely forget what's happening in the match.

The tea break wasn't without its moments of apprehension. I didn't take my pads off; just changed my shirt. The first ball after tea, however, brought relief when I glanced Shastri for a single. Brenda had been watching my progress on TV. Unfortunately, racing from Ascot was being shown at the time I reached the landmark and she was told of the fact by David Lloyd of the Press Association on the telephone.

The ultimate test target for batsmen is Sir Gary Sobers' 365. I was half-way towards it on the final assault on cricket's Mount Everest when I played a lazy drive and Prabhakar hit my off stump. Nobody can be unhappy with 333, but slowly a feeling of anti-climax enveloped me because I'd got so close and probably would never have the chance again. But that innings has put me on the map. Nobody will ever again be lost for words when they see me. Geoff Hurst lives nearby and says that not a day has gone by since the 1966 World Cup without someone mentioning that hat-trick in the final. That's how he's remembered. My trademark now is 333. Sobers' 365 represents the number of days in the year; my three threes is the best hand in brag – it even beats three aces. I don't think I'm a better batsman because of it, but it has certainly elevated me to a higher plane in some strange way. There's a list of records I broke at the back of this book; that's been for others to research. The headline in *The Times* read: 'Gooch makes triple century and attains greatness at last.' I'm not sure about that, but that 333 has given Graham Gooch an everlasting identity inside and outside cricket.

Of course, the easy wicket, Azharuddin's blunder in fielding first and the lacklustre Indian bowling started to eat into my achievement in some eyes. I resented that. The runs still had to be made and I could only score them against those playing. Memories play tricks on some of the older followers. When Sobers hit his undefeated 365 at Kingston in 1958, the Pakistanis had only two uninjured specialist bowlers in their attack, but nobody thinks any less of that innings because of that. I know some of the Indian bowling was mediocre, but that's not my fault. It was my job to take advantage of it, which I did. One factor not mentioned by those waving the damp cloth was that while Sobers was 21 when he set the record that beat Sir Len Hutton's 364 (Hutton was 22 at the Oval in 1938), I had celebrated my 37th birthday the week before. I wasn't as exhausted as I'd been on Thursday, but I was still pretty weary.

I don't want it to appear as if nobody else was playing for England in this Test. We had great knocks from David Gower, Allan Lamb and Robin Smith, the last two hitting hundreds. The only Englishman to suffer on account of my innings was John Morris who had to wait nearly two days before walking out to the wicket – and then had to walk back in almost immediately when I declared. In an ideal world he would have batted out the day, but we needed to get at the Indian batsmen. We had shown what a good wicket this was and the Indian batting line-up might well take full advantage of the favourable conditions, just as we had done.

If we thought the Indians were going to dig in and fight a dour rearguard action, we were in for a nasty shock. Attack was their form of defence and they weren't badly placed at the end of the Saturday with a total of 376 for 6, and with Azhuraddin and Kapil at the wicket. The Indians had batted magnificently, a tremendous effort considering our total. Even though I was on the receiving end, I could still appreciate the marvellous shots being played. Mohammad Azharuddin's innings was out of the very top drawer. His century came up in only 88 balls, a remarkable achievement as he was batting to save the Test ... or so I thought! His dazzling, wristy strokeplay was the day's star attraction, but Ravi Shastri's ton, a more solid knock, gave the tourists a good start. I took the catch at mid-on when he mis-hit Eddie Hemmings. Earlier I'd had Manjrekar caught behind in my opening over. It was my only dismissal of the season. I may not get many victims, but I make sure to choose classy victims! (My only success in 1989 had come during the third Ashes Test, when I picked up the wicket of Mark Taylor.)

Devon Malcolm, after a good series against New Zealand, had begun to lose form. Sometimes he gave the impression that he was not quite with it. But he was still inexperienced at Test match cricket. Devon's capable of bowling aggressively and of taking wickets at the highest level. Ideally, he needs two steady bowlers to support him – dependable types to act as foil to his 'wild card'. Asking him to bowl tight is, basically, to misuse him. He had proved at Port of Spain and at Edgbaston that he could be the quickest man on show. Chris Lewis bowled a good spell on the Saturday, but his only success was when Tendulkar stepped to leg to hit him through cover, à la Viv Richards, and was bowled. I was criticized for not bringing Eddie Hemmings on until the 57th over, but I felt we had more chance of success with our pace attack.

We began on Monday with India needing 78 runs to save the follow-on. Once they reached the safety of 454, a draw looked the likely result. The tourists certainly didn't edge their way to safety: they got there – by one run – in just 65 minutes, with Kapil plundering 63 of them. It could have been so different, because I was convinced I had picked him up at second slip in Angus Fraser's first over of the day. The ball went straight into my hands, but Kapil stood there waiting for the umpire's decision. Nigel Plews was unsighted at the bowler's end and consulted with Dickie Bird who was standing at square leg. But he couldn't help and Kapil was given not out. You can't give a decision if you can't see it. I wasn't angry with Kapil, he was quite within his rights to stand there. But something's amiss when neither of the two officials on the field can see what's happened.

Enforcing the follow-on still looked a distinct possibility when we had reduced India to 430 for 9 and Hirwani, an authentic number 11, wandered out to partner Kapil. The newcomer survived the final ball of Gus Fraser's over, leaving Kapil to get the 24 runs needed for safety. Kapil blocked the first two balls from Eddie Hemmings – then smashed the next four into the building works at the Nursery End for six apiece. It was the most amazing piece of hitting I've ever seen in a Test Match and summed up India's whole approach to our huge total. That Kapil's onslaught was not only justified but absolutely vital was apparent when Hirwani was out leg before to the first ball of the next over, giving Gus a well deserved 5 for 104. I kept waiting for this match to revert to some sort of normality, but something extraordinary kept happening. If Kapil had failed, one of two things would have happened: either the match would have headed to an uneventful draw, or we would have won easily. Now that India had saved the follow-on, the match was still alive.

We went for quick runs to add to our 199 first-innings lead and were able to declare 471 ahead during the final session on the Monday. I was in the runs again, making 123 this time, and that gave me a record aggregate of 456 in a Test, beating Greg Chappell's 380. No one before had scored a triple century and a hundred in the same first-class match. I was surprised by that. Mike Atherton continued his good form with 72 as we put on 204 together, then the middle order batted unselfishly and that allowed us an hour's bowling at the Indians. This was proving such an incredible Test that it crossed by mind more than once that the tourists could pull it off. But Devon and Gus each dismissed an opener and India finished the day at 57 for 2.

The course of the final day was probably the most predictable of the five, and England duly achieved victory just before three o'clock. Well, the final act was not quite predictable, because the win was sealed when England's mid-on pounced on the ball and flattened the middle stump at the bowler's end, leaving Sharma stranded. The fielder was me and I don't think I've done anything so spectacular in the field since my school days. It had been a solid team performance on this last day. The four bowlers had chipped away at the Indian batsmen. Manjekar, Vengsarkar, Azharuddin and Tendulkar all got starts, but none reached 40. The run-aggregate of 1,603 was a record for a Lord's Test, beating the 1930 Ashes clash by two runs. England, and especially I, were on top of the world, but it would be wrong to forget the contribution Azharuddin and his team had made to this Test. Without their positive approach, it could easily have been just another Test match. Now it's my Test. I like that. It's not something you can plan or work for. But they can't take it away from you once it happens. My 'new life' as a celebrity began the following day when Littlewoods asked me to present a cheque for £1,556,070 to that week's treble-chance winner.

Second Test, Old Trafford

That night Brenda and I travelled up to Linden Hall, outside Newcastle, to prepare for the Callers'-Pegasus two one-day matches between England and the Rest of the World at Jesmond. The Caller brothers, Ian and Roy, had done a great job in bringing international cricket to that part of the world and I certainly enjoyed my visits there. It was always a sell-out and I'm sure that that enthusiasm will be reflected in the support Durham receive when they enter the county championship.

I led England in the first match and we won by nine wickets. At the dinner that night, which marked the Callers' last sponsorship of this event, I handed the captaincy over to Allan Lamb and, jokingly, added that I hoped he would make a better job of it than the previous time I had transferred leadership to him in the West Indies. He didn't, because England lost by 10 wickets, though I think he suffered a Rest of the World backlash after their heavy defeat on the first day.

I'm often asked if it isn't an anti-climax going from an occasion like that Lord's Test match to the run-of-the-mill county scene. It's not run-of-the-mill for me and I feel sorry for any cricketer who thinks that way. Cetainly, we all relish the big-match atmosphere, but the county matches have their own special rewards. I enjoy playing for Essex just as much as I do for England. By now our march up the 1990 table was gaining real impetus when we returned to Southend to face Nottinghamshire. It had been a Southend wicket that had cost us the 1989 championship with that 25-point penalty. This time, however, we gained 24 points as we won by 10 wickets and improved our position.

Then I was off on England duty again. It's not ideal for a county captain to keep disappearing, but Essex are a close-knit community. Derek Pringle, my appointed deputy, was suffering from back trouble, so Neil Foster took charge. And Keith Fletcher was never far away to offer a guiding hand. That's the Essex way and it's certainly paid dividends during the time I've been at the club. I couldn't imagine being anywhere else, and hope to be involved there when my playing days are over.

Not surprisingly, England picked the same squad for the second

Test at Old Trafford, but later Neil Williams came in for the injured Phillip DeFreitas. The same side took the field as at Lord's, but this time we batted first because I won the toss. The Lord's Test may have belonged to a 37-year-old veteran, but the Manchester match became the property of a 17-year-old Indian batsman, who saved the Test for his country and kept the series alive.

Our first day wasn't up to Lord's standards, but it was not far off it. We closed at over 300 with three wickets down. Mike Atherton again helped to get England off to a great start and we put on 225 for the first wicket. Batting with him was becoming an enjoyable experience. He's so solid and, after a bad start, had come through his first year of the big-time with flying colours. It was obvious to one and all that Mike had a high-class career ahead of him. He'd taken his chance well. Maybe his inclusion had been fortuitous (Wayne Larkins having been the original selection for the Texaco series against New Zealand, and replacement David Gower having failed), but Mike grabbed his chance with both hands. He was being hailed as the new Geoff Boycott, but Mike Atherton is clearly his own man. There are similarities; both have excellent techniques and temperaments and neither likes to give it away. Mike is definitely one of the best players to come into the England side since I've been playing. When I've failed, he's usually got runs, and vica versa. That's one of the qualities of a good opening partnership.

Mike and I lasted until the first over after tea, when I was given out, caught behind. I thought the ball had only brushed my shoulder, and I rubbed the offending area to help the umpire make up his mind. But John Holder had no doubts, and I was on my way. These gestures by batsmen, like the West Indies' Gus Logie lifting his bat when there's an lbw appeal to indicate he's hit the ball, are creeping into the game and put more pressure on the umpires. As well as trying to tell the umpire what to do, the batsman indicates to the crowd what he thinks. If he's a local favourite, his dismissal may then spark off crowd trouble. I wasn't trying to tell Holder his job, although TV replays suggested I might have been unlucky.

We were bowled out for 519 on the second day, the first time the Indians had managed to do that in eight first-class games on the tour. Robin Smith became the third century-maker and remained undefeated at the end, after a 60-run last wicket stand with Devon Malcolm, who is not the greatest stroke-maker but who now made ample amends for leaving Robin stranded on 99 in the West Indies during the game against the President's XI. Curiously, Robin was on 76 both times Devon came out to support him. In the Caribbean, our number 11 had not been able to resist temptation and was bowled while swinging ambitiously. This time Devon kept his nerve for a Test-best score of 13, allowing Robin to get his ton. Gus Fraser put us right on top at the end of day two by removing Shastri, Sidhu and Vengsarkar.

Azharuddin now set about dominating a Test match Saturday for the second time in a fortnight. Manjrekar supported him as the pair put on 189 for the fourth wicket; Tendulkar joined his skipper to add 102 for the fifth. That stand took India past the follow-on mark, and when they were all out at the close the tourists were just 87 behind. Azharuddin's 179 was not quite as fine as his inspirational masterpiece at Lord's, but it was just as important. He scored 103 between lunch and tea. Our bowlers fought back well, capturing their last six wickets for 74 runs. Gus Fraser was again the best of them, with another five-wicket haul, while Devon Malcolm and Chris Lewis had their problems.

It hadn't been a bad day's work. Life's easy when things go your way. It does no harm to see how your players cope with adversity and to shake off any complacency that might have crept in. That was important because I'd just been named captain for the Ashes tour to Australia; that was going to be no picnic. I was delighted to get the job. It had been 10 years since I had toured there with England and, after our problems in the 1989 Ashes, I was keen to make amends. I'd scored only 168 runs in that series, and I had never really performed at my best against them, making only one century in 27 Tests.

There was still plenty of the 1990 summer left, however, and this news wasn't going to distract me from winning the Indian series. I didn't last too long on Monday morning and was caught glancing down the leg-side for seven; then David Gower pulled a short ball from Hirwani onto his wicket via his boot. Mike Atherton once more provided the anchor while Allan Lamb got his own back on those who claimed he couldn't play spin. Nothing spurs Lambie on as much as being written off, and one of his sixes crashed into the seats below the press box in a defiant gesture. Lambie can play spin. He's a fighter, he's got a good technique and he's a match-winner. Here at Old Trafford, once again, he had put England in a winning position. We batted on for five overs on Tuesday morning, although a bruised arm kept John Morris out of action (he had got in the way of a fierce Robin Smith drive the previous evening). The Indians were left 408 for victory, which on the evidence of Lord's they would pursue with vigour.

As things turned out the tourists had virtually lost the game by tea; they had been reduced to 183 for 6. Some of the senior Indian batsmen had pressed the self-destruct button. Shastri edged a wild drive off Devon's bowling, Kapil charged down the wicket to Eddie Hemmings and missed, and Vengsarkar was bowled by Chris Lewis offering no shot. John Morris's injury allowed his Derbyshire colleague, Chris Adams, two moments of glory as the substitute fielder. His dramatic dive from short square leg removed Sidhu in the second over; then he claimed Manjrekar in the same place off Eddie.

Young Tendulkar and Prabjakar were left holding the fort at tea, and an early breakthrough in the final session would undoubtedly have given us the match and the series. But Tendulkar rolled forward the years and batted through to the close for his maiden Test century to prolonged applause that echoed around Old Trafford. Prabhakar was still there, too; the pair had added 160 in two and half hours and India ended up only 65 short of victory.

Mushtaq Mohammad is the youngest player to score a Test century – 17 years and 82 days. Tendulkar was a month older; but his hundred came at such a time of crisis – with India on the ropes because of the irresponsible way several of their senior batsmen had played – that it will rank with the great Test innings. He'd shown himself a remarkably mature player. It was interesting to ponder whether he would have been playing Test cricket if he'd been English. The answer is almost certainly 'No' – he'd still be waiting for his chance: we are inclined to mistrust precocity in our sportsmen. Tendulkar was not ruffled by fast bowling nor intimidated by the situation. Selectors have to make a judgement on whether a player is ready or not, whether they might destroy a talent by exposing it too soon. In England we probably err on the side of caution. Some believe that if you're good enough, you're old enough.

Much as I admired Tendulkar's innings, I was annoyed at not winning the second Test. We had had our chances: I missed Prabhakar at slip, and Eddie Hemmings failed to hold on to a caught-and-bowled drive by Tendulkar. Instead of making the series safe, we'd let India off the hook and now they had a chance of making it 1–1 at the Oval.

Our younger players had a chance to impress when the Test & County Cricket Board's Under-25 XI took on the tourists at Edgbaston after the second Test. Essex didn't have a game, and three of our batsmen, Nadeem Shahid, Nasser Hussain and John Stephenson, were included, the last as captain. Most were candidates for the winter's A tour. Originally, the West Indies had been the destination, but costs had ruled that out. Pakistan was the next alternative, but at the last minute the Gulf War intervened and England's A tour found sanctuary in Sri Lanka. The A team is not an England second XI; that was never to be its function. I'm sure England will see the benefits over the next few years as the younger players come through.

Essex had beaten Yorkshire by an innings at Middlesbrough during the second Test and I returned for the Surrey game at Chelmsford, which we won by 283 runs. Neil Foster was in great form and the driving force behind our championship challenge. Not only did he take 11 wickets as Surrey were dismissed for 114 and 120, but he top-scored in our first innings with 58. It's been unfortunate that his career has been troubled by injuries. He's such a great bowler that I'd have him in my England side every time if I could. Unfortunately, he's currently serving a five-year Test ban for joining Gatting's South African tour. England's Test side never saw the best of him, just odd magic moments: he was always struggling to secure his place. His knee problem is a degenerative injury, but Fossie is still a class performer. He can be a difficult, rather abrasive character at times. But it was his magnificent bowling that was maintaining Essex's championship challenge. In the second week of July we'd been third from bottom, but six wins in nine matches had put us just two points behind Middlesex, who had lost their early season momentum, and with a game in hand.

Third Test, Oval

England picked the same squad for the final Test of the summer at the Oval, with Neil Williams retaining his place. Much of the newspaper talk was now about who was going to be selected for the Ashes tour, always a popular pastime. Much debate centred on David Gower. He had not really joined in the run feast since his return and was definitely under some pressure at the Oval to justify selection. John Morris, too, was under pressure, though that was not his fault: he'd had very little opportunity in the series. Certainly over the previous few weeks I'd been keeping a close eye on the performances of the leading candidates and taking stock.

The Oval had changed somewhat. Not only was the new West Stand next to the pavilion ready for use, but Cornhill, the Test sponsors, had their logo painted on the outfield.

For the first time in the series, we found ourselves on the back foot. Azharuddin won the toss and didn't repeat his Lord's mistake. We lost Chris Lewis before the start with a dizzy spell and Neil Williams made his Test debut. After a couple of early setbacks, India settled down and had reached 324 for 4 by the close. Shastri provided the platform with an undefeated century. It was the second hundred of the series for the makeshift opener, who's one of the most versatile cricketers in the Test arena. For most of the summer I'd been accused of not using Michael Atherton's leg-spin. I would have liked to bowl him more, but my job's to bowl those I think will win England the Test match. It's not a game just to give everyone a bowl. But it's true that the only way he'll improve as a Test match bowler is to bowl in a Test match. And in two spells at the Oval, Mike showed that there is certainly room for improvement. He seemed to lose the confidence that all leg-spinners need somewhere between the county and the Test scenes. His seven overs went for 60 runs. Vengsarkar became his first Test victim when he smashed a full toss straight back to a grateful bowler. Azharuddin looked on course for another hundred until Jack Russell took a brilliant one-handed catch to give Neil Williams his first Test success.

Friday saw us toiling in much the same manner as Thursday, as India went on to their highest total against England. Azharuddin eventually declared at 606 for 9 and we lost Mike Atherton in the final 12 overs of the day. Shastri had gone on to make 187 and Kapil Dev, certainly not the bowler he was, showed his batting had lost none of its vigour and skill by reaching the 14th century of the series.

Our reply was less than wholehearted and half the side had gone for only 139 runs. David Gower, John Morris (moved up the order) and Lambie all failed to reach double figures, and we went into the rest day 113 runs short of the follow-on target with three wickets left. It was not the sort of performance the selectors wanted before picking a touring party; several players had it all to do in the second innings.

India asked us to follow-on on Monday morning, after we finished 266 runs in arrears despite an Eddie Hemmings fifty. I'd hoped to bat all day, but fell in the final hour to a one-handed catch at backward short-leg by Vengsarkar. But David Gower hit six fours in those final 40 minutes and England went into the last day 50 runs behind, with nine second-innings wickets remaining.

I'd played my final Test knock of the summer. Not only had my 88 on Monday taken me past Sir Donald Bradman's record 974 runs for an English summer, but I became the first man to reach 1,000 Test runs in an English season – 1,058 to be exact. By this stage, records seemed to be falling like confetti around me. I was proud to beat Bradman and be the first to 1,000, but it was of secondary importance. After our solid summer, I was desperate that we didn't fall at the final hurdle. And I was gratified that that feeling was shared by the rest of the side.

The final day belonged to David Gower. His undefeated 157 ended India's hopes. David spent the morning session in uncharacteristically cautious mood as he accumulated 39 more runs. After lunch, he looked more relaxed and more like his old self, on his way to his 16th Test century. By the close he'd ended all doubts about his place in the winter party. The case for John Morris wasn't so clear-cut; his 32 runs had not answered all the questions.

England had taken their second series of the summer. This final Test was useful because we were under pressure for the first time and had to play some good cricket to save the game. Most cricketers look good when things are going their way; how they react in adversity is usually far more relevant, especially for an Australian tour. We had dominated the first Test and a couple of dropped catches cost us a win at Old Trafford on a pretty flat wicket in the second. We had fought back at the Oval; the pressures were different, but I wasn't unhappy to see how we had dug ourselves out of a hole. Our batting was at the heart of the wins over New Zealand and India. We hadn't had a great bowling attack in 1985 when we regained the Ashes 3–1, but we posted big scores – just as the Aussies did to us four years later. When you're making 500-plus totals, things tend to happen for you. I've seen it time and again. The opposite is also true. Fail in the first innings, and you're struggling to save the match.

England in Australia, 1990–1991

Essex's charge for the championship had continued during the Oval Test against India with victory at Derby by an innings and 94 runs inside two days of a four-day game. Curiously, Derbyshire had just been docked 25 points, like us in 1989, for producing a pitch that was 'clearly unsuitable for first-class cricket' in the previous game against our rivals Middlesex, who had lost after being bowled out for 99 in their second innings. Our young left-armer Mark Ilott was providing Neil Foster with good support and the pair took 15 wickets in the match. But Middlesex went back to the top, though only by a single point, when they ended their run of six games without a win by defeating Yorkshire at Leeds in the same series of matches.

I travelled to Northampton after the Oval Test to join the Essex lads for the three-day game there. We batted first and when Winston Davis thumped my pads with the fifth ball of the day, I knew it was close. I was quite prepared for umpire Kevin Lyons to raise his finger. He didn't. But I wasn't prepared for Davis's reaction. He stood in the middle of the pitch and didn't move. It was only when the umpire called up Allan Lamb, their captain, from first slip and he trotted over to Davis, that the bowler returned to his mark. Even then he spent a fair time composing himself before delivering the next ball. However upset he was, there was no need to behave like that. Northants announced the following day that he'd been fined for 'blatant dissent,' and Kevin Lyons received an apology. The incident can't have upset me too much because I hit 174, my 11th first-class hundred of the season. The Test series might have finished, but apparently I could still collect all sorts of records. It was nice to be told about them, but they played no part in my preparation for matches.

Our bowlers took a battering on the second day as Lambie, Rob Bailey and Wayne ('Ned') Larkins all hit hundreds; in Ned's case it was a double one. After having most of his summer ruined by his finger injury, I was pleased to see him among the runs again. The match was drawn because Lambie didn't give us a chance. That's fair enough, but tactically he knew we had to go for the win. That meant scoring quickly and then giving ourselves enough time to bowl them out. A loss or draw was no good to us – we would try anything to get the victory. I hit another hundred to pass 2,500 first-class runs for the season. I received £1,000 as the first player to do that – with another £1,000 for the club. That would increase by £10,000 for both of us if nobody else managed it by the end of the season. (One other did: Jimmy Cook of Somerset.) John Stephenson, my opening partner, was enjoying his best season, scoring 76 and 82 in this match as we became only the third pair in history to make two double-century opening stands in the same game. But the match fizzled out into a draw, although with Middlesex not playing, we had returned to the top of the table with a lead of four points.

Northants headed straight for Lord's afterwards to face Lancashire in the NatWest Final. I don't think that last day in the field against us did them any favours: to all intents and purposes, they'd lost the final inside an hour when Phillip DeFreitas reduced them to 39 for 5. Northants recovered to reach 171, but it was never enough as Neil Fairbrother again showed us what England was missing with a flashing 81.

That weekend I travelled up to Tyneside to take part in a Single Wicket competition with Graeme Hick, Mark Greatbatch, Malcolm Marshall and Ravi Shastri. I wasn't an original choice, but a late replacement for Ian Botham. The competition took place on an artificial wicket in the middle of the National Garden Festival. It was done on a round-robin basis with everyone bowling at everyone else. You lost points if you got out, but if you didn't take wickets, you were struggling. I grabbed the runners-up spot by dismissing Mark with my final delivery, but Graeme walked away with the competition.

The following day I learnt that a second member of Essex was to join me on the Ashes trip: our county scorer Clem Driver. I didn't even know that he'd applied to go until Micky Stewart mentioned it during the Oval Test. Clem had expressed an interest in the job, but didn't want me to know – he didn't want any favours. Clem had become something of a legend at Essex. I'd first noticed him when he ran Keith Fletcher's Benefit in 1973; later he took over as scorer and had been doing the job for 12 years. Since he'd started announcing the bowling figures and other useful information on the loudspeaker, Clem had become essential listening with his little comments and deliberate mistakes. When I was walking to the wicket with Brian Hardie, Clem would announce that Graham Gooch was the one in the white helmet. True, I was wearing a white helmet – but so was Brian! The crowd began to respond and now he plays up to it.

Clem has his drinking days and his non-drinking ones – on the latter he sticks to wine instead of Scotch. He's called the Abbot because he's president of a travelling cricket club called the Pilgrims; the emblem on the tie is a green Friar Tuck. Clem thought it hilarious when he was kitted out with the full England touring gear, tracksuit and all. The tracksuit was never worn, but the trainers would occasionally be seen in various hotel cocktail bars around Australia. By the end of the tour Clem was rightly proud of being one of only two in the party that had not made a claim on the medical insurance. Not bad, considering the Test & County Cricket Board had refused to insure him. He'd driven all the way to Birmingham for the medical and was not impressed by the verdict that he was overweight and had a dicky heart. 'I knew that before I set out,' was his reaction. As it was, he was more resilient than the rest of us and had the final laugh.

Wednesday 6 September was the day English cricket had been waiting for: the naming of the Ashes squad. Sadly, it also brought some unwanted news, the death of Sir Len Hutton. Sir Len had been captain when England won in Jamaica in 1953/4 and I was delighted to become the second England skipper to win a Test there.

My 333 put me in the record books alongside Sir Len, Sir Don and Sir Gary, though I don't consider myself in the same street as them. I've got ability and have done well, but they are legends. It's not just age or even a knighthood which turns a great player into a legend. Of my contemporaries, Ian Botham's a legend, so are Viv Richards and Sir Richard Hadlee. There are other great players about, but they are not legends. I don't know what makes a player cross that line. I just don't consider myself in the same breath. I'm proud to have hit the sixth-highest score in Test cricket. I'm not an emotional guy, maybe I look at my achievements rather cold-bloodedly. In the fullness of time, perhaps, my outlook will change. When all is said and done, players are always remembered in their best light. It's the great shots and great knocks that remain; like childhood memories, in which only the sunny days survive.

People use other events as a calendar of their own days. Everyone knows where they were when they heard the news of President Kennedy's assassination, John Lennon's shooting and England's 1966 World Cup victory. I watched Geoff Hurst's hat-trick on a wonky TV while at a holiday camp on the Isle of Wight. I wonder if people will one day recall what they were doing when Goochie hit 333 at Lord's.

Picking the Ashes squad hadn't taken long. The England Committee – Ted Dexter, Micky Stewart, Alan Smith (Chief Executive of the TCCB) and Ossie Wheatley (Chairman of the Cricket Committee) – were joined by myself and Raman Subba Row (the outgoing Chairman of the TCCB), with tour manager Peter Lush and Tim Lamb sitting in. I was certainly a lot less rushed than the previous year, when I was named captain for the winter tour and didn't realize I'd be helping to pick the squad the same afternoon. That task was made even more difficult because of our poor showing in the Ashes. But England had performed well in the summer of 1990 and the results had confirmed this. That makes selection a lot easier and more of a formality.

The side that finished the season, with Chris Lewis included instead of Neil Williams (Chris was absent only because of illness), were almost automatic choices. There was no doubt that Chris had the potential; what he lacked was consistency. He's a brilliant all-round cricketer and we were investing for the future. Mike Atherton had produced the goods straight away; but sometimes it takes young talents longer to find their feet. If he was going to make it at the highest level as an all-rounder, Chris was going to have to take more responsibility for his batting and move higher up the order. He was important to us: for one thing he was a brilliant fielder in a side that was not notable for its fielding. I hoped and believed that hard work and enthusiasm would sharpen us up and compensate for our lack of athleticism. David Gower had settled any doubts over his form with that big hundred at the Oval. There was some discussion about John Morris, who'd not yet settled in at Test level, but he'd had little chance in his three Tests and had done nothing to deserve omission.

That left five places: an opener, a reserve wicket-keeper, two fast bowlers and a second spinner. We talked about the all-rounders, but didn't feel there was one good enough. David Capel wasn't bowling at the time. Lancashire's Mike Watkinson is a good cricketer, but I couldn't see him batting at six in a Test. Gladstone Small was picked for one of the bowling spots. He'd been dropped for the India series after some erratic displays, but had regained his form with Warwickshire, was an experienced Test player and had done well in Australia on Mike Gatting's tour. Phil Newport, Phillip DeFreitas and Martin Bicknell were in the frame for the final fast-bowling spot. Daffy had a great NatWest final, winning the Man of the Match award after taking the first five Northants wickets; but we went for Martin because he was the youngster in form, would benefit from the experience and we wanted someone to swing the ball regularly. Philip Tufnell and Richard Illingworth were the two left-arm spinners talked about. Philip had impressed me every time I'd played against him. He always bowls aggressively and makes you hurry your shots – the sign of a good bowler. He was the best I'd seen. Alec Stewart was the perfect choice for the second wicket-keeper – a front-line batsman who keeps. I believe that's the right policy if there is a player of that type available: he becomes the side's all-rounder.

I didn't feel there was an outstanding candidate for the third opener's spot. Eventually, we went for 'Ned' Larkins ahead of Hugh Morris and Darren Bicknell. Hugh had had a great season, scoring ten hundreds, but it was one good season in six or seven – and in a summer when everyone was scoring runs. If Hugh had another good season, he would merit serious consideration. Darren, like 'Ned', had missed a large part of the season through injury. In the end, we opted for the guy we knew. That was our squad picked. You try to get it right, but are bound to make mistakes. At the end of the day you have to trust your judgement. It's all very well being wise after the event. The selection of 'Ned' probably attracted most press criticism, but generally the party was well received and our policy of picking the best young faster bowler and spinner in the country was warmly praised.

My good friend, Middlesex's former England captain John Emburey, rang me before the final three championship matches and we agreed that two wins would be enough to win the championship. We had two home matches, so I was fairly optimistic. We started well, bowling out Northants for 196 and getting within 11 of their total with five wickets down at the end of the first day. I made 92, but we found ourselves on the back foot as Northants made 636 for 6 and left us to make 589 to win in eight hours. Alan Fordham, Bailey and Lamb were the century makers this time and the Northants batting was certainly doing its best to deny us the title. We were bowled out for 312, suffering our first defeat for three months after seven wins and five draws. Middlesex beat Notts and went back into the lead by 14 points.

We had been moved out of the driving seat and needed a positive performance against Kent at Chelmsford. I wanted 254 runs from my final four innings to become the first batsman to score 3,000 first-class runs in an English season since Bill Alley in 1961. That's not something you plan for at the start of a summer, but having got this close, I was keen to make it. I didn't make that public at the time because it becomes distracting, but opportunities like that don't occur very often.

In the event, I was already as close as I was going to get: I broke my left thumb attempting to catch Trevor Ward off Neil Foster at second slip. Initially I came off and told Keith Fletcher that it didn't feel too bad. But ice brought no response, so I waited until lunch, went to the hospital, got the X-rays and brought them back to the ground. I was becoming an expert after my experiences in the West Indies, and I could clearly see the two breaks. That meant a plaster job.

My immediate concern was for Essex, just two games away from the championship. But I rang Micky Stewart to tell him that, although the injury would keep me out for six weeks, I should be ready by the start of the Ashes tour. I was as disappointed as I'd been in the Caribbean. Again, I was denied the chance of seeing the job through to the finish. I'd always prided myself on not missing games through injury.

My summer was over. I was going to have to sit it out and watch the final two crunch games, just as in the West Indies. I'd missed out on those 3,000 runs, but I had become only the third batsman after Sir Don Bradman and Geoffrey Boycott to finish an English season with a three-figure average. It was only six months later that I discovered it was such a special achievement: I had assumed it was fairly common. The championship wasn't going to be decided until the final round of matches. Our Kent game was drawn, the bowlers tried as hard as they could but the wicket defeated us in the end. Middlesex drew at the Oval, where we were to play our final match, and they claimed six bonus points, as we did; so Middlesex held on to their 14-point advantage.

Middlesex headed up to Edgbaston for the Refuge Assurance Cup Final, where they beat Derbyshire. That night the Cricketers' Association (the players' union) held their annual dinner in Birmingham. Mike Atherton was voted Young Player of the Year, while I was named Player of the Year. Being honoured by your fellow professionals, whatever you do, is the highest tribute you can get. They know the pressures and problems; if they respect you, it's something to be proud of.

We took on Surrey without Derek Pringle (injured back) and Mark Waugh (septic finger) as well as myself, while Middlesex travelled to Hove to meet Sussex, who were propping up the county table. Early on the third morning, Essex had Surrey following on after Neil Foster had claimed six wickets; but Middlesex were in an even stronger position at Hove and the championship was theirs just before tea. Although we had fought to the end, we had only ourselves to blame. In the three games prior to this, we must have dropped more than 20 catches. We just kept shelling them out and you can't sustain a challenge with fielding like that. Our general cricket let us down badly.

I felt most sorry for Neil Foster, who had led from the front in the final matches and had bowled magnificently. No one could have asked for more. 'Fossie' was maintaining a remarkable strike-rate. In the past five seasons his wicket tally has been 105, 86, 80, 92 and 94 – 457 in all. That's top-drawer bowling.

During that Surrey game, I had an appointment with Paul Gascoigne at the Spurs training ground. We were doing some promotional photographs for Stuart Surridge, but afterwards had a kickabout where I was able to astonish him with the full range of my soccer skills. You have to speak as you find: as far as I'm concerned he was great fun, totally natural. That night I went to Upton Park with several of the Essex lads to see the Hammers 'thrash' Ipswich 3–1.

The 1990 summer ended with more hundreds scored than in any other season. There were 428 three-figure scores compared with 248 in 1989. Alan Lee of *The Times* wrote that I'd 'begun and ended the summer in plaster – and broken batting records and bowlers' hearts in between'. The first is fact; I'm not sure about the rest. I think it was the groundsmen who broke bowlers' hearts in 1990. Anyone who could pick up a bat made runs. Batsman v bowler had become an unfair contest, and that wasn't doing anyone any favours.

Later that week I headed off to North America with Brenda and the kids. I had agreed to captain England in two one-day games in Toronto and New York against the West Indies. Since it was also going to be a family holiday, I attended the matches even though my broken thumb kept me on the sidelines. The trip had caused a bit of a rumpus because the TCCB would have preferred us to stay at home before the Ashes tour and not risk injury. But we had been approached during the summer and had made a commitment to play at a time when we weren't under contract.

The controversy highlighted a problem that needed resolving. The Board wanted to control the Test players during the winter; the only way that would work would be if the players signed winter contracts and were paid accordingly. Then the board would have every right to tell players what they could and could not do, as far as cricket was concerned. Ted Dexter had tried to introduce the winter contracts in 1989 when there was a threat of a South African rebel tour, but it had been rejected by the counties. Now it had been agreed in principle and started for a small number of players in the winter of 1991/92.

We watched the first game in Toronto with a crowd of about 5,000. England lost easily by seven wickets and then went down by 53 runs in New York the next day. The second game was better attended, but I'm not convinced that cricket will ever really take off in the Big Apple. Even the organizer was rather confused by it all. He introduced the most famous cricketer in the world at the big dinner before the matches as 'Vince Robinson, captain of the West Indies team'. Viv was not amused and I don't blame him. We stayed on in the United States for 10 days and took the girls down to Florida to see the wonders of Disney World.

The day after I arrived back the plaster came off my hand and I drove up to Lilleshall, where the tour party was gathering for three days, getting kitted out and going through various fitness tests and exercises. My thumb was a bit stiff, but I was going to be fit for the start of the tour. I had a week at home before leaving for Australia. That's always a difficult period because the imminent departure is uppermost in every-one's mind and you are only really marking time until you leave. It's not as though it's a normal business trip. This England tour was scheduled to last 18 weeks, and that's a very long time to be away from one's children. It was going to be my first Christmas away from Hannah and the twins. I'd been banned when England went to India in 1984/5, was unavailable for Mike Gatting's Ashes trip in 1986/7, and the Indian tour in 1988/9, for which I'd been appointed captain, was cancelled. Brenda and I looked at the possibility of the family coming out to Australia, but with Hannah at school, it would have been extremely difficult to fit in. Much as I would have loved to see them, we decided it was more sensible and less disruptive if they didn't fly to Australia.

I was a bit angry when the TCCB insisted that we get together early in the evening of Wednesday, 17 October, as we weren't flying out until four o'clock on the following afternoon. I complained to Micky, but he pointed out that there were various meetings to attend.

I said goodbye to the kids and my dad drove me round to the

Excelsior Hotel at Heathrow. He stayed for a drink and I could hardly believe it when I saw Allan Lamb in the bar. We were scheduled to have a meeting at six, but Lambie was there first and early – and that had never happened before. We walked down a corridor where all the lads were waiting in their collars and ties. Someone else was there, too – Michael Aspel – and as he produced the Big Red Book, saying 'Graham Gooch – This is Your Life!' suddenly everything fell into place. That's why we had to meet early; that's why Brenda's mum had been all dressed up when I left the house; that's why the kids weren't too worried about my leaving. All that day I'd felt something fishy was going on, but there had been nothing I could put my finger on.

It was a good night – I really enjoyed it. I was carted off in a chauffeur-driven limo to Teddington Studios, where they set me up in a mobile home. I recognized all the voice-overs and it was good to see some old but familiar faces; Douglas Kemp, my old schoolmaster; Graham Hammond, the only school chum I've kept in touch with; and Bill Morris, who played for Essex in the 1950s and had coached me at Ilford Cricket School. There were other well-known faces, among them Allan Border, Geoff Boycott, Ian Botham and John Emburey. And, of course, Lambie – who seemed to have some trouble keeping to the script. It was quite an emotional evening, and it made leaving the family for four and a half months an even tougher wrench.

Perth was our first port of call. We were to be based there for nearly three weeks while acclimatizing, practising and playing our opening matches. That suited me. The weather there is usually warm and predictable; the practice facilities are good. Also, the flight to Perth is shorter than it is to Sydney or Melbourne; and the less time in the air the better. Lots of British people have emigrated to Perth; there's an English feel about the place, it's very relaxing. And there's space – loads of it. Perth's a sprawling city, spread around the Swan River. That has produced more of a sleepy, small-town feel than the normal hurly-burly atmosphere of a big city. Perth is separated by 1200 miles of semi-desert from the east and south-east parts of Australia and there's more than a friendly rivalry between Western Australia and the cities to the east. Critics say that very little happens in Perth: and that's exactly what we were hoping for as we prepared for the tough series ahead.

These hopes were soon dashed by an injury to an important member of the party – me! I was becoming something of a liability on the injury front. After 17 years without a hitch, I had received more than my full quota of trouble over a 12-month period. At least this time it wasn't a break. We had split the squad into two sides, with the help of some locals, in order to play a practice match in the Perth suburbs. Robin Smith had just belted two of my long hops into the car park, and I thought I'd better pitch it up. This I did, but Robin was in the groove and smashed the ball back. Instinctively, I stuck my hand out for the catch, and the ball just ripped open my ring finger between the two joints. The best way to describe the injury was that my finger resembled a sausage that has just burst open in a frying pan. My first worry was that it was fractured, but a local doctor confirmed there was no break. Rather than stitch it, he decided to pull the skin together using butterfly tape. I was relieved that the injury wasn't as serious as first thought, but it was impossible to say when I'd be back in action. My own target was the opening first-class fixture with Western Australia in 10 days' time.

Lilac Hill was the venue for our tour opener against a Western Australia President's XI. The local officials had taken a lot of trouble to create a festival atmosphere, reminiscent of an Arundel Sunday game. Several of the current WA side were included – as was one D. K. Lillee. Australia's leading Test wicket-taker, now 41, had been training hard for this one-off 'comeback', but much of the hard work was undone by an evening out with Robin Smith the night before the match.

Dennis's wicket-less nine overs cost 47 runs: Robin, who wasn't playing, had accomplished his mission. We were however, struggling at 63 for 4 in reply to their 205 for 7, which included a fierce Tom Moody century. But Alec Stewart and John Morris brought us home without further mishap. For Alec, Lilac Hill was a second home; he'd spent seven winters there playing for the Midland-Guildford and one of the temporary stands displayed a 'Welcome back Alec' banner. Afterwards, the teams enjoyed a leisurely return to the Hyatt hotel by boat, although 'D.K.' made his excuses, saying that he was not allowed out with us again.

We flew up to Geraldton the next day for the weekend match against a Country XI. My finger was on the mend, but fielding would have been a problem: I could bat, but couldn't catch. After agreement from their skipper, I decided to play, but only as a batsman. The wicket was not ideal for a touring side desperate for batting practice – it was slow and low. The locals, for whom this was a rare opportunity to see a touring side, hadn't come to watch batsmen struggling on a bad pitch. They wanted to see runs, not top-class batsmen playing and missing, or taking risks just to get the ball off the square.

I managed just 10 on the Saturday as we made 197 for 8 before declaring; but I felt better the next day, with 47 including eight boundaries. The finger wasn't troubling me and I was glad to be out in the middle after a seven-week lay-off because of that finger and my earlier broken thumb. Mike Atherton and Wayne Larkins were also in the runs, while Devon Malcolm took a wicket with his very first ball of the tour. But the biggest morale-booster of the weekend came as the Great Britain rugby league side overcame the mighty Kangeroos at Wembley. We stayed up late to watch their 19–12 victory on TV. I'm keen on both rugby codes, slightly preferring the union game. In Australia there's no debate: rugby union comes a poor third to league and Aussie Rules in the football stakes. But in all games, as in everything else, the Aussies are fiercely competitive. It's part of their nature. The Kangeroos had been the best rugby league team in the world for a long time and it was a fantastic performance for the Brits to go one-up in the three-match series. Cricket and rugby league may be worlds apart, but when you're in Australia, any English success should be relished. You can be sure the Aussies won't miss the chance to crow when the boot's on the other foot.

Back in Perth, half of our party got ready for their first cricket under lights by practising at the WACA. It was freezing and the night-time seemed to make it even colder, but the lads had to familiarize themselves not only with the lights, but also with the white balls. Red and white balls are like chalk and cheese. There shouldn't be a difference, but there is. The white ball is harder and comes at you much quicker. It's not just an illusion; the white ball does 'ping' off the bat and goes much farther. We noticed that

Man of the Match Allan Lamb celebrates his first Test century on foreign soil in Jamaica, or so he thought. Actually the scoreboard had got ahead of the scorers and Lambie had only reached 99! But he went on to make 132 in the opening Test against the West Indies.

Nasser Hussain hooks Curtly Ambrose in the Barbados Test. Nasser did well to latch on to this one because Ambrose didn't bowl too many loose deliveries, taking 10 wickets in the match.

Ian Bishop was the destroyer in the final Test with eight wickets at the Recreation Ground, Antigua. Bishop was missing when the West Indies came to England in 1991, recuperating after a back operation.

A familiar Hadlee pose. And a typical response from the umpire. I'm out first ball lbw to Richard Hadlee in the Trent Bridge Test, jogging memories of my 1989 Ashes ordeal when Terry Alderman caused me so many problems.

Allan Lamb hits John Bracewell to the boundary during the Lord's Test. Like Trent Bridge, the second Test against New Zealand was badly disrupted by the weather.

Jack Russell sweeps John Bracewell at Edgbaston. Behind the stumps is Adam Parore, just 19, making his Test debut because of Ian Smith's hamstring injury. But he finished on the losing side as England won for the first time in a home series since 1985.

Tea-time at Lord's on the second day of the Indian Test as Robin Smith and I go off for the break. If I look slightly apprehensive, it's because I'm on 299!

India captain Mohammed Azharuddin, with umpire Dickie Bird in the foreground, perhaps reflecting on his decision to ask England to bat as we piled up 653-4 declared.

My third century in a row against India, 116 in the second Test at Old Trafford. Fellow opener Mike Atherton hit 131, only the second Lancastrian to score a Test hundred on his home ground, as we put on 225 for the first wicket.

The ups and downs of cricket. David Gower hardly enhanced his tour prospects after being lbw for 8 in the first innings of the Oval Test against India. But an undefeated 157 after we followed on quickly brought the smile back to his face.

The lads soon realised that Eric Clapton is just as comfortable with a bat in his hands as a guitar after his concert in Adelaide. Unfortunately, I was confined to St Andrew's Hospital and missed the show, although Eric kindly popped in the following morning for a chat.

My first tentative net in Perth after my hand operation. I had planned to return in the game against Victoria just before Xmas, but circumstances dictated an earlier comeback.

Australian Bruce Reid celebrates after I'd been caught down the legside in the Sydney Test. Reid made us suffer in the Ashes series, but it was genuinely pleasing to see a world-class bowler back after his serious back problems.

Wayne Larkins hits Greg Matthews for four in the Sydney Test. 'Ned's' selection came in for a fair amount of criticism, but his two half-centuries at Melbourne should have provided the platform for England to level the Ashes series.

You're allowed to smile after 22 years. That's how long it had taken us to beat the West Indies in England. Celebrating on the Headingley balcony with me are *(l-r)* Robin Smith, Devon Malcolm, Allan Lamb and Philip DeFreitas.

\ different balcony, a different result. /iv Richards is the one smiling this ime as the West Indies take a 2-1 ead in the series with just the Oval Test to come.

A great end to the season for Alec Stewart. He was the man in the hot seat at the Oval when we gambled on a wicket-keeper batsman for the final Test. That match won, Alec salutes the crowd after hitting his maiden England ton against Sri Lanka at Lord's.

Botham's back. Even the darkest, mirror, mafia-type sunglasses aren't going to hide the most famous cricketer in the world. And they haven't impaired his sight either as Ian Botham takes another slip catch in the Sri Lanka Test.

The infamous reverse sweep. Not normally in my repertoire, but played properly it can be very effective and this one helped me to my seventh Test century in 13 months against Sri Lanka at Lord's.

at fielding practice, 'Ned' Larkins was hitting some catches to fielders in the deep, but the ball kept on soaring over their heads and clattering into the stand seats. Yet the white ball's certainly easier for spectators to follow. I remember watching the Surrey-Warwickshire NatWest final in 1982 from the back of the old Mound Stand and it was only by identifying the shape of the shot that I could follow the ball.

The WA XI weren't going to allow me to bat and not field, so I passed a rigorous fielding test on the Monday night. We chose 'Ned' ahead of Mike Atherton; he had done well for England in one-day games and was a destructive batsman. This match brought me back into confrontation with Terry Alderman; the WA team had been boosted with three 'guests'. Dean Jones and Mark Waugh were already known to us, but Darren Lehmann was Australia's rising batting star. I had dinner with Mark before the match. He had returned to Sydney with that septic finger injury which had kept him out of Essex's last match with Surrey. It took quite a time to heal – he had missed the first three weeks of the Australian season. Now he was keen to put himself back on top of the waiting-list for a Test place.

It was Lehmann who took first honours, with a half century that helped WA ease home by three wickets. The simple truth is that our 180 was not a big enough target on that wicket. Despite that, our bowlers fought back well, especially Martin Bicknell, who claimed three wickets in 15 balls on his debut. Alderman was again my undoing, though this time it was his safe hands at slip that sent me on my way. After we had slipped to 57 for 4 a typical Lamb knock, with support from Jack Russell and Chris Lewis, took England to a respectable but hardly inspiring total.

The match proved a triumphant return for Bruce Reid, who'd been out of the game for two years with a serious back injury that had required four operations. The tall, willowy, left-arm fast bowler had been a thorn in Mike Gatting's side on England's 1986/7 tour, but had missed the last successful Ashes visit to England. His 10 overs cost just 15 runs.

Bicknell's form was impressive: he swings the ball, and this pitch was responsive. Others would not be. Martin was still learning his trade. His problem was inconsistency: control, accuracy and moving the ball in the air were the areas he needed to work on. His pace is not going to worry high quality batsmen. There's no point trying to blast batsmen out. Sir Richard Hadlee learnt that the hard way and worked out a style of bowling that suited him best and worried the world's leading batsmen. Alderman had been very quick when he started, but had had to adapt after dislocating his shoulder when he rugby-tackled a fan who had run onto the WACA during the Test with England in 1982. I think the fast bowlers you face early in your Test career appear quicker because you're less equipped to cope. Lillee and Thomson seemed like express trains on my Test debut. Now, if I came across them, I might not think they were that quick. The fastest I've faced was Patrick Patterson in 1986 at Sabina Park, when everything was in his favour, notably the 'corrugated' pitch. That's one of the few times I've been apprehensive when going out to bat. But, as ever, your mind must contain only positive thoughts.

The WACA pitch is one of the most sporting I've encountered. A lot of runs are scored square of the wicket; but there's usually something there for the bowlers in the first session, so I put WA in when I called correctly at the start of our four-day state game. Angus Fraser found the pitch responsive, though he had little luck; but with Devon Malcolm taking two wickets in three balls, we had the home side struggling just after lunch, and half their side went for less than 100. But Graeme Wood, a former Test opener who had dug in against English bowling in the past, again refused to yield and his dogged century helped WA to 289, with Mike Atherton's leg-spin collecting the final three wickets. Wood batted well, but our bowlers had let WA off the hook by bowling too short.

It was the batters' turn to give an unprofessional display on the Saturday, when England were bowled out for 246, after reaching 163 for 3. Actually, we weren't bowled out: most of our wickets were given away by injudicious attacking shots. We couldn't afford such carelessness in state games, let alone the Tests. Even Lambie, who looked a dead cert for our first century of the tour, fell 16 short when he spooned a catch to cover.

WA, especially their skipper Geoff Marsh, who hit 151 in the second innings, made us pay by setting a target of 373 to win in

80 overs on the final day. After avoiding the close-fielding positions on the first day because of my hand, I had moved into the slips on the third day – and cost Gladstone Small the wicket of his former Warwickshire team-mate Tom Moody. The chance went straight into my hands – and straight out again. Those hand injuries were definitely affecting my confidence in the field, especially when catching. Before the West Indies tour I'd been happy with my form in the slips, but it fell below the required standard during the 1990 season. I enjoy fielding in the slips and take a high percentage of chances. I wasn't ready to quit and retire to the outfield just yet, so I was working doubly hard on my close catching.

England's attempt to win was little short of a disaster, although we salvaged some pride by holding out for a draw after collapsing to 90 for 6 with 54 overs remaining and with Allan Lamb off the field with a suspected broken arm. That we survived was due to Robin Smith's heroic 4½-hour undefeated 98 and stern support from Gladstone and Gus, who each batted for over an hour, and Devon who lasted 43 minutes – an eternity for a batsman of his ability. The final six and a half overs were negotiated by Smith and Lamb, who had earlier said there was no chance of his batting, even though X-rays discovered his elbow was only badly bruised. But we'd got so close that Lambie couldn't throw in the towel, and it was typical of his fighting spirit that we managed to escape.

Allan had been to see a specialist in Perth about growths on his eyes. It wasn't a new or unusual complaint, and it is quite common in Australia, South Africa and the West Indies. Allan had first noticed the problem in the Caribbean in 1986. It hadn't impaired his vision, but his eyes became sore in strong sunlight. There was also the threat of the growths spreading over the pupils. An operation was recommended, although it could wait until the end of the tour.

We had scraped a draw, but had performed well below standard. At least the newer and younger members of the England party might now be aware of what we were up against in Australia. State games bear no relation to the games tourists have with the England counties. For a start, there are only six states and every player is a candidate for the Test side. The match against the touring side is a big event and a golden chance to get noticed by the selectors. Add to that the Aussie's natural aggression and competitiveness and you have a game on your hands. The equivalent game in England is more of a non-event; it's way down the list of priorities for an English county; often key players are rested. The Tetley's Bitter challenge, offering prize money to the counties who beat the tourists, has at least helped improve the standard and given the games more purpose. In Australia, money doesn't need to be offered as an inducement to bring out the best in the home side. So our three-week stay in Perth ended in something short of glory, and we headed off for the other side of the continent with more than ample room for improvement.

Every member of the touring party will take one particular memory of our match against a South Australia County XI to the grave: the flight from Adelaide to Port Pirie, where the match was to take place. The journey lasted only half an hour, but it seemed a lifetime as turbulence set up by an electrical storm threw the plane all over the sky. These short flights in small planes are all part of a cricketer's life abroad, and nobody expects the smooth passage of a jumbo jet. But this was something else, even for hardened travellers like David Gower, Allan Lamb and myself. Tour manager Peter Lush has undergone some of the more extreme delights of internal travel in India, but I've never seen his knuckles as white as they were on this trip.

Still, every cloud has a silver lining. For the first time in three weeks, Philip Tufnell had nothing to say for himself. 'The Cat', as he was known (for his fielding, he insisted; for his sleeping habits, claimed others) was establishing himself as one of the tour characters, 'Ned' Larkins having taken him under his wing. But I've never seen anyone as petrified as Philip was when the plane began to be tossed about; he grabbed hold of the seat in front and didn't let go until we landed.

All this came on top of a five-hour flight from Perth. The lads weren't too happy when they discovered that the journalists who'd driven up from Adelaide to Port Pirie had done the journey in under two hours.

Our flight had been delayed leaving Adelaide anyway, so we arrived late for the official function, where I was introduced as

Peter Gooch. Norman Tully, the organizer, apologized for his error – and then called me David!

Port Pirie was that sort of town. Local garage mechanic Simon Fuchs had an afternoon to remember when his leg-breaks claimed the wickets of David Gower, 'Ned' and Alec Stewart. But our young bowlers, Philip Tufnell and Martin Bicknell, matched him with three wickets apiece and the touring side won by 111. 'Ned' was Man of the Match with a hard-hitting century. That earned him an Akubra hat and an authentic Drizabone Long Riders coat. I already had one of the hats and got a coat, too, when the *News of the World* photographer took a picture of 'Ned' and me with coats, hats and shotguns. We really looked the business – mean and dangerous. That's more than I could say about our cricket. We now had two more four-day games before the first Test in Brisbane, and we had to start getting our act together.

The match against South Australia was the perfect opportunity. The Adelaide strip has the reputation of being one of the best batting tracks in the world and our opponents were the only Aussie state side without a current Test player, although David Hookes was still on the scene. The simple facts of day one were that I won the toss, put them in and they finished up at 316 for 3. It could have been worse: two of the wickets fell in the final half hour.

With a total like that, I faced a fair amount of flak for not batting on such a good surface. The wicket was greenish and I believed our bowlers could have got the upper hand in the first session. We didn't and Glenn Bishop and Paul Nobes punished England and me with a record second-wicket stand of 275. We didn't bowl well in the first period. Martin Bicknell, eager to take his chance, tried to bowl too quick and ended up bowling too short. By the time he and Chris Lewis got their acts together, the batsmen were well settled and the pitch less responsive.

Having put them in, I was looking for three wickets by lunch; when that hadn't happened, I knew the rest of the day would be a struggle. When I decide to field in a county championship match, I aim to dismiss the opposition for under 200; anything over 250 means my decision to insert was a bad one. But, having made your choice – good or bad – you get on with it.

My finger had been improving steadily, but it had felt sore when

I took a couple of practice catches before the SA game. The pain went, however, and I turned up on the Saturday, the second day of the SA game, looking forward to getting some runs on the famous Adelaide Oval wicket. I arrived early for my net as usual. That had become my routine since taking over as captain. There's a lot to do when you're in charge, especially with a county side.

I don't think I appreciated that when I took over at Essex in 1986. I was trying to do everything, rushing around, trying to fit in my own net and then arriving back in the dressing-room just before I was expected to go out and bat. I found myself taking the first ball of a game without feeling ready or composed. That's when I said the captaincy was affecting my batting. I couldn't give my best in those circumstances, so I handed back the Essex captaincy to Keith Fletcher. Consequently, when I was given the England job in 1988, my failure to last as county skipper was brought up as a sign of my unsuitability. But the solution, for me, was simple. I now arrived early and, with help from Micky or Eddie Hemmings, got my net out of the way. I knew if I didn't do it then, I wouldn't do it at all.

Once my personal requirements had been attended to, I could concentrate on the problems of captaincy and be in the dressing-room half an hour before the start. It gives me time to change out of my sweaty clothes, have a cup of tea, listen to my portable CD and compose myself for batting. After all, that's the reason I'm in the team: scoring runs is my job. I need time to gather my thoughts, otherwise I don't feel ready for the contest ahead.

After my net with Micky before the start on Saturday, my finger felt sore when I took off my glove. It hadn't been hit, and I wondered whether holding the bat tightly might have been the reason. But, as I changed my gear for the warm-up, the finger really began to trouble me and the pain had moved into my hand. Half an hour after my net, there was no way I could catch a ball, and I just threw the ball for the slip-catching practice. I couldn't take any further part in the fielding and it was obvious something was wrong. I was in real pain by the time I saw Laurie. He correctly diagnosed that the finger had become infected. So I took some antibiotics, put the finger in salt water and waited for some reaction while the lads took to the field.

Dr Don Beard, South Australia Cricket Association's medical officer, dropped in to have a look and said he'd return later in the day. The only other time I'd had a pumping pain like it was when I had had an infected knee. When Doc Beard returned I couldn't bend the finger. He was sure the tendon was infected and put me on an antibiotic drip at the St Andrews Hospital while he tried to track down a hand specialist. That man was Randall Sach, who was just sitting down to his dinner. Thankfully, he came to see me straight away. He ordered an immediate operation to drain the pus. I called Peter Lush and Micky to the hospital and told them of the situation. It meant my missing the first Test for sure – but, as Randall explained, the alternative was a missing finger or hand. It was only in the days following the operation that the severity of the condition became apparent; even a delay of a few hours might have had serious repercussions. The hand had been poisoned by a very destructive, fast-acting virus.

My own future wasn't uppermost in my mind that Saturday night. Here I was out of action – and with no guarantee of when I would be able to play again. But it was different this time. With a broken hand or finger, it's all matter-of-fact – you know roughly how long it will take to mend, and there are several stages to go through to achieve full fitness. My poisoned hand was much more a step into the unknown. I kept telling myself that I'd be back for the second Test, starting on Boxing Day in Melbourne. But if that proved over-optimistic, was there any point in my staying in Australia? The third Test followed on almost immediately. Although my fractured finger on the West Indies tour was heartbreaking, with England on the verge of glory, this was worse. In the Caribbean the standards had been set, the tour was well on the road. Here in Australia, by contrast, the side was still finding its feet. We had not performed up to standard so far, and several key players were struggling to find their form. Moreover, the first Test is the key match of a series: it sets the tone for the rest of the tour. Sadly, I had to come to terms with missing the first act of this 1990/91 Ashes battle.

My more immediate problem was getting through the Saturday night after the operation, which had gone well. Despite a T-shirt, sheets and blankets, I was freezing. Unfortunately, I was also sweating and running a temperature. The nurse came in every hour to change my drip and take my temperature. The blanket was the first to go; next she relieved me of my T-shirt, as I was apparently too hot. I was left with a single sheet and thought conditions couldn't get any worse – until she switched the fan on! The arctic conditions certainly took my mind off my finger, especially when she started washing me down with a cold flannel.

I was pretty wiped out on the Sunday – and our latest attempts on the cricket field didn't help my recovery. Despite rain washing out half of the Saturday, half the side were out for 149 by the close, chasing SA's 431. We failed to save the follow-on with a bit to spare, but put up a better show in the second innings. Then, just as England poked their heads through the escape hatch, our final four wickets went down in five balls from Denis Hickey. At 325 for 5 we had been 111 ahead with just over a session left before Hickey struck. Our bowlers – without Devon Malcolm who had limped off after being hit on the foot when yorked by Hickey – made South Australia work hard before the state side recorded only its second ever win over an England touring team.

It's demoralizing to keep losing. I'd arrived in Australia with the intention of trying to win every game. Allan Border's 1989 side came to England with that determination and beat nearly all the counties. It gave them a boost and sharpened their competitive spirit. Winning does count for a lot.

The team headed off to Tasmania the next day without me. Just as annoying was the fact, before leaving Adelaide, they were able to get to an Eric Clapton concert, again without me. Eric is a keen cricket fan and he had visited the Adelaide Oval during our match. He also took time off to come and see me twice; it was much appreciated. Sadly, his plans for me to watch, (complete with drip!), from the side of the stage were scuppered by the usually tolerant Randall Sach.

Another visitor, this time uninvited, paid me two visits at St Andrews Hospital. A photographer from the local paper just wandered into my room and asked if he could take a picture of me on my sick bed. A ban had been put on interviews and photographs, so I said 'no', adding that he wasn't supposed to be in my room anyway. Yet, three-quarters of an hour later he was back. I told him to go, but as the sister starting pushing him out of the door he raised a camera above his head and took one shot before being shunted out. It was enough and the picture of a rather startled England captain on his sick bed was flashed around the world.

I regarded this as an invasion of privacy. I had quite clearly refused him permission to take the picture and asked him to leave. He simply disregarded what I had said. His newspaper wrote a letter of apology which, considering they'd got and used what they'd sent the photographer to get, was pretty hypocritical. I may be a stickler, but I like a few common courtesies when it comes to the press. What gets my goat more than anything is when a reporter rings me up and starts firing questions without even bothering to ask if I mind being interviewed. To stop being pestered in Adelaide, I gave an interview to David Lloyd of the Press Association and that was passed on to the many visiting and home journalists.

Originally I was to stay at St Andrews for four days, but I ended up being in for over a week. Randall Sach had sliced my hand open during the operation and the wound required 30-odd stitches. The injury had been infected by a rare but lethal organism. The bug had got sealed in before the original cut had healed, but we never discovered how and when. Randall wanted to be absolutely sure there was no further infection. It would have done his reputation no good at all if the England cricket captain had returned home minus a finger. He was extremely attentive – and his post-operative care included Sunday lunch at his house with his wife Robyn and children Jamie and Melissa. Their hospitality was most gratefully received, and there were others in Adelaide who went out of their way to make my enforced stay pleasurable. David Norrie, a friend who also happens to be cricket correspondent of *News of the World*, had stayed behind in Adelaide to drive me around. We spent a couple of afternoons at the South Australian Open golf championship, an evening at the Adelaide Casino, and went to a Beaujolais Nouveau dinner at the Chessar Cellars. That week convinced me of the need to carry on playing cricket for a few more years: the round of socializing had wiped me out. I'd put on half a stone, and I needed to get back to cricket for a rest and to get fit again. The visit to the Chessar Cellars had also landed me in trouble at home. Brenda rang the St Andrews the following evening and, when told I was out, enquired when I might be back. The sister did me no favours when she said: 'I don't know; he didn't get in until half past one last night.'

The news from Tasmania was encouraging. Allan Lamb had led England to a six-wicket win over Tasmania with four overs to spare in the one-day game. The bowlers pegged the home side back to 173 in their 50 overs, while Mike Atherton provided the cornerstone of our reply with an unbeaten 88. But the key fixture in Tasmania was the four-day contest against an Australian XI, which was led by David Boon and contained several players trying to break into or return to the Test team. We had another disastrous start – Mick Atherton, 'Ned' Larkins and David Gower had all gone before we'd reached double figures. But Allan Lamb, with 154, Robin Smith and Alec Stewart rescued the situation, before yet another spectacular collapse saw our final six wickets go down for six runs. However, Devon Malcolm, just when we were beginning to wonder about him, rediscovered his Caribbean form with 7 for 74 after his first two games had produced four wickets at an average of almost 60; and Lamb hit his second century of the match. The result was a draw, but at least England had begun to show some of the previous summer's form. Not before time.

First Test, Brisbane

The Australian 12 for the first Test was announced during the match. There were recalls for Bruce Reid, who'd bowled well for Western Australia at the Oval while I was in Adelaide, and Greg Matthews, who had not played in a Test since Mike Gatting's tour. Otherwise, it was the team that had inflicted such damage on English cricket in 1989.

I rejoined the party in Brisbane three days before the first Test. It was good to be back, but I was aware that I'd become something of an outsider. All I had to offer for the moment was advice. My aim was still to be fit for the second Test, but that date was no more definite than it had been a week before. Returning home for a spell was never really a serious option. If the second and third Tests were ruled out, I would go home and not return. But to go home for three weeks would have had a disruptive affect on the family. The girls would wonder what was going on, and I doubt if I would have been left in peace for a quiet holiday with the family. The only advantage of that option was that I would have been out of the way. I still considered them my players, but it was Lambie's show for the moment. If there was a selection disagreement, Allan would get his way. I had to be careful not to get too involved. He was the one who had to raise the team's camaraderie and self-respect. It was an awkward situation. I tried to concentrate on dealing with players on a one-to-one basis. I didn't see that as undermining the skipper's authority, and Lambie knew what I was up to.

Both teams attended a Benson & Hedges 'Clashes for the Ashes' party in Brisbane. Everyone appeared relaxed, although you could sense an underlying tension. The Ashes are a big event in every cricketer's career. Whether it's for your first or your fifth series, you always feel as if you are about to become part of cricket history. I sought out Bruce Reid to congratulate him on his fightback, and had a long chat with Allan Border. My Essex colleague John Stephenson, who was playing cricket on the Gold Coast, had joined the England party as cover in Brisbane, and later we were joined by Graeme Hick at the pre-Test nets. Zimbabwean-born Graeme, who was spending the winter playing for Queensland, would be eligible for England in April 1991, after his seven-year wait.

The Gabba at Brisbane has a reputation for producing results in Test matches. Allan Lamb wrongly called 'heads' and Allan Border put England in to bat. That was no surprise: it had been the custom in recent Tests here. England played four fast bowlers, with Eddie Hemmings missing out. 'Ned', 37 years old the day before, took over my opening spot with Mike Atherton, and Alec Stewart's form earned him the sixth batting spot ahead of John Morris. Carl Rackemann was made Australia's 12th man.

I had my 30-odd stitches removed the day before the Test; at least I felt I was making some progress towards returning to the fray. I visited a specialist the next day and he confirmed that I was on course for my Boxing Day date with the Aussies, although it was decided to send for Glamorgan's Hugh Morris, who was to lead England A to Pakistan, just in case.

First blood went to the Aussies as England were bowled out for 194 on the first day. At one stage, we'd been 117 for 2, but Reid was already causing the senior batsmen problems. In a triumphant return to Test cricket he captured four of the top six batsmen, including David Gower, who had lived dangerously for his 61, Robin Smith and Alec Stewart in the space of 16 balls. The tail soon followed and we were left with a fight on our hands. You needed an above average slice of luck to survive or succeed on that wicket on the first day. Basically, you had to use your ability and ride your luck to score. David's innings was typical Gower: brilliant, exciting – yes; reliable – no. But on his day he can still take apart any attack in the world.

The Aussies started the second day at 16 without loss. Just after tea, they were all out and England had an unexpected first-innings lead of 42. These are the bare facts. It was a fantastic fightback. Our bowling was very good, and our fielding was even better. Angus Fraser, whom I later described as a 'captain's dream', made the initial breakthrough and he, Gladstone Small and Chris Lewis took three wickets each, with Devon Malcolm ending Greg Matthews' defiant knock. Whenever the ball went in the air, an English hand was there to grasp it. Mike Atherton took two stunning catches in the slips, and efforts from Chris Lewis, Gladstone and Robin Smith were just as spectacular.

Our outstanding effort gave us a problem Australia had not had to face in the evening session of the first day, when their openers had been left with only 23 minutes to survive. Now England had to face 90 minutes and 20 overs of hostility. I said to Mike Gatting, who was covering the tour for Sky and the *Daily Express*, that this hour and a half would determine the result of the match. If we could get through with the loss of only one wicket, it would give us a great chance.

Unfortunately, 'Ned' went first ball when he played over a swinging yorker from Bruce Reid. He had been struggling with a mouth abscess, which had just been drained. He refused to make excuses, but it must have had a weakening effect and he eventually needed six stitches inside his mouth after completion of his dental treatment. Mike Atherton and David Gower had got within sight of the close when Terry Alderman delivered an unplayable ball to

Mike. I was in the press box at the time. As we watched the replay on TV, Greg Chappell remarked that the delivery would have been too good for him. Worse was to follow, David playing on to Merv Hughes.

England finished the day at 56 for 3, a lead of 98. It could have been even worse. Allan Border, who'd taken a diving two-handed catch to remove Chris Lewis in the first innings, had sunk to his knees with his head in his hands after dropping the simplest of catches off Allan Lamb. Border was as aware as anyone how delicately balanced this Test was and knew that Lambie has a habit of taking advantage of opportunities like that. AB admitted afterwards that he would have swapped his position for ours at the end of the second day – and he dropped Lambie another 200 times before he went to sleep that night!

I would certainly have swapped our position for his at the end of the third day: England had lost by 10 wickets! Once again, that man Terry Alderman had done the damage. In retrospect, I think the Test was probably decided with the last ball of the first over of the third day, when Alderman skidded through Lambie's defence to trap him lbw to begin a devastating spell in which he took 5 for 16.

England had effectively started the day at 100 for 3. A minimum target was 200, and if we set Australia anything over 250, at least one of their batsmen would have to make a big score. We were in a promising position – but we failed to deliver. It was crucial to get through the morning session reasonably unscathed because the wicket was getting easier. Jack Russell, who had come in as nightwatchman, was the only one who got his head down; he batted for nearly two hours. If either Robin Smith or Alec Stewart had stayed with him, things might have turned out differently, but both were out to attacking shots, a quite unnecessary extravagance in the circumstances. England's last nine wickets fell for 72, and the final total of 114 was our lowest score in Australia since the Centenary Test of 1977.

Australia required 157 runs to take a 1–0 lead in the series. It was a low-scoring match, but by now the pitch had lost much of its venom and the home team could take it as carefully as they liked. Mark Taylor and Geoff Marsh showed just how near to safety we were by finishing the job that afternoon and seeing Australia home by 10 wickets. The last time Australia had beaten England in three days was at Leeds in 1938. I felt sorry for Allan Lamb. Three games as my stand-in captain – and three defeats. Lamb stood up and was counted afterwards, blaming himself for not providing the big score England needed and confessed that 114, with the pitch as it was today, was just not acceptable. Once again, Terry Alderman had tormented England's batsmen, but this time with a difference. Previously, English conditions had suited him best; now he was able to silence his critics at home. In 13 Tests against England, Alderman had collected 91 wickets.

Our Ashes challenge had got off to the worst possible start. The scale of the defeat was as stunning as its speed, and it left all of us rather shell-shocked. I felt helpless. There's not much to say when you get rolled over like that. Talk is cheap; what we needed was answers on the field, not off it. Micky decided little would be achieved by rushing out to practise the next day, so the team was given the day off. The press thought we'd done little to deserve the rest and should have been out in the nets, paying penance. That's exactly what we did the next day, but, once again, the press was far from happy.

The trouble arose after Mike Gatting, banned from Test cricket for five years after taking a side to South Africa at the start of 1990, had offered his services as a net bowler and we had accepted. The fact that Mike was serving a Test ban didn't bother me, but it was seized upon by the press. As far as practice went, we couldn't win: it was wrong not to work; and it was wrong to use all the facilities at our disposal. In general, I believe it's a good idea to have a day off after a Test match, whether you win, lose or draw.

The press hadn't finished with England – or rather Allan Lamb – for his part in our defeat. It was revealed that he'd paid a visit to Jupiter's Casino, 50 miles up the Gold Coast, on the second night of the Test in the company of Kerry Packer, Tony Greig and David Gower. I felt sorry for him. He'd done his best, but it just wasn't happening for him. At first, Lambie foolishly denied he'd been there; there was no chance of his not being noticed, in view of the company he was keeping.

The question to be considered, as far as I was concerned, was whether he really wanted to put himself through that two-hour round trip when he knew he was batting first thing next morning. My answer would have been 'no': I would rest up and do nothing. But Allan Lamb isn't me – he's full of energy and always has been. Curfews smack of treating grown men like schoolboys; I don't believe that's the best way to bring out the character in the side. Most players respond to responsibility. I'm sure the evening out had no effect on his performance the next day. Lambie assured me he was back just after midnight and I saw no reason to doubt him. But the great danger was that he laid himself open to attack if anything went wrong. Allan Lamb visiting a casino the night before England crashed to a sensational 10-wicket defeat was meat and drink to a gluttonous press corps.

So now we had to pick ourselves up. The Ashes series was put on hold for a month as the Benson & Hedges World Series got underway. We were to play eight one-day matches against New Zealand and Australia, with the top two countries competing in a best-of-three final. For a side whose first-class form is poor, the limited-overs game is not the ideal way back. Batsmen can't hang around too long in the middle trying to get in the groove, and bowlers are more concerned with keeping the runs down than taking wickets. Our opening game was against New Zealand in Adelaide, so I was able to consult Randall Sach on my hand's progress. He was more than satisfied, and I was allowed to resume light training. I was also able to discard my sling and the finger was now protected only by a splint.

We had arranged two one-day games against the Australian Cricket Academy at St Peter's College. We won both games comfortably and Hugh Morris shrugged off his jet-lag to get among the runs. After that bad Test defeat, we needed to bounce back quickly. There was only one first-class match before the second Test, but a successful World Series campaign would help restore confidence. There are no draws in the one-day game and a couple of victories were what was urgently required.

Unfortunately, our form in the World Series opener could best be described as 'pathetic'. I was upset to see us outplayed by a team of part-time cricketers. If you compared the credentials of the two sides on a man-to-man basis, we were clearly superior.

But it was England who looked like the amateurs at the Adelaide Oval that day. The Kiwis did nothing outstanding – and we crumbled under the pressure.

New Zealand had been easily beaten by Australia in the opening match. We put them in and they struggled to reach 15 after 10 overs. John Wright was caught in the gully off Devon Malcolm, but the square-leg umpire had called no-ball. It was a delivery that Wright had to play at, but the rule down-under in one-day cricket prohibits balls that pass above the batsman's shoulder when he's in his normal stance position. (I believe the 'above-head-height' rule used in England is better.) Wright hung around to anchor their innings and take the Man of the Match award.

In a match reduced to 40 overs because of the rain, the Kiwis averaged six runs an over during the final 30 as England's performance in the field deteriorated rapidly. If ever a team looked like they were suffering a heavy Test defeat hangover, it was us. Our bowling was at best ordinary, catches went down and the ground fielding was sloppy. Despite that, the target of 200 to win was nothing special – it's a common enough target in what for us had now become a Sunday League 40-overs thrash.

David Gower hit the second ball of our reply for six – and was out two deliveries later. Mike Atherton dropped anchor, and the whole innings got bogged down. When England tried to apply the accelerator pedal, wickets fell. Only John Morris's brave 63 off 45 balls kept us alive. The final margin of defeat was only seven runs, but it never felt that close and we certainly didn't deserve to win.

Micky Stewart, Lambie and I had been critical after the Test defeat, but now was the time to read the riot act. If England carried on like this, the tour was going to be a disaster. It had been not merely a poor performance, but an unintelligent one. Nobody plays as much limited-overs cricket as we do, but we'd played like novices. Even if we had sneaked through at the death, the players would have received an earful behind a closed Adelaide Oval dressing-room door.

Our main concern was the general lack of competitiveness and application. Lambie, playing in his 100th one-day international, confessed that he'd rarely taken part in such an inept performance. The players, if they hadn't realized it already, were left in no doubt as to what was now required. It saddened me that talented players had to be reminded that they were playing for their country. I had assumed that this was a cricketer's ultimate ambition and that all the motivation necessary would come from within.

Next day, New Zealand lost to Australia. It was a rest day for us and we had planned a trip to Geoff Merrill's winery at Mount Turtle. Geoff had established a reputation as one of Australia's top wine-makers and he loved his cricket. That was good news for us, as Geoff's generosity kept us well stocked throughout the tour; his Chardonnay was a particular favourite. Our trip to Mount Turtle was postponed for a few hours while an extra practice was arranged for Sunday morning. I'm not in favour of 'naughty-boy' nets (as they became known), but nobody could deny we needed the practice. We were beginning to realize that we faced two problems – one of form, one of attitude. Hard work could overcome the former. The latter was a new experience for me, and one I had never expected to encounter on an England tour.

Our loss against New Zealand was the first of eight successive one-day games on the schedule for us in December. Six were in the World Series; the other two were against a Prime Minister's XI in Canberra and a Sir Donald Bradman XI at Bowral, the great man's birthplace. Between the first and second Tests, England had to travel from Brisbane to Adelaide to Canberra to Perth to Sydney to Bowral to Sydney to Brisbane to Melbourne to Ballarat to Melbourne – a pretty arduous schedule. The Prime Minister's match is a traditional fixture; the present Prime Minister, Bob Hawke, has become something of a fixture himself, having been in office for a decade.

Normally, this match has a leisurely, festival atmosphere about it, but our performances so far demanded that we win and win well. Even that proved beyond us, and we went down by 31 runs. The PM's side, led by Allan Border, scored 226, helped by the 34 runs we conceded in the final three overs. Our problems mounted when David Gower cracked his thumb in stopping a fierce drive from Border in the gully; he returned after X-rays to bat at number 8. Despite an opening stand of 57 between John Morris and 'Ned' Larkins, our challenge fell away feebly.

At this stage, we could have done with a four-day state game.

I'm not making excuses: the itinerary had been agreed. But it's very difficult to recover batting form when you're hopping around from town to town, pitch to pitch, in a series of limited-overs slogs. Normally, the one-day internationals are at the end of the Ashes tour, but this time the schedule had been changed because Australia were leaving immediately after our last match for their West Indies tour, and it was advantageous for them to finish with the last two Tests against England. It was the same itinerary for the Aussies, but they also had their domestic cricket. If England had been winning, the problem would not have been so acute. But having slipped, we were finding it almost impossible to find a way back. This itinerary was very different from the ones when I first toured Australia. Then, all the Test matches were preceded by a state game in the same place. That meant that we would be in each Test venue for two weeks before the match, and enable us to get settled and used to the conditions. For me that's a much better way of doing things. Few people come to the state games, anyway. The state matches would not have to be on the same grounds as the following Tests, but I would welcome a return to the old system. As it is, touring teams are moved from pillar to post – and Australia is an enormous country.

Touring is still a great experience, but these days it consists mainly of three things: travelling, practising, and playing. We had only eight free days in 16 weeks of touring – an average of one day off a fortnight! Nowadays, we spend much less time away from home, and there was no one-day cricket in the old days. So much more is cramped into less time, and sacrifices have to be made. Touring used to be much more relaxing, with most of the travelling done in comfortable trains. Today even an hour's flight can effectively take a whole day. Bags have to be packed and bills paid. Then there's the bus to the airport, often a delay, then the flight, and a bus at the other end before checking in at the new hotel. It all takes its toll – especially when the tour is going badly.

The Perth legs are the most tiring: there's a two-hour time change and a five-hour flight; it always seems to knock you out. David Gower and Eddie Hemmings, who had twisted his ankle in Adelaide, joined me on the sick list, while Mike Atherton was left out of the squad for the next, floodlit, clash with New Zealand.

Mike had taken 26 overs to score 33 at Adelaide and was struggling to find his England summer form. We considered it best for him to concentrate on getting himself right for the Tests and didn't become even more distracted trying to cope with one-day requirements.

England achieved their much-needed victory over New Zealand, but ours was hardly a convincing batting performance. We dismissed the Kiwis for 158, and our bowling and fielding were much nearer what was required. New Zealand reached 94 for 2 before losing their next six wickets for 34 runs in 15 overs. All five bowlers, including Philip Tufnell on his international debut, kept a tight line and our catches were held. 'Ned' and John Morris then continued their promising opening partnership with a stand of 72, but what should have been a gentle amble to victory became a frantic charge as England collapsed to 129 for 6 before Alec Stewart (who was named Man of the Match) and Gladstone Small settled the nerves and the match.

Nothing had really changed. We'd moved off the bottom of the table, but our batting was still liable to crumble at the first sniff of hostile bowling. But at least the victory had improved our position in the World Series. Maybe we would perform better now that the pressure had eased slightly.

Fat chance! Within two days England were back at the bottom of the table and Australia had opened a yawning gap between themselves and the other two sides competing for the World Series. For the third time in the competition we failed to reach 200 after deciding to bat. Had it not been for a spirited 31 from Martin Bicknell at the end, England would have fallen well short of our meagre total of 192. Once again a promising position was thrown away: at 128 for 3 we had a good platform from which to attack in the later overs – but five wickets went for 28 runs.

You can't sustain a challenge with collapses like that. Australia didn't have to break sweat and won by 4 wickets, with Dean Jones top-scoring. The one bright spot in our out-cricket was a magnificent two-handed diving catch by Chris Lewis to give Philip Tufnell his wicket. But it was depressing to watch the home side move relentlessly and efficiently towards their target.

Earlier, I'd gone to the practice ground for some gentle catching.

My finger was on the mend, and my return couldn't come too soon as far as I was concerned. Our injury problems increased when Gladstone Small broke down mid-way through an over with a groin strain. It was impossible to tell when he would be fit again. And so, as we were approaching crunch time, we sent for Phillip DeFreitas. Daffy had just missed out on selection and would be keen to prove we had been wrong if he got the chance.

I stayed behind in Perth to see a specialist while the rest of the party flew to Sydney. I probably wouldn't have been as desperate to return if the side had been performing adequately. But, with David Gower injured and Allan Lamb bothered by fibrositis, England were in danger of losing their entire trio of senior players. Our combined total of Test appearances was close to 300, while no other member of the touring party could boast even 20 caps. But I was also aware of the dangers of coming back too soon. That over-eagerness may well have been the reason why my finger became poisoned. By not keeping the original wound covered, it's likely that I encouraged the infection to take hold. However, I was confident that I was now ready to return to the fray.

Where better than Bowral, the birthplace of Sir Donald Bradman? If I thought the mere sight of G.A. Gooch back in the England team would work miracles, I was in for a shock. The Bradman XI was captained by former Aussie Test star Doug Walters, but it was young Darren Lehmann who stole the show with an undefeated century. Our 229 for 7 in 50 overs contained half centuries by Allan Lamb, Alec Stewart and Hugh Morris – I chipped in with 7 batting at number five – but our innings still lacked conviction and the home side won with nearly eight overs to spare.

We seemed incapable of getting both departments of our game on song at the same time. On the odd occasions that our batting functioned effectively, the bowling would let us down; when we bowled well, we batted badly. I thought things might look different from the middle; maybe it wasn't as bad as it seemed from the dressing-room. Now, I knew. It was, and I told the players so behind locked doors after the match. The way we were playing, we never looked like winning matches. Heads were dropping. We weren't going to find a way back by staring at the ground. I don't like watching cricket at the best of times, but the past month had been torture.

Thursday night brought some respite when we beat New Zealand under lights at Sydney by 33 runs. It was our most competent performance in the World Series so far and I felt that at last we'd taken a step forward. Allan Lamb got us out of trouble with one of his typically forceful one-day knocks, making 72 after England had been 23 for 3. Once again we failed to make 200, but the SCG wicket was not the easiest to score runs on. Martin Crowe was the main threat to us, but New Zealand's challenge faded when Angus Fraser had him lbw.

We bowled and fielded like an international side at last. Some claimed that the Kiwis had let a winning position slip, but that usually happens because the batting side is put under pressure by tight bowling and keen fielding. We showed some fight, and that pleased me just as much as collecting another two points.

Australia now had a maximum of eight points from four games, we had four from four and the Kiwis just two from six. The 10,000 Sydney crowd was a noisy lot and during our night match there had been outbreaks of violence more reminiscent of the antics of a soccer crowd in England. It's certainly one of the most intimidating cricket arenas I've played in.

We headed for Brisbane for a weekend in which our progress would be tested with two World Series games in two days. By Sunday night England were back to square one, having lost both matches and let New Zealand back into the competition. There was no excuse for that. The Kiwis were without the injured Ian Smith and Mark Greatbatch and their Hadlee-less bowling was ordinary by international standards. But too many of our key players were struggling to find their best form after two months on Australian soil. Robin Smith made 41, but was dropped twice and looked a shadow of the batsman that had taken the fight to the Aussies in 1989. Chris Lewis had managed just 15 runs in five World Series knocks, and back trouble forced him to drop out of the Sunday game. But our biggest problem was Devon Malcolm, who was whacked all over the Gabba. Devon's opening six overs cost 43 runs and his bowling had lost all its rhythm. We wanted him firing on all cylinders at the Melbourne Cricket Ground for the second Test, but time was running short. And it was too risky to play him in the one-day match against Australia on the Sunday: if Dean Jones had got hold of him, it might have finished him for the rest of the tour.

My worries about Jones were spot on. He was on the crest of a wave and hit 145 from 136 balls. Jones is a player who will back himself against anyone, and he makes the most of it. That afternoon he amply justified his reputation as the best one-day batsman in the world. Jones and Geoff Marsh put on a record 185 for the second wicket, and with 90 coming off the last 10 overs Australia ran up a massive 283 for 5. One-day cricket concentrates the mind wonderfully; there's no dithering in a situation like that. Our options were clear. Go for the runs. We failed by 37 runs: a commendable effort – except that we might even have won if we had not shot ourselves in the foot once again. Both Alec Stewart, who was batting beautifully, and Robin Smith were run out. That made it six run-outs in three matches, all involving top order batsmen. It's hard enough chasing a target of nearly 300 without throwing your wickets away.

My weekend scores were 48 and 41; nothing to write home about, but at least I was back and spending some time in the middle. My hand wound had opened up while I was fielding on the Saturday, but it wasn't serious. Other pluses were the batting form of Alec Stewart and the bowling form of Philip Tufnell.

Our two defeats hadn't dropped us to third place in the World Series table – yet. That came on Tuesday in Tasmania, when New Zealand ruined Australia's spotless record with a one-run win after the home side had rashly experimented with their batting order. A high run-rate was no good to us now; we had to win one of our two remaining games against Australia to qualify for the final, otherwise the Kiwis, who'd flown back to New Zealand, would be returning to Sydney and Melbourne for the finals in mid-January. Our last two World Series qualifiers would follow the second and third Tests. So it was time once more to concentrate our attention on that famous little urn.

Second Test, Melbourne

Ballarat is an old gold-mining town about 60 miles from Melbourne. After all the racing around we'd done in the previous few weeks, it was pleasant to return to an old-fashioned touring venue for the state game against Victoria. W.G. Grace had played here and rated it the best pitch in Australia. The locals were genuinely pleased to see us and it was one of the most enjoyable stops of the tour. But our injury problems mounted still further when a ball smashed into the back of John Morris's hand during fielding practice and, more seriously, Allan Lamb tore a calf muscle running back to the motel after play. John's hand was badly bruised and the X-rays did not rule out a break. Lamb's damaged calf put his place for the Melbourne Test in doubt; it was giving him as much trouble in 1990 as my hand was to me. Lamb had just hit his third hundred of the tour and maybe it wasn't wise to attempt the five-mile run after three hours at the crease. It was a more serious injury than the one he had sustained in Barbados during the West Indies tour. On top of that, Micky Stewart, who had been suffering from a chest infection in Brisbane and now was experiencing numbness in his right leg, had to return to Melbourne for tests and was detained overnight.

The match started badly for us. Dean Jones hit another century off the England bowlers as Victoria reached 441 for 7. Then Mike Atherton and Robin Smith gave the first signs of emerging from their batting doldrums, and when Victoria went in again, Devon (whose wife Jennifer had just arrived) took three wickets in a 13-ball spell on the Saturday evening. During dinner on the Friday night David Gower had wondered whether it would be wise to order duck. It wasn't: he was out first ball when he missed Merv Hughes' full-length slower delivery! He vowed never to tempt fate again.

It was pleasing to see Mike Atherton back in the runs because he was taking quite a while to adapt to Australian pitches and conditions. That wasn't surprising for one so relatively inexperienced. But it was the Lamb injury that was the most serious consequence of our visit to Ballarat. England hadn't been able to put David Gower, Allan and myself on the same field since the opening state game; the way things were going, that might be the first and last time we played together on this trip.

There was the small matter of Christmas to celebrate before the second Test began. That Boxing Day date was always at the back of my mind during the festivities. We had had little time to prepare for the traditional fancy-dress parade because the England party didn't arrive in Melbourne until Christmas Eve. David Gower was chairman of the Social Committee and had warned the fancy-dress shop of our needs. Every player is given a letter; he chooses a theme starting with that letter and finds an appropriate costume. I had ordered nets for Christmas morning, so the press cocktail party was switched to Christmas Eve at the Windsor Hotel, where they were staying. It was a fairly chaotic party, but the best ones often are. Cricketers are nowadays a lot more wary of the press than they used to be. There seems to be a greater turnover of cricket correspondents these days, so you don't always have time to get to know them. In any case, you'd be a card or two short of a full pack if you didn't realize that a certain element among them would stuff you if given the chance. But this was the season of goodwill to all men – even pressmen!

Practising was not the ideal way to spend Christmas morning, but we needed to sort a few things out before picking our Test team. Lambie had failed his fitness battle, so we were doubly keen that David Gower, troubled by a bruised right wrist, would be available for selection. A TV crew got rather close when he was in the nets and David let them have both barrels. David has this reputation for being laid back, but he can blow a fuse quicker than anyone I know. No decision on David was forthcoming as yet, so we were going to have to wait until the morning of the match. After the nets it was back to our hotel, the Rockman's Regency, for the fancy-dress parade. My letter was R, but my appearance as an England rugby player carrying a rugby ball got very low marks. Lambie looked sensational as a bunny-girl, though as far as I know few bunny-girls sport a bushy moustache. Daffy DeFreitas was the spitting image of Prince. David's letter was B, and he turned up as Biggles, jodhpurs and all. (I didn't know then that this wasn't going to be the only appearance of that particular costume on this tour.) Our Christmas lunch was the usual noisy affair, but, with the match starting the next day, I took it easy. I didn't lay down any set rules; you have to rely on people's judgement. This was my first Christmas away from the girls. Although we'd been away for 10 weeks, we still had four Tests to play. I rang home twice and regretted not being there to share in their enjoyment, but now I had to turn all my thoughts to the task ahead.

Resolving the Gower situation took a fair amount of time on Boxing Day morning. David said that he was not 100 per cent fit. Lambie and I wanted to know how near to fitness he was so that we could make a judgement on whether to take a calculated risk or bring in someone else. David reckoned he was about 85 per cent fit; batting would not be too much of a problem, but he thought he'd struggle in the field. (Actually, because of his shoulder problems, David's fielding had been restricted over the past few years. He was still one of the best catchers in the game, but his arm had 'gone'. We had to send relay teams after David if he chased a ball in the outfield to make sure the batsmen didn't take two for the throw.) We decided to take the gamble. His experience was vital. Lambie would be absent and this would be only my second first-class game after injury.

There were 50,000 fans inside the MCG that morning, all packed into only half of the stadium. The building on the far side of the field, including the infamous Bay 13, had been demolished to make way for a new stand. Chris Lewis was still troubled by his back, so Daffy came into the side; Philip Tufnell's recent displays won him a place over Eddie Hemmings. It looked a flat wicket and I had no hesitation in electing to bat after winning the toss. Mike Atherton's bad trot continued with a duck, and Terry Alderman made it 30 for 2 when I padded up, offering no stroke. At Ballarat, I had felt rusty and ill at ease. Here I was happy with the way I was batting, everything was moving right. Then I made a serious error of judgement. It's my job to pick the line of the ball and I got it wrong. That was annoying because I'd been in no trouble until then. 'Ned' Larkins, who was playing only because of Lambie's injury, hit a patient half century, while Robin Smith had just begun to look settled when he was given out caught behind. At 152 for 4, our innings was in the balance, but David and Alec

Stewart enjoyed an undefeated fifth-wicket stand which reached 87 by the close. After our recent troubles and poor start, that was a good recovery.

The second day went Australia's way. David and Alec took their stand to 122 – but then our last six wickets fell for 78 runs, giving us a total of 352. The highlight was a 100, exactly, from David. Our gamble in playing him had come off. As usual with David, it was a mixture of agony and ecstasy to watch; or rather, the other way around. He looked in good nick on the first evening and next morning gave a vintage Gower display, with flowing cover drives, to reach his century. The way he was playing, a really big score from him would have put England in control. But then a delivery from Reid 'stopped' on him and the bowler stretched his lofty frame to take a return catch in his left hand. Reid was enjoying his re-entry to the big time and finished with another six English wickets. Our 352 was 50 runs short of my target, and Australia had reduced the deficit to less than 250 by the close for the loss only of Geoff Marsh. The fierce wind played havoc with our bowlers and Angus Fraser struggled to cope with the conditions. Chris Lewis had trouble of a different sort. A specialist had discovered a stress fracture in his back. There was no reprieve and he had to return home for an operation. Chris had got his chance in the Caribbean when Ricky Ellcock had to return home with a bad back. Daffy, brought out as cover when Gladstone injured his groin, was the beneficiary this time and he joined the party for the duration.

Gus carried on from the night before when he turned over his right ankle as he bowled his second ball of the day. If he had cried off then, we would really have been in trouble. As it was, his opening nine overs were typical Gus, costing only five runs. The Middlesex youngster wasn't finished and his nagging accuracy exposed Australia's batting to bring him a fantastic 6 for 23 spell. He had bowled his guts out, and he nearly collapsed on his return to the dressing-room. Australia, at one time 133 for 1 and later 224 for 3, were all out for 306, giving us a lead of 46.

That was a real bonus. On this wicket, you had to bowl well to get wickets: straight and accurate. The home batsmen played some rash shots, but that was because they had been put under pressure.

Gus wasn't the only one to claim six victims – Jack Russell picked up six catches behind the stumps. Daffy and Devon, with two wickets apiece, did their job well and Philip Tufnell performed admirably without much luck on his debut. This was much more like it. We had turned a far from comfortable position into potentially a winning one by doing the simple things well. Our heads were high that Friday night. But only 24 hours later they were back in our boots after one of the most incredible passages of play in cricket history.

As at Brisbane, our bowlers had got England back into the game. And as at Brisbane, our batters cost England the Test. The pitch had started to become uneven and was misbehaving a bit, and we were confident that anything approaching a target of 250 was going to test the Aussies. Mike Atherton went early again but 'Ned' and I took the score past 100. I was feeling good and looking to move the score along when I chased a wide one from Reid and was caught behind. It was a risky shot, but we needed to capitalize on our advantage if we were to win. We suffered a slight hiccup during the afternoon session. David was out for nought for the first time in a record 120 Test innings – that duck on the menu in Ballarat had a lot to answer for! – but 'Ned' and Alec were together at tea.

Our overall lead was now 193, with six second-innings wickets left. My instruction during the break was that we mustn't lose quick wickets. With 30 overs left that day, we were looking to bat safely for 15 overs, then to review the situation and go for quick runs if we had wickets in hand. We were still one-down in the series and were after that win that would level things. The Aussies, and Reid in particular, had other ideas. The home side turned the game on its head with the most decisive 12 overs of the series. I couldn't believe my eyes. At tea, the worst we could do was draw the Test. An hour later we were staring defeat and a 2–0 deficit in the face. Reid's post-tea figures were six overs, six maidens, no runs, four wickets. That made it 7 for 51 in the innings and 13 for 148 in the match. Greg Matthews was the expensive bowler after tea: his six overs and two wickets cost three runs! Australia, instead of fighting for survival with a 300 target to intimidate them, needed 197 runs for victory. That still wouldn't be easy, but their confidence had been boosted by our collapse. And time, which should have been an extra pressure on the Australians, was no longer a factor. It was worse than the first Test, much worse. I've never seen anything like it. And, while the home side had been boosted by our failing, it had the opposite effect on us. I felt sorry for our bowlers. They'd delivered when the pressure was on, and our batsmen had let them down.

And our bowlers did, in fact, give us a lifeline by reducing the Aussies to 28 for 2 on that fourth evening. Afterwards, I had a drink with Ted Dexter, the chairman of the England Committee who had flown out to Melbourne. England were still in with a chance, but we had to get amongst the wickets early on. Sadly, not a single wicket fell on that final day as Australia strolled home by eight wickets to go two up in the Clashes for the Ashes. Devon had a confident lbw shout turned down early on; that apart, Boon and Marsh gave nothing away. We made them fight all the way: after three and a half hours' play, only one boundary had been scored. But once Australia had reached tea and safety, Boon opened up and Marsh pushed the winning single at five o'clock. Philip Tufnell felt Boon was lucky to still be there: our left-arm spinner was not alone in his conviction that Jack Russell had taken a thickish edge as Boon had attempted to cut when Australia were still 31 short of victory.

All Philip's frustrations came to the surface as he argued, snatched his cap, wandered to the boundary muttering and carrying on the argument with umpire Peter McConnell. I don't care if McConnell had got it wrong, you have to accept the umpire's decisions. At the end of the match, I went over to McConnell to ask what had happened. He explained that Tufnell had made a fuss about the decision, which was obvious to everyone, and McConnell had had a go back – which he regretted. McConnell added that he would not be reporting the matter.

Players have to learn to control themselves. I find it sad to see them acting like that, whatever the provocation. Another, more serious problem was that Gus had left the field with a hip injury and it looked pretty serious. We had finished the West Indies series without our most reliable bowler; was it going to happen here, too? I was still a bit bemused to be on the losing side after we had played the better cricket for three and a half days. Full credit to the Australians, though. They showed all their fighting qualities to conjure a win out of nothing. They had been almost out of the match, but fought their way back. It wouldn't have been so bad if I thought my side was capable of doing the same. But, frankly, after watching the way we folded under pressure here and in Brisbane, I didn't think we had the bottle.

That's a hard and painful thing for a captain to admit, because it means he's failed. And I found that conclusion difficult to shrug off over the final weeks of the tour. But at least the problems on the field hadn't spilt over to cause any rifts in the touring camp. Many wives and families had arrived by now. Robin Smith had been introduced to his first-born, Harrison, who had arrived early in December. Earlier plans for him to fly home about the time of the birth had to be shelved because of our various injuries and losses of form. There was still a good atmosphere within the group, although the two Tests and the World Series failures had inevitably taken a toll of morale.

One of the advantages of touring in Australia is that we don't live in each other's pockets. In the Caribbean the touring cricketers tend to gravitate to the same spots in what, apart from Jamaica and Guyana, are quite small islands. Australia is a vast place, with more and bigger attractions. Eating and drinking is one of the favourite pastimes. The major cities are located on or very near the coast, and the seafood available in their restaurants is of top quality, while Australia's wines are now recognized as among the best in the world.

I was able to enjoy both at Doyle's on New Year's Eve with the lads. There had been a big firework display in Sydney Harbour to welcome 1991. In some ways, I was sorry to see the old year go; I had played some of the best cricket of my career, enjoyed many personal and team highlights and had been awarded an MBE in the New Year's Honours list (one smart alec Aussie broadcaster reckoned the initials stood for 'Massively Beaten England!') But I hoped the new year would herald a change in fortune for this particular touring party.

Third Test, Sydney

I didn't have long to wait. Our clash with Australia under lights at the SCG on New Year's Day was our penultimate match in the World Series qualifier. But, once again, we hit the self-destruct button. Our bowlers were certainly getting a raw deal. Simon O'Donnell and Mark Waugh had come to Australia's rescue with a record sixth-wicket stand of 112 after half their side had gone for less than a 100. 'Ned' and I made inroads into the 222-run target with an opening stand of 65 in 16 overs, but that was the beginning and end of our challenge: 10 wickets fell for 88 and the Aussies won decisively. We were at the point of no-return. Not only did we have to beat Australia in our final match, but our run rate had to improve if we were to make the finals. After this woeful performance, the chances of that looked remote.

Gus Fraser had surprised everyone by playing in the one-day game in spite of his hip problem. But he played that night only because he realized he had no chance of lasting through a five-day Test. With Allan Lamb still unfit, the loss of Gus was a major blow, especially after his heroics at Melbourne. Daffy was left out of the Test squad because we decided to include two spinners. In recent Tests at the SCG it's been the slow bowlers who have generally done the damage. This time was no exception – except that the damage done by Philip Tufnell and Eddie Hemmings here was mainly to their own reputations.

Allan Border won the toss and batted. Although their openers were removed cheaply, the rest of the day was something of a slog, although I picked up the wicket of David Boon with the three-card trick. He hit me for three fours and I bowled another delivery that should have gone the same way, but he smashed it straight to backward point. Boon is a good little player. At the time his place in the team was under threat, but he finished as their top run-getter in the series. Border also had his heart set on a century – he'd gone more than two years without one – and looked distraught when Eddie bowled him round his legs, sweeping, in the seventies. AB is not the dominant player he once was, but he is still one of the hardest men in Test cricket to get out.

Australia were 259 for 4 overnight and they doubled their score to make that Saturday, 5 January, the worst day of my cricketing life. The previous Saturday had been bad enough when we surrended the second Test, but we lost our pride and dignity here at the SCG. The England cricket team had become a laughing-stock. Our poor bowling exposed our pathetic fielding. This was the worst fielding side I'd ever been in. It was a total disaster. I felt helpless, responsible and embarrassed. I would never have believed that any side I was in charge of could be so inept. Even Clem, our scorer, who had never made a negative comment on a day's play in all the time I've known him at Essex, admitted he was embarrassed, too. It was obvious that not everyone was pulling their weight. You can't afford to play Test cricket like that, especially against the Aussies. The way they were playing, we couldn't afford to be anything less than at our best. Greg Matthews had a field day, hitting his fourth century for Australia, and even Terry Alderman shot way past his previous Test best and batted for an hour and a half.

My day was made complete when Eddie Hemmings reacted angrily after umpire Peter McConnell turned down an appeal for a catch at short leg. After Alec, the catcher, had tossed the ball on to the ground, Eddie swung at it with his boot towards McConnell and it hit the stumps. I knew how frustrated everyone was getting, but there was no call for dissent or tantrums. The trouble with a flare-up like this is that the captain has no chance to intervene. I didn't get much response from Eddie when I went over to try and calm him down. I wasn't in Philip Tufnell's good books, either. He hadn't been very happy when umpire Tony Crafter refused his appeal for a catch off Alderman. His long-awaited first Test wicket came after 74 overs and 191 runs, when Matthews skied a full toss to Eddie in the deep. I went over to offer my congratulations, but all I got was Phil's back as he turned towards his fellow spinner. Eddie's outburst could not be ignored and both he and Alec Stewart were spoken to by manager Peter Lush that evening.

But in the middle of all this mess there was a flash of genius that hopefully will linger longest in the memories of this Saturday at Sydney. Jack Russell, who was, remarkably, standing up to Gladstone Small, sent Dean Jones on his way with a lightning leg-side stumping. He was a lone master craftsman at work who hadn't been dragged down by the performance of the rest of the team.

Just as our bowlers had brought us back into the contest in the opening two Tests, England's batting line-up at last paid its way and gave us a slim chance of victory at Sydney. David Gower's century was breathtaking, his runs coming at an alarming rate on the fourth morning, but Mike Atherton's hundred was the rock on which our challenge was built. Mike hadn't had an easy time, but had stuck to it; his innings allowed people to flourish at the other end. Mike is a steady rather than a quick scorer, very reminiscent of the late Ken Barrington. Alec was intent on making the number six spot his own and followed his 79 at Melbourne with a brave 91 here that deserved those additional nine runs for his maiden Test hundred.

In order to press for victory, I declared 49 behind Australia. I couldn't leave the deficit any larger, and this gave our bowlers nearly an hour to get at Australia on the fourth evening. Again we removed the openers cheaply, and Australia went into the final day with a lead of 87 with eight wickets left. Despite our poor form, poor attitude, Australia's lead and the lack of time, I believed we could win on that final day. By the close, many more felt we should have won. At one stage the home side were 166 for 7 – a lead of 215 – with four hours remaining. Australia's batting heroes were Ian Healy and Carl Rackemann, who went for 75 balls before scoring his first run. It was left to Devon Malcolm to knock over Rackemann's stumps. Our target then was 255 in 28 overs.

That was Devon's first over of the day, and I faced a lot of criticism for not using him earlier to dislodge Rackemann. Before play, Devon had told me that he wasn't fit to bowl. I told him to come out with us: if Devon didn't field, then he wouldn't be allowed to bowl. If his injury eased during the course of the day, then he might have a chance. With hindsight, it was an error not to bring him on earlier, but my fear was that one loose over from an injured bowler like Devon might cost us 15 or 20 runs – and runs, as well as time, were a vital commodity at this stage. The spinners weren't being hit and looked as if they might break through at any moment. Philip Tufnell bowled well, taking 5 for 61 in his second Test, but he has a lot to learn. There's a bit more to Test cricket than just bowling.

Our last real chance of victory had now gone. Everyone assumed that we would have reached a total of just over 200 in around 40 overs if we had wrapped up their tail quickly. I'm not so sure. Allan Border wouldn't have made it easy. But David Gower and I came out with guns blazing and put the wind up them with 84 runs in 12 overs. It was great fun. There was no point in the draw: only a victory would give us a chance of regaining the Ashes. It was a very slim chance, so we made the effort. But sustaining that run rate was impossible without taking chances – there were no one-day regulations to hamper Allan Border's field placings – and we finished at 113 for 4.

And so the Ashes, my main objective in Australia, slipped beyond our grasp. We'd had our chances but not taken them. The Aussies responded positively to pressure and we did not – and that was the vital difference between the sides.

Two days later our last chance of a trophy – a bigger one but much less significant than the Ashes – vanished in the debris of yet another batting collapse in our last one-day qualifier. The final margin was only three runs, but it took the confident hitting of a bowler, Angus Fraser, to get us that close. Again the Australians were in trouble early on at 127 for 6; again they took their total well past the 200 mark as we faltered under the pressure. That target ended any problems of run-rate. If we won, England would qualify for the finals; if we didn't, New Zealand would return to Australia and England would head out to Albury to face New South Wales.

Our Sydney form had not been lost on the home crowd, and one banner proclaimed 'Phil Tufnell Fielding Academy'. From a promising 93 for 2 England slipped to a hopeless 146 for 8. Our last pair put on 43 runs from 33 deliveries, leaving Phil Tufnell needing to hit the final ball for four for victory. He heaved and missed. The match highlighted the batting problem that had troubled us all through the World Series. Some players were making a good start, but then they failed to consolidate. And I was the biggest culprit. It's not usually a problem for me, but I kept on stuttering in the 30s and 40s when feeling well set. I've always enjoyed one-day cricket and have always been successful. Going in first is the only place to bat; you've got the time and you can dictate from there. If I reach 40-odd, I would expect to take my score into the 80s at least three times out of five.

Allan Lamb was fit again and took the side to Albury, while I remained in Melbourne for a few days' rest. It had been non-stop and none too pleasant since my return from injury three weeks earlier. The side's attitude, even more than their form, was getting me down; I wanted time to consider what the real problems were and to prepare for the final two Tests. Australia kept up their charge by beating New Zealand 2–0 in a one-sided World Series final. I watched Ivan Lendl and Mary-Joe Fernandez at the Australian Open; I tracked down two of the British women challengers, but they didn't last long. I also played some golf. But the Gulf war deadline was approaching and was occupying ever-increasing media attention.

The war started on the day I flew from Melbourne to the Gold Coast and joined up with the squad again. They'd lost to the Sheffield Shield champions NSW by six wickets after being bowled out for 164 in their first innings. Mike Atherton then hit a century in the second, but found no support. This was our fourth defeat in eight first-class games, with four draws. We were in grave danger of becoming the first England side in cricket history to leave Australia without a single first-class victory.

England did win and, after the trouble we'd had in the previous three months, it should have made sporting headlines. But, no. Those were reserved for David Gower and John Morris, who celebrated Robin Smith's first century of the tour with a fly-past in two Tiger Moths. I was sitting on the balcony with John Stephenson when someone pointed to one of the planes and said: 'that looks like Lubo'. You must be joking, I thought. The link with his fancy dress at the Christmas party hadn't registered with me yet.

Peter Lush, our tour manager was rather taken aback at the daily press conference when he was asked if David and John had been given permission to leave the ground and salute Robin's innings in such a spectacular way. It was the first he knew about it. But that wasn't the end of it. When Peter returned to the dressing-room to find out exactly what had gone on, our David was missing again. It turned out he had gone back to the airfield to pose for pictures, Amy Johnson-style, for some eager photographers. That, for me, was the most astonishing part of the incident. David's decision to return to the scene of the 'crime' for the photo session showed a lack of respect for the way things were. I assumed he hadn't asked me for permission to leave the ground because he knew I would refuse. It might have looked like a bit of fun, but it set a bad example. David thought he was harshly treated, but in my view he let the team down badly. I was disappointed – he should have known better. So should John Morris, even though he was making his first tour. The tour was going badly and the management were pretty annoyed. The disciplinary committee consisted of Peter, Micky, Lambie and me. I don't like fining players, but something had to be done. I was in full agreement with the £1,000 fine.

Our approach was much less cavalier on the field. Queensland were bowled out for 286, with Phil Tufnell collecting another five wickets. Centuries from Robin Smith and John Morris, plus 93 from me, took England well past 400. The home side then struggled to make 175, and we romped home by 10 wickets. For some reason Queensland didn't seem to play with the same competitiveness as the other state sides. Graeme Hick scored 45 and 14, but Stuart Law, who was named Shield Player of the Season, looked an exciting prospect with 74 and 44. John Morris batted well and he was unlucky that Robin Smith, the batsman most under threat in the Test line-up, matched his century. All in all, after our fight back in Sydney and this victory on the Gold Coast, England travelled to Adelaide in a more positive frame of mind for the fourth Test.

Fourth Test, Adelaide

The Adelaide Oval is not the easiest place to force a victory. Batsmen traditionally have the upper hand on this true track. There was also little likelihood of Australia relaxing, now that the Ashes were safe in their possession. It's not in their nature. Anyway, their selectors were getting ready to pick the tour party for the trip to the Caribbean. The men in possession were in a strong position, leading 2–0 in a five-match series with two Tests remaining. However, they made two key changes for the Adelaide match. Steve Waugh, after his brilliant summer in England in 1989, had struggled in this series and was now replaced by his twin brother, Mark. That did not weaken them materially. Mark had played for Essex for the past two seasons and was clearly a top-class cricketer and competitor. Carl Rackemann, despite defying and denying us at Sydney, was also dropped and Craig McDermott returned. 'Billy the Kid', as he is known, was only 25, but his star had faded since a successful Ashes tour of England in 1985. But he had returned to his best form with Queensland and was desperate for another shot at the Poms.

We also had some team changes to make in Adelaide, and one of them was, for me, the hardest of the tour. It was the correct cricket decision, but I hated having to tell Jack Russell that we were going to alter the balance of the side and that meant Alec Stewart taking over the wicket-keeping spot. Jack would lay down his life for England and his commitment had been unstinting from the first day of the tour. He was also the best wicket-keeper in the world – yet I had to tell him he'd lost his job! But we had to take whatever steps we thought necessary to save the series. Angus Fraser, though not 100 per cent fit, had to play. The hard grounds of Perth weren't going to suit him, so this was kill or cure; otherwise there was little point in his staying on. He was the one class bowler we had and I noticed it when we wasn't playing. We had to include an extra seam bowler in case Gus broke down, so the one guy with a great attitude had to miss out on this particular occasion. Jack's batting form had deserted him over the past year and, with an extra bowler, we couldn't really see him coming in at No 6.

Ian Botham had always given the selectors the advantage of picking an England XII: six batsmen, including Beefy, and five bowlers, including Beefy, plus a wicket-keeper. When Ian wasn't around, choosing an XI became a little more difficult. At Adelaide, David Gower, Allan Lamb and I were finally in the same team again; it had been 82 days since that last happened. Lambie returned in place of 'Ned' Larkins and took over the number three spot. That had been England's problem batting position over the years. David had spent a lot of time going in first wicket down, but I didn't think he was suited to it. In recent years Mike Gatting had been the only one who had really fitted in there. That's where he bats for Middlesex; it suits his game and his temperament. Going in at number three is the hardest batting job; you can be walking out to take guard during the first over of the day – or hanging around in your pads for five hours.

Before the Test I went to the airport to pick up a couple of special visitors from England, Alf and Rose Gooch. Mum and Dad had never seen me play in a Test abroad and the 31-hour journey was a bit of an ordeal for them. Alf loves his cricket and has driven me all over the place. But he had never travelled this far before, so I was determined to put on a bit of a show for them.

Allan Border chose to bat, but our dismay turned to hope when the Australians stumbled to 124 for 5. Mark Taylor was run out (as he would also be in the second innings). The left-hander had batted four times in Tests at the Adelaide Oval – and had been run out every time! That must be one of the more obscure cricket records. Daffy DeFreitas removed AB and then Dean Jones for a duck. 'The greatest one-day player in the world' had been struggling badly since that weekend in Brisbane in mid-December. But our attempts to dismiss Australia cheaply were thwarted by Greg Matthews and Mark Waugh, who hit a remarkable century in his first Test innings. I knew he could play and had been glad their selectors had resisted the temptation to bring him in earlier, but I was surprised at his level of self-confidence. When Philip Tufnell came on, Mark took the attack to him. He didn't bowl badly, but Mark wanted to dominate and came down the wicket to him. In your first Test with your side in trouble, that's a brave thing to do. Mark said afterwards that it was one of those innings in a thousand where every shot seems to come out of the middle of the bat; it seemed that way to me, too, out there. There were no nervous 90s: he moved from the 70s to his century with speed, confidence and inevitability.

Greg Matthews was the perfect foil; he'd been a thorn in our side, batting-wise, all through the series and he batted 318 minutes for his 65, while Mark took under four hours for his 138. Craig McDermott also batted for nearly three hours, and the Aussies got out of jail once again with a total of 386.

Gus Fraser limped out of the attack on the second day, so we went looking for a cover for Perth. Essex's young left-arm bowler Mark Ilott was playing club cricket in Adelaide and had helped us out in the nets to counter the threat of Bruce Reid. But we decided to send for Phil Newport, who was with England A in Sri Lanka, and he flew to Perth. Phil Tufnell was also in trouble with a throat infection and only a last-minute drop in his temperature of 104° stopped him being carted off to hospital. This England cricket team was certainly putting a strain on the medical resources in Adelaide. I had introduced mum and dad to Randall Sach and his family; Randall kindly hosted another Saturday night dinner for us, the Lushes and the Stewarts. Randall took a few days off from his consultancy work to watch this match. But such is the hospitality and congenial atmosphere of an Adelaide Test that, after five days, *he* looked the one in need of attention!

Our first innings got off to a bad start. Mike Atherton and Allan Lamb were both out for ducks on the Saturday evening. Robin Smith found some form at last, but England suffered that familiar collapse again on Sunday. After we had got to 160 for 3, our last seven wickets capitulated and Australia had a lead of 157 runs. On this pitch, that effectively ended our chance of winning.

The worst moment came when David Gower lazily pulled the last ball before lunch into Merv Hughes' hands at widish long leg. It had not been David's week. The jokes about Biggles and his Tiger Moth joyride continued; the crowd laughed as he cast his eyes skyward when a plane flew over the ground on the first day. I, for one, wasn't laughing when David fell to this the sucker punch just before lunch. Martin Johnson, the amusing but often cruel cricket correspondent of the *Independent*, wrote that it was that shot which should have earned David his £1,000 fine, and that I took so long leaving the field at lunch in my dismay at David's carelessness that by the time I reached the pavilion it was almost time for me to come back out again. I was rather stunned, I must admit. I didn't say anything to David in the dressing-room. There was no point. He knew what he'd done: the Aussies have been feeding him that ball for years and, more often than not, he has taken the bait. They bowl him a couple an over with a leg slip and a long leg, who's at 45 degrees. If he hits it perfectly, it goes straight to the fielder on the boundary. It's not a controlled shot, and it's just not worth the risk, but David can't curb the habit. It was disappointing from his point of view because he was getting close to Geoff Boycott's record number of Test runs for an Englishman and because he had been our outstanding batsman in the series so far. I know the risks in selecting him. When I put David Gower in my team, I have to accept the way he plays, the good with the bad.

McDermott was the bowler on this occasion, and he picked up four more England wickets to take five in the innings to crown a successful comeback. Allan Border then batted us out the game. Boon, as he did against Gatt's side at Adelaide, scored a hundred, and the skipper was undefeated on 83 when he declared. Our task was daunting: 482 to win in a day and 10 overs. But, again, we had nothing to lose. We batted confidently in the first session and went into lunch at 115 without loss.

I chatted with Lambie during the interval and we decided to have a go. As at Sydney, the odds were heavily stacked against us, but we added 88 in the hour after the interval to make the impossible look just conceivable. I scored my first Test century in Australia at last and was really pleased that Mum and Dad were there to see it. I should have brought them down under earlier. They'd been here less than a week, and now I had the hundred that I'd been searching for since 1978!

Even when Mike Atherton and I had gone, Lambie kept up the charge. But when he, David and Alec went in the space of three overs and 10 runs, we had to call a halt, and Robin Smith and Daffy batted through to the close for a draw. AB had been criticized for batting on too long before declaring, but our charge silenced those comments.

It was a brave effort and emphasized that, in terms of ability, there was little to choose between the teams. In all four Tests, we'd had more than a sniff of victory – but we still had nothing to show for our efforts. That was the difference between this tour and our 1989 Ashes attempt. We'd hardly had a single good day that summer as the Aussie tourists got the upper hand and regained the Ashes. But here in Australia the sides were about level on a day-to-day basis; if anything, we had a slight lead. No wonder I couldn't shake off the conviction that we had thrown away a great chance.

The Aussies' squad for the West Indies tour was announced on the final day of the Adelaide Test. The entire Adelaide XII was picked along with Mike Valetta (opener and second keeper), Peter Taylor (second spinner), Steve Waugh and Mike Whitney (left-arm back-up for Bruce Reid). Reid had made a tremendous return to international cricket, but the Aussies were aware of the need to protect one of their most valuable assets and they decided not to risk him in the Perth Test, when he was suffering from a bruised heel.

Fifth Test, Perth

We travelled to Perth with the Aussies by a rather roundabout route. The fuel controllers in Australia were striking and we hurried to leave Adelaide before getting stranded. Nobody fancied making the journey to Perth by any other means. The flight was delayed and then we headed up to Alice Springs for refuelling. We had only enough fuel to get there, but it meant that we were still as far away from Perth as we had been in Adelaide.

We arrived after midnight (Perth time), and after my Test hundred and five hours in the air with all the delays, I was ready to crash out. Not that anybody was rushing around Perth either. Wednesday, 31 January – the next day – was the hottest day in Perth's history. The temperature reached 45.8°C, almost 115°F, and practising at the WACA was a draining experience. The only consolation was that the heatwave was scheduled to break on Friday when the Test started. The city was almost at a standstill. Thousands of cars broke down in the heat and you could see bush fires raging in the distance. Most of us took shelter in the air-conditioned Hyatt hotel.

Gus Fraser failed his fitness test, and Phil Newport came in for his third Test match. This was a shame for Gus because Perth was one wicket he would have enjoyed bowling on – it had pace, bounce and moved sideways a bit. I rate Phil as a bowler, but some days he can seem to 'disappear'. Because he's such an attacking bowler, he can be in trouble if the ball doesn't swing. AB overcame his groin strain to make his 117th consecutive Test appearance for Australia – a tremendous record.

Australia had batted us out of the last two Tests, so I was grateful to win the toss and get first use of the WACA wicket. Just before tea, we were 191 for 2 with Lambie and Robin Smith going at full belt, helped by the Aussies' worst bowling of the series. After all that had happened, I was taking nothing for granted – which was just as well. Our last eight wickets disappeared for 53 runs and McDermott, with figures at one time of 2 for 72, finished up with 8 for 97 – the best Ashes bowling figures since Bob Willis's epic 8 for 43 at Headingley in 1981. David Gower, needing 67 runs to pass Boycott's Test total, was left stranded on 28 not out, having come in at number five. Marsh's wicket before the close was some consolation, but we had squandered yet another glorious chance. I'd never been in a side that had such a propensity to self-destruct. It wasn't that we weren't any good; the way we manoeuvred ourselves into possible Test-winning situations proved that. But, the hard work over, our generosity towards the opposition was often fatal.

Our bowlers gave us another fighting chance when the home side was reduced to 168 for 6, but that man Matthews again dropped anchor to provide Australia with a first-innings lead of 63. That was the story of the tour: England, having got to 212 for 3, made only 244; Australia, reduced to 168 for 6, made 307. Matthews had certainly outstayed his welcome as far as we were concerned: he spent more than 18 hours at the crease in this series, an average of over $2\frac{1}{2}$ hours every innings, and only David Boon bettered his total of 353 runs. Ian Healy batted for about half that time. Australia had benefited handsomely from such stubbornness from their number seven and eight.

The ball flew all over the place that third morning and we did well to get through to lunch for the loss only of myself and Lambie. We needed to set the Aussies 250 to have any chance. The Aussie bowlers only had to put it in the right spot and something would happen. The wicket quietened down after lunch, but you wouldn't have noticed it if you had seen our batting. Another seven wickets fell, this time for 69 runs, and it was all over with England at 144 for 9. Phil Newport, with an undefeated 40, and Devon Malcolm, battled long enough to ensure the match would move into the fourth day. David Gower finished 34 runs short of his Boycott target when he tried to attack his way out of trouble and edged a wide ball to second slip. Alec Stewart had followed his 91 at Sydney with 35 runs in five knocks. (Some people believed that switching to wicket-keeping duties caused his loss of form, but I don't accept that.) Only Robin Smith looked like occupying the crease for any length of time.

Australia were left needing to make 120 to win. Mark Taylor completed a disappointing series when he was caught off the final ball of the day; that was the seventh time in a row he'd been out for less than 20. He had made a record 839 runs in the 1989 Ashes battle in England; this time his tally was 213. He'd struggled when we started bowling round the wicket to him; it's not so easy to leave the ball and he often got caught in the cauldron. But he's a quality batsman who will work out how to beat that problem. His runs in 1989 weren't a flash in the pan; he's a good player who happened to have a bad series in 1990/1.

We enjoyed our first official Test rest day in Perth. We were bound to get another one because the match was never going to last five days. Our Press XI met the Aussies at Melvista in the Clashes for the Ashes, but lost by four wickets after the sort of batting collapse they had been criticizing us for over the past four months.

The following morning the Aussies collected the 81 runs they needed for victory before lunch. It was, frankly, a fitting finale to our tour: we bowled badly, fielded sloppily and dropped two catches. I was in no mood to offer excuses at the press conference afterwards. I'd failed as skipper, and we'd failed as a team. I wasn't kidding when I said I was seriously considering my future as captain; it had got that bad. One thing was certain: I and we couldn't go on like this. The 10-day trip to New Zealand to play three one-day games was an addition we could have done without. But it was going to be an important time for me. I intended to make a thorough analysis of the past four months and decide whether I had a future as England's Test captain.

The West Indies, 1991

The English summer may have come and gone since that final Aussie press conference, but my statements at the time still hold true.

'I have known only one way to play cricket and that is to compete in every game and every situation. At this level you have a right to assume that the players have the right attitude. One of my faults is that I am intolerant of players who are not putting in as much effort as I think they can. I suffer because I expect everyone to try as hard as I do. I also dislike playing on losing sides – it's not the way I was brought up. At the time you select who you think are the right personnel, but you find out things about people as you go along. We all make mistakes. It's fair to say that a lot of players' careers will be on the line when we get back. Everyone has to look at their own performances honestly and decide whether they have given their best. It is my belief that some have not.'

After repeated questioning about the West Indies series, I said: 'I would like to play, if selected, and I am available to be captain.' I meant that, too, but there would have to be changes – I wasn't in the business of leading 'no-hopers'.

Our trip to New Zealand had brought little respite. We won the opening one-day international in Christchurch, when the Kiwis collapsed in a manner more typical of us that winter. Our total of 230 for 7 – with runs from Allan Lamb, Robin Smith and Alec Stewart – looked well within New Zealand's reach when they needed 69 off the final 10 overs with five wickets left. By the time the final three overs arrived, no more wickets had fallen and just 19 were needed. Nobody would have swapped their position for ours, but Martin Bicknell grabbed the wickets of Ken Rutherford and Chris Harris, after their record sixth-wicket stand of 122, in the 53rd over – and the Kiwis folded. It was a great relief to be on a winning one-day side again after four successive defeats, but really we should have lost.

And then, despite the fact that we were in a winning position in the last two games, England managed to lose both with consummate ease. Some of the party had gone white-water rafting on the Hurunui river after the first match, but I ducked out – my life was full enough of ups and downs as it was. Wellington was the venue of our next game. I asked New Zealand to bat and was pleased to restrict them to 198 for 8. Angus Fraser and Phillip DeFreitas were the pick of our bowlers. We made a good start and were cruising to victory at 147 for 3. The final 12 overs left us with 41 runs needed and six wickets left. We lost by 9 runs! I should have been used to our collapses by now, but they still got me upset and angry. It wasn't even a particularly tight situation. Just the hint of pressure and we folded like a pack of cards.

There was just one match left in our 125-day tour. Most of us had had enough and were keen to get home. I'd hoped we might depart in style, but that was too much to ask. Victory would be ours if we scored 55 runs in the final 10 overs, with seven wickets remaining. Our response was to lose all those wickets for 46 runs in 55 deliveries. I was beginning to wonder what target might be within our grasp. That defeat, yet again, wasn't only the fault of the middle order and tail: the top order batsmen, especially Lambie and I, had failed to finish what they started. If just one of us had put a big innings together, we would have won that series in New Zealand. Nobody plays more one-day cricket than we do, yet England had given a totally inept performance in a series of 11 matches in Australia and New Zealand. Despite losing the Ashes 3–0, we had played our best cricket in the Tests.

We did make mistakes regarding selection. But that's unavoidable – you just hope to get it right most of the time. It's easy to be wise after the event. It was our attitude that disappointed me more than our performance. Too many of our players went about practice as if it was a chore. I've always enjoyed nets and training – it's part of the life of being a professional cricketer for me. I feel lucky to be out there; and, if you work hard, you'll improve your game. England aren't the only problem. I've noticed county teams that seem to warm-up simply because they're told to, because it's the done thing.

Fielding is the one occasion when a side acts as a team, when the players are all together. You must look the business, a tight-knit unit. We did in the Caribbean; we did not in Australia. You field with your brain as well as your body; the golden rule is to believe that every ball is coming to you, and act accordingly. I knew some of our players weren't the best of fielders – that wasn't my complaint. What angered me was that they weren't paying attention or making an effort. I tried to explain to them that fielding practice is organized so we can improve our performance. The irony is that our fielding in Brisbane was outstanding, as good as I've seen from any England side: we caught everything, and you could see our bowlers respond.

In the end I concluded that our trouble came down to personnel. 'Fitting in' hadn't been a problem in the West Indies, but it certainly was in Australia. The character of the individual must come into selectors' discussions. I'm not suggesting that a player's ability should be disregarded or that someone merits a trip just because he's got a Union Jack on his chest. But the balance must be right. In the future, we must look a lot more carefully at the problem of compatibility between players and at the way individual players respond to the concept of collective effort. I've learnt the hard way that cricket's a team game and you can't afford to have players not pulling their weight in that respect.

I got upset and angry about our whole performance in Australia because I wanted my team to perform in the right manner. I can accept losing; I can't accept not competing, not being in the game. For the first time in my career, I'd failed as a captain because players hadn't responded to my leadership. No one likes being slaughtered. Once we lost confidence, we didn't do ourselves justice. We weren't unlucky: our cricket in the one-day and state matches was abysmal. We weren't so bad in the Tests: while we threw away a winning position in Melbourne, we fought back well in Sydney and Adelaide – although that Saturday in Sydney remains the worst of my cricket life.

The few weeks off at home before the start of the new season were rather hectic. Apart from the official functions, lunches, dinners, speaking engagements and cricket shows, it takes time to settle back into the bosom of one's family. The problem is that you've got into a touring routine while the family have settled into a home-life routine without you; both sides need to adjust to the return to normality.

Our visit to Buckingham Palace for my New Year's Honours OBE caused a little problem. The official invitation allows the recipient to bring three guests, so Brenda and I had to make a choice: we left the twins at home and took Hannah. The most embarrassing moment came after meeting Her Majesty, when Brenda dropped the award in the gravel. A few days earlier the Brentwood District Council had given me a civic reception and I was presented with a parchment scroll. All my achievements were recorded in the council minutes and it was rather embarrassing when the clerk stopped after every specific item to let the 80-odd audience clap in appreciation. It was a great honour, but at one time I felt the ceremony was going to take as long as my 333. Afterwards, Brenda and I shook hands with everyone there. A series of speaking lunches took me around the country, including Manchester, Belfast, Birmingham and Stoke. Cricket shows are another part of pre-season life; local retailers invite their customers along and the equipment manufacturers show their wares. Brenda and I did manage to get away with the family – to Portugal – then we went up to Linden Hall, near Newcastle, for Essex colleague Alan Lilley's wedding; Neil Foster, Brian Hardie, John Lever and Geoff Miller also came along.

I met Ted Dexter and Micky Stewart early in April. I told them I would be happy to carry on as captain; they told me they were happy at my decision. I hadn't been completely despondent on the Australian tour. You have to live with whatever happens and be as optimistic as you can. I have learned a lot in the past few years and one important lesson is that you must try and think positively, no matter how bad everything seems. Even when the tour was going so wrong I could console myself with the sheer enjoyment of playing cricket.

I've always been at my happiest practising and playing. My

motive for wanting to be captain of England had nothing to do with the status. I didn't even think about that. I've noticed it now, of course: when I'm out in the street, people nudge and point. They want to talk to you when you are captain; you are in demand. There are others who relish all that, but I would rather get back to playing. I picked up the inaugural England Player of the Year award at the pre-season Cornhill Lunch and said at the time: 'I'm looking forward to one more shot at the West Indies and, despite what happened in the winter, we do have the talent to beat them.'

While it's nice to be wanted, I'm a bit concerned about the lack of outstanding candidates for the captaincy. Not everyone is in favour with the powers-that-be – for a while, I wasn't considered suitable. Captains are normally picked from players of high Test experience. The county game is much less of a captains' nursery than the Test team: the selectors are much more likely to pick a Test player with limited leadership experience than an experienced county skipper with only a few England caps. When Mike Gatting lost the job in 1988, there were several players – John Emburey, Allan Lamb and myself – with the right experience. The West Indies have Desmond Haynes as their official vice-captain, but Richie Richardson, Gus Logie and Jeff Dujon could all do the job. Experience is a vital ingredient for the job; so is the ability to handle pressure. I don't believe skippering a county team gives you much preparation for the real Test.

The week of my appointment for the West Indies Test series was dulled by the news that two of our class performers were going to miss the Texaco one-day internationals. Robin Smith went in for a pre-hernia operation and would be out for six weeks. Far more serious were the problems Angus Fraser was still having in overcoming the hip injury he sustained during the second Test at Melbourne. I've called Gus a 'captain's dream' and I meant it. Not only is he a class bowler, but he's a hungry one – he wants wickets badly. What annoyed me was that it seemed to take an eternity to diagnose what was really wrong. It was during the first Test at Headingley that it was decided he would have to take a complete rest for the whole summer.

Gus took part in our England get-together during the MCC match against the county champions at Lord's in mid-April. The

34 players who had gone on the two tours, plus Graeme Hick (now eligible for England after a seven-year qualification period) and Ricky Ellcock, were in attendance. A week later Lord's announced the introduction of winter contracts for six players: Allan Lamb, Jack Russell, Devon Malcolm, Angus Fraser, Mike Atherton and me. Robin Smith, after proving his recovery from his operation, was added during the first Test. These players were reckoned to form the nucleus of the England team over the next 12 months. The contracts not only give the top players more security, but give Lord's control over their cricket activities out of season. The England team has a much more professional approach to winter touring and there is now an extensive pre-tour programme supported by a £1 million sponsorship by the city firm, Whittingdale. It's only fair that professional sportsmen are paid for their time and efforts. Hopefully, the scheme will expand: with an A tour as well as a senior tour every winter, most of the top England players will be required on duty somewhere.

Essex welcomed a new overseas star – Pakistan's Salim Malik. Around Christmas time in Australia I had spoken to Mark Waugh, who had been with us for the previous two seasons, and he had told me he wouldn't be returning to England as he wanted a season off. Mark was, of course, a certainty for Australia's upcoming Caribbean tour. Essex would have waited for him, but he fancied a rest. With a one-year contract to offer to someone who had never played county cricket before, our choice of a replacement was rather narrow. The two contenders were Salim and New Zealand's Mark Greatbatch. I'd seen Salim at first-hand on England's tour of Pakistan as well as on his visits to England; he's a world-class batsman. He denied us a place in the 1989 Nehru Cup Final when he smashed England's bowlers all over Nagpur with some of the most ferocious hitting I've ever seen.

Tracking him down in Pakistan was about as easy as bowling to him that day, but I eventually made contact by phone from Perth during the final Ashes Test. He seemed keen to come, and we knew he'd fit in well. That's important for us at Essex. If there was any doubt about an overseas player's temperament or character, we'd probably shy away. Once again, we got great value for our money, and I'm sure he'll be a key player for Pakistan next summer. Salim's very quiet, but he has friends all over the country. He faced the West Indies last winter and we asked him how he coped with their four-man pace attack. Salim replied that he just played his natural game. 'I like to drive,' he told us, then paused before adding: 'Wait very long time!' I was glad to discover that it's not only England's batsmen who struggle against the world's best.

About the same time, the West Indies announced their party for the tour to England. It was going to be more of the same, although Ian Bishop was out after a back operation. Two young bowlers, Hamesh Anthony and Ian Allen, were brought in to give them experience. Amazingly, 13 of the 1988 squad were returning – it would have been 14 if Bishop had been fit. Gordon Greenidge and Viv Richards were making their fifth West Indies tours to England. The small number of players they have to choose from only partly explains that consistency of selection. Once they believe a player has talent, the West Indies persevere with him through thick and thin. One of English cricket's selectorial failings has been impatience at a player's lack of immediate success. But that's understandable because there's always another player to put in his place. Just below the highest level there are many excellent players of similar standard, and county cricket doesn't always tell you all you need to know about them.

Ricky Ellcock was a young fast bowler we took to the Caribbean in 1990. Unfortunately, he broke down with a recurrence of an old back injury and had to return home for an operation before bowling a ball for England. That put him out for a year, so it was pleasing to face him when we took on Middlesex in the Benson & Hedges zonal match at Chelmsford at the start of May. He bowled pretty quick, but his condition then deteriorated as some of the screws in his back worked loose, and he had to sit out a second English summer. The cold weather could not have done his back any good. I no longer get too upset at the vagaries of our climate. But it was so cold for such a long time – and when it finally warmed up, the rains came. It was certainly the worst start to a season I could remember, and that's saying something. I'd sneaked an early-season century off Cambridge University but, that apart, the runs were hardly flowing.

The double-sided bat had reappeared at the start of the season. As far as I'm concerned, a bat is good because of the quality, not the shape, of the wood. There has been a variety of designs in recent years, but I don't believe any are better than the conventional one. The weight of bats has gone up. That's been an advantage for me: it makes them stronger and widens the 'sweet spot'. But the biggest change has been the introduction of the laminated bat made of two pieces of wood. Such bats are no better in performance than the traditional type, but they are stronger and last longer. The best wood is soft and breaks quickly. Whereas I used to go through three old-style bats in a summer, a laminated one may last me through the season. That's no reflection on the bats I used before – I was with Gray Nicholls in 1975–8 and Duncan Fearnley in 1979–86. Today I'm with Stuart Surridge. The Gray Nicholls bats were lighter, but all three have made good bats for me.

Nasser Hussain could have done with a laminated car when he ran into me on our way to the Sunday League game at Nottingham. We were playing a county match at Northants and had been advised to steer clear of the roadworks on the M1. On the Market Harborough Road I was driving my new Toyota Celica (registration H15 BAT) with the Essex secretary Peter Edwards alongside. Nasser was following with Nadeem Shahid in his Sierra. After a long rise, over which you couldn't see, I had to brake sharply at a Stop sign immediately over the crest, where men were painting white lines in the road. A few seconds later, Nasser came over the crest and was unable to stop in time. My car was drivable, but his was a mess and we pushed it off the road. While we were waiting for a taxi to take them to Trent Bridge, the same thing nearly happened again, the following car missing by inches. There was no warning of the impending danger on the uphill approach, which struck me as pretty stupid. Nasser was pretty shaken up. And, just to make his day complete, we lost the match.

Lord's had earlier announced that white balls and coloured clothing were in plans to jazz up the Sunday League for 1992, although a move to split the League into two divisions of 50-over games to allow free Sundays for other matches was scrapped. Some see the Sunday League as a great evil. I've always enjoyed it. It's an entertainment specific to Sundays and has provided many counties with a much-needed source of revenue over the years. But I don't agree with mucking around with the rules: either play it or scrap it is my view.

My first England duty of the summer was to help select the squad for the three Texaco matches against the West Indies at the end of May. Robin Smith had made a quick recovery from his operation, but these games are physically tough and it was decided to let him work his way back gently to full fitness. The squad was picked with the 1992 World Cup in Australia and New Zealand very much in mind. This was an ideal chance to look at some of those in contention. It was also important to generate a good spirit after the winter problems. You have to have a spirit of camaraderie; without it the whole team performance is crippled. It was missing in Australia – and it showed.

Graeme Hick came in, along with Richard Illingworth, Mark Ramprakash and David 'Syd' Lawrence. Chris Lewis recovered from an early-season injury and edged out Devon Malcolm. Neil Fairbrother was recalled, as was one I.T. Botham. The West Indies are the one side that haven't felt the force of Ian Botham at his best: he's never really done himself justice against them. But he'd already one century under his belt for Worcestershire in 1991 when the news came over the tannoy at New Road, where the West Indies were the visitors, that Botham was back. Beefy hadn't been at the wicket long, but he proceeded to celebrate his return with a blistering 161. It was his first-ever hundred against the West Indies and it took him only 83 balls. As ever, the great man's instinct for the big occasion was spot on. Even Graeme Hick's long-awaited entry to international cricket had to take second place to Ian's return.

Texaco Trophy

The Texaco series was not only won 3–0 but went as well as we could have expected or hoped. The critics were quick to remind us that this was the same score as in the 1988 one-day series – and that the West Indies had gone on to win the Tests 4–0. I'm the first to admit that these limited-over games are no preparation for

Test cricket. They give no pointers to what's going to happen. But our performances were significant as indicators of the extent of our recovery since the disasters of the Ashes tour the previous winter. They boosted our confidence, individually and as a team. The atmosphere had been so different and depressing the last time we had played a one-day game, in Auckland. Suddenly, the atmosphere was just right. That translated into a good fielding performance and that, in turn, lifted the bowlers.

All three victories were different. The opener at Edgbaston was a low-scoring game, and we had to dig in to come through. The match at Old Trafford featured heavy scoring on a goodish wicket. The West Indies chased our total and we held up well under pressure – a distinct change from the winter. The final game at Lord's was another high-scoring affair, but this time England had to chase, and made it. Our batsmen Mike Atherton, Allan Lamb and Neil Fairbrother took the three 'Man of the Match' awards, but it had been a great team effort, with everyone pitching in at some stage.

Mike Atherton did well to grab the award from Ian Botham in the first match, at Edgbaston. It's not that Ian's just a great cricketer; he's also a lucky one, and no sportsman I know of has a greater sense of the big occasion. I remember catching New Zealander Bruce Edgar at the Oval in 1986. Ian had been suspended for most of the season, but dismissed Edgar with his second ball on his return to the England team. Ten balls later, Beefy had a second wicket – and so passed Denis Lillee's world record of 355 Test wickets.

So it was no surprise that he dished up something special on his first appearance for England for nearly two years. Richie Richardson was his first-over victim this time, and Ian got Edgbaston going with 4 for 45 as the West Indies were restricted to 173 for 8 in their 55 overs. The overcast conditions were certainly helpful and the ball was swinging all over the place. Bad weather forced the match into a second day with England needing 76 for victory with six wickets left. I'd lasted just two balls, but Mike Atherton was in stubborn mood and saw England home with five overs and one wicket to spare. But the win had come at a price. Botham had torn a hamstring going for a quick run – and was out of the one-day series. Warwickshire's Dermot Reeve was called up as replacement. Injuries like that take longer to overcome the older you get. I should know; even now I can't catch with my broken hand as well as I used to. Mike Atherton finished undefeated on 69 and received valuable assistance from Richard Illingworth in a last-wicket stand of 23. Everyone in this England side could bat and had at least one first-class century to their name. After the many batting collapses in Australia, Edgbaston made a welcome change.

So did Old Trafford, where we found ourselves defending a large total on a good wicket. As at Edgbaston, the West Indies were generous in their wides and no-balls; they conceded 43 extras in Birmingham and 40 in Manchester. They eventually lost by nine runs, so a little more care might have made it tighter. Mike Atherton and I put on 156 for the opening wicket, but the key to our 270 for 4 total – our highest-ever against the West Indies – was Allan Lamb's 50-ball 62. Lambie is a brilliant judge of a one-day innings, knowing instinctively when to accelerate and put on the pressure. In this game, he also helped Graeme Hick find his feet against the West Indies. Mark Ramprakash had come in for Ian Botham – and that meant a full 11-over bowling stint for me.

The tourists opened their reply with Phil Simmons and Jeff Dujon. Desmond Haynes was sitting out the one-day series with a sore back, while Gordon Greenidge had injured his knee fielding. For years the sight of Greenidge limping out to bat has made bowlers' spirits sink; but this time his injury was serious. He came out with a runner near the end; but, sadly, this was the end of his 1991 tour to England. Viv Richards appeared to be rather subdued and not too bothered about getting behind with the rate, but we couldn't relax: when he's at the wicket, anything can happen. Then Chris Lewis trapped him lbw and it was all over bar the shouting. We eased home by nine runs.

That gave us the Texaco trophy, but I was still keen to make it a clean sweep at Lord's. I put the West Indies in and 'Syd' Lawrence gave us a perfect start when his first ball to Jeff Dujon smacked the off-stump. Jack Russell then took a great catch off Simmons' inside edge, but the rest of the West Indies batsmen chipped in, Gus Logie top-scoring with 82.

I hadn't planned it that way, but this mini-series was testing all aspects of our game. England now needed 265 runs for victory. We got them and the hero was Neil Fairbrother, who at last reproduced his Lancashire form for his country. He went on the rampage and smashed the first England home century against the West Indies in a one-day game with 113 off 109 deliveries. At the other end Graeme Hick made steady if less spectacular progress and finished with an unbeaten 86. Hick's confidence grew the longer he batted and the more he watched Fairbrother's assault. Neil has as good a record in one-day cricket as anyone – and the whole of England was able to relish what Lancashire had been telling everyone about for years.

Fairbrother had moved up the order because Allan Lamb had been forced to drop out after being hit on the foot by a Curtly Ambrose yorker at Old Trafford. An X-ray showed nothing broken, but Nasser Hussain was added to the squad and Dermot Reeve made his debut at Lord's. This Texaco series hadn't been a great time for Lambie. We had dinner in Birmingham when the first match was held up by the weather, and he wanted to know why he hadn't been appointed vice-captain for the summer, as he had been the year before. I had to apologize for not telling him sooner, but it had been decided not to name a vice-captain. As he had fulfilled that role for the previous four series with England, he took this as a demotion, which was not the case. The decision was made for a number of reasons, not least the great shortage of candidates to do the job.

Lambie and I are of similar age, and England needed to look elsewhere for the future. At this stage of the summer, it was by no means certain that I would be available to lead the side to New Zealand and the World Cup. There's no easy way to tell someone that he's no longer in a certain position. Part of the problem was that Lambie's appointment the previous summer had created a precedent: it was the first time England had named a vice-captain at home. Ted Dexter also spoke to Lambie about it. Basically, he had not been asked to do the job because it had been decided to do without a vice-captain. As far as we were concerned, that left a possible future appointment in the balance. Lambie felt differently. He announced that he would not be available to captain

England again. We've all been through that sort of disappointment. I was captain when Ted Dexter replaced Peter May as chairman of selectors, and I lost the job without even getting an interview. I believe I deserved that at least. But David Gower regained the captaincy after Mike Gatting was vetoed by the TCCB's chairman of cricket, Ossie Wheatley. Had I been injured, Mike Atherton would have taken over at Lord's. But with no Lambie now to step in, we had a problem. There aren't many candidates of test level who fit the bill. Not appointing Lambie would not have ruled him out of leading England again, as far as I'm concerned. But his own decision, after we discussed it on the dressing-room balcony at Lord's, ended that possibility.

Getting back on the winning trail was a great relief. Our one-day form had been even worse than our Test record during the winter. Before this 3–0 victory, England had won only four games in 21 since the start of 1990. It was important to improve, and not only for the forthcoming World Cup: it had been announced that England would play a five-match Texaco series against Pakistan during the 1992 summer, with two games before the tests and three afterwards.

My one-day form continued as Essex put out Hampshire in the Benson & Hedges quarter-final at Chelmsford. Essex seemed to have played Hants a lot in cup competitions recently, usually ending up on the losing side. I thought we were heading for another defeat until Neil Foster got rid of Chris Smith near the end of his allotted 11 overs and the rest of their batting collapsed to Don Topley, who had just been appointed coach to Zimbabwe for the World Cup.

The semi-final draw gave Essex a home tie against Worcestershire after the first Test. That would give me a chance to judge Ian Botham's fitness. Sadly, his hamstring had removed him from the frame for the Headingley Test – a shame after his impact at Edgbaston. Yet, without that injury, Derek Pringle might not have made the squad; and he was to have a great summer; that's the way things happen. Derek has always done well against the West Indies. His previous best Test bowling had been against them at Leeds in 1988.

Devon Malcolm returned for 'Syd' Lawrence, while Robin

Smith replaced Neil Fairbrother. With Robin back, we decided on Mark Ramprakash ahead of Neil: the Lancs left-hander had had his chance the previous summer. There was a delay in announcing the side because I wanted to tell Neil personally, but the Old Trafford switchboard was jammed during my lunch-break at Bristol. Eventually, Micky broke the news to him. As I was at Bristol, changing in a Portakabin for the first time in my career, 'Syd' was close at hand, but it's not true that his bowling me second ball was revenge for his omission from the Test side – he had not yet been given the bad news! Mark Ramprakash wasn't the only Test newcomer: Graeme Hick and Richard Illingworth joined him. Then Glamorgan's Steve Watkin was added to the squad when Derek Pringle had a recurrence of a back problem.

Derek was not fit to practise on the Wednesday and looked doubtful, but in the event it was Chris Lewis who failed to start. When you have a squad of 13 – and one of those is a late call-up – you want to be able to pick from everyone. Otherwise the whole selection is thrown into turmoil. If Chris had been fit, he would have played instead of Steve Watkin. This wasn't the first time Chris had dropped out on the morning of a match – nor was it the first time he'd complained of dizzy spells. We had no alternative but to omit him again. Had Steve Watkin not been there, we would have had to go into the Test with a spinner, which we didn't want to do at Headingley.

The Windies had their own problems. After over a decade, the old firm of Gordon Greenidge and Desmond Haynes would not be opening for business as usual. Haynes had recovered from his back strain, but Greenidge was out of the tour after an operation on his injured knee. That was a big loss. Losing a player of that quality for an entire series must affect a side. Haynes and Greenidge were a solid, settled, top-class opening pair and one of the reasons for the West Indies success in the 1980s. Greenidge has one of the best techniques I've ever seen. He is more free-scoring than his partner. Both have all the shots, but on his day Greenidge is capable of destroying the best bowling in the world. They are the best opening combination I've come across. Phil Simmons was given the almost impossible task of stepping into Greenidge's shoes.

First Test, Headingley

Our Texaco successes had created a surge of excited anticipation for the Tests. The bookies had even cut the odds against us winning the series from 6 to 1 to 9 to 2. Headingley usually produced a result: there hadn't been a Test draw there since 1980, and I agreed with those who suggested that if we were going to cause an upset, Leeds was the place. The omens weren't good when Viv called correctly and, after some delay, invited England to bat. We finished the day at 174 for 7, and it could have been even worse. Allan Lamb was out to the last ball before lunch to leave England 64 for 4. Robin Smith and Mark Ramprakash then came to the rescue with a gritty partnership, although both were out before the close. Ramps batted nearly 2½ hours for his 27: a very mature knock in difficult circumstances. Robin showed no ill-effects from his operation with a typical fighting 50, although he failed to beat Ambrose's throw going for a second run. He came into the dressing-room looking for some sympathy, thinking he had made his ground. But all we could say was 'Sorry, Judgy, it was out.'

It was England's turn to look sharp in the field on Friday as the West Indies reached 166 for 8 in reply to our 198. Viv was still there on 73, but we had fought our way back. Steve Watkin's first Test wicket was the prize of Desmond Haynes, and then Mark Ramprakash rattled the tourists with two brilliant pieces of fielding. The Middlesex youngster caught Simmons with a spectacular two-handed diving catch to his right at cover, then ran out Carl Hooper with a textbook pick-up and throw in one movement from the same position, the ball hitting the stumps at the bowler's end. It was such moments of inspiration and opportunism that had been missing in Australia. Even I caught the mood and ran out Richie Richardson going for a third run.

Derek Pringle crucially removed Viv at the start of the third morning, and England had a valuable first-innings lead of 25. But Ambrose soon made short work of that as we crashed to 38 for 3, and later to 124 for 6. Curtly took all six wickets and was twice on hat-trick; more to the point, he removed both Lamb and Smith first ball. Jeff Dujon showed all his catching skill to hang on to an edge from Mike Atherton.

I managed to survive to the close with Derek Pringle. My score was 82, but I knew I was going to have to add quite a few more if we were going to win this Test. I found a willing partner in Derek. I'd scored 74 when he came to the crease, and we were to add 98 for the seventh wicket. He helped us to a total of 252, leaving the West Indies to score 273 for victory.

I ended up on 154 to complete my set of centuries on England Test grounds; Geoff Boycott, Kenny Barrington and Ian Botham have also managed that. It had been very hard work, and I fully agree with the cricket writers who rate it as one of my best Test innings, especially in view of the state of the match and the strength of the opposition. Batting against the West Indies always offers the toughest examination of your skill, courage and patience; but this was a bowlers' pitch and the overcast conditions suited the men with the ball. It was pretty obvious to everyone that I had to stay there. If I'd have been out early on the fourth morning, England would have lost the Test.

That was still possible, of course, when the West Indies came out to bat. Simmons went first ball to Phil DeFreitas, and the tourists started the last day at 11 for 1. The weather posed as much of a threat as the Windies: the dark clouds seemed to be approaching Headingley quicker than our victory. Steve Watkin made the crucial breakthrough with the wickets of Hooper, Richards and Logie. Daffy claimed four wickets, but the final one went to Devon Malcolm as Walsh slashed the ball high to cover. It should have been Ramprakash's catch, but Atherton raced in from gully and made a desperate dive.

That was it! England had won by 115 runs: our first victory over the West Indies at home since 1969. Five of the side had enjoyed that triumph in Jamaica 15 months earlier, this one was just as important – perhaps more so after our winter experiences. English cricket was making good news on the front pages again. Everyone was trying to remember what they were doing in 1969 when the first man had landed on the moon and we had last beaten the West Indies at home. I had been in East Africa on tour with London Schools and John Emburey. (During our game in Nairobi, one of the spectators was a little 10-year-old by the name of Derek Pringle.)

Freddie Trueman (who had been sharing centre stage with Raquel Welch at his daughter's wedding during the Leeds Test) kindly named me Man of the Match for my sixth century against the West Indies and my 14th Test ton in all. Considering my tally a year earlier had been eight, I was enjoying a great run. My Headingley innings was not a fluent knock. I rarely felt as though I had hit the ball right in the middle of the bat. That might sound strange after scoring 154 not out, but it wasn't until the Sunday that the occasional ball hit the sweet spot and went for four. It was one of those situations where you just had to hang in there and pick up runs where you could. I've always said I find it particularly pleasing to score runs against the West Indies because it is such a hard school. It's the best attack in the world, and that is the reason why a 50 against them is worth a hundred against anyone else. But this victory was no one-man show. Smith and Ramprakash had batted well, while Daffy, Pringle and Watkin all took vital wickets. Someone made the comment that my mood must be somewhat different from that at my last post-Test press conference in Perth. True, I'd been depressed and annoyed four months earlier. Now English cricket had rediscovered its pride and no one could have been happier than me.

Usually a Test win is celebrated only in the sports columns of the papers. Occasionally, though, a victory catches a mood and becomes a national event. That had happened after our success in Jamaica the previous winter. While you're abroad, it's difficult to catch the mood back home. But there was no mistaking the pandemonium that followed our Headingley triumph. Players sometimes find it puzzling why some wins are bigger news than others, but not this time. The combination of the 22-year wait, beating the world champions and our recent winter of discontent was a genuine cause for national celebration.

Second Test, Lord's

After our champagne party on the balcony, some of the lads decided to make a night of it and stayed in Leeds as they had no cricket the following day, with only the Benson & Hedges semifinals on the Wednesday. I did go back home after the game, though, to prepare myself for Worcestershire and Ian Botham. That proved a waste of time, however, as Essex were rolled over for 104 and Worcs had made the final by mid-afternoon, losing only one wicket.

Ian bowled superbly and took the Gold Award with figures of 11–6-11–3. The wicket did a little bit early on, as it does at Chelmsford. We got to 26–0 before collapsing. Our meagre total was obviously insufficient against Worcestershire's formidable batting line-up and Tom Moody saw the visitors home with an undefeated 72. Despite his fine bowling effort, Ian admitted the hamstring was still troubling him, so he was a non-starter for the Lord's Test.

Despite that Headingley win, the total of 31 runs collected by Allan Lamb, Mike Atherton and Graeme Hick, plus Devon Malcolm's waywardness, were a worry. But those three batsmen are all quality players, and Devon had to be allowed one poor game after all his efforts over the past year; so we merely added 'Syd' Lawrence to the squad for the Lord's Test – it never does Devon any harm to know there's someone pushing for his place.

Unfortunately, Micky Stewart's attempt to provide Devon with some specialized coaching after he'd dropped out of Derby's game against the West Indies didn't go down too well with the Derbyshire committee. The reason for his county absence, it emerged, was the arrival of his first child. We'd been worried that Devon was going into the second Test with no cricket after a poor performance in the first. Micky, who was less concerned when the reason for Devon's withdrawal was revealed, still got in touch with Derby and arranged a special session with Devon on the Saturday between the Tests. The wet weather meant the pair had to work indoors, so Micky arranged a tutorial at Lord's on Monday.

One of the strengths of the current England set-up is that it allows us to have our fingers on the pulse, to know which players are having problems and trying to sort them out before they become too serious. That's part of Micky's job; England's Test bosses must have some input. He had gone through the formalities, informing Derbyshire; there's no way he would have pitched up at Derby otherwise; that's not his style. I was rather surprised to read that the Derbyshire chairman Chris Middleton had described the exercise as 'a totally wasted journey.' Hopefully, county and country are pulling in the same direction. Middleton continued: 'It implies that we don't know how to look after Devon.' The incident got rather messy and Mr Middleton was subsequently fined £750 by the TCCB's disciplinary committee.

I made a trip of my own before the Lord's test, to Thoiry in France. The event was part of David East's Benefit year. The Essex team and supporters, about 80 in all, raced from our Sunday League game at Chelmsford to Stansted Airport for the champagne trip and a little cricket. We beat France by 70 runs, being careful not to suffer the same embarrassment as MCC had two years earlier, when they lost. Derek Pringle and I came back early the next morning to prepare for the Lord's Test, but the rest of the lads enjoyed two more days sampling the wares of the Laurent Perrier champagne house in Rheims. The trip had been organized by Lay & Wheeler, old-established wine merchants of Colchester. It was the first time Essex had ventured abroad on a benefit trip. I hope it won't be the last.

Lord's had taken nearly £2 million in advance bookings. Test matches there are always special. There's no better place to bat and, if things go well, there's no better place to succeed. It engenders a real sense of achievement. After considering including a spinner, we took the field with the same XI that had won at Leeds. We stuck with Steve Watkin because he'd done well at Headingley and the Windies didn't seem to play seam bowling particularly well. As things turned out, a specialist spinner might have been useful, but we did have the services of Graeme Hick. The Windies were forced to make one change: Patrick Patterson was suffering from a calf injury, so Ian Allen came in for his Test debut.

Viv won the toss and, again after some deliberation, decided to bat. Lord's wickets are always good, even though groundsman Mick Hunt was forced to make a late switch after damage to the original pitch. The Windies batsmen certainly had no problems on it during the first day: England were restricted to one success per session. We bowled well from the Nursery End, through Daffy and Pringle, but not so well from the Pavilion End where Malcolm and Watkin operated. Daffy's first eight overs went for eight runs:

Devon's for 44.

Our only success in the morning came on the lunch break when Hick had Simmons caught at slip off his third ball in Test cricket. Lambie took a brilliant catch and, with the score at 90, we had badly needed the breakthrough. Pringle produced a beauty to find Haynes' bat edge in the afternoon session, and Hick induced a false stroke from Richie Richardson after tea.

At the 317 for 3 the tourists were handily placed, with Richards and Hooper threatening. Hooper went on to make a superb 111; but we fought back well on the Friday to dismiss them for 419 by mid-afternoon. Pring was the pick of the bowlers with 5 for 100. The West Indies brought out the best in him: his control was first rate, and he had learnt to swing the ball in the past couple of years, instead of just being a seam bowler. By the end of the series Viv was telling me: 'He's really improved.'

I was pleased for Derek. He's a genuine all-rounder, but he had suffered from comparison with Ian Botham over the years. Like Ian, people expected him to bat at No.6, but that's too high a position for him in a Test line-up. I've been critical of Derek in the past. If he had the aggression of Angus Fraser or Neil Foster, he would have played a lot more matches for England. 'Suggsy', as he's known (after the lead singer of the pop group Madness), is still easygoing, but has worked hard over the past couple of seasons. Despite his back problems, he is much fitter now. He's taken a fair amount of stick in his time, so I was pleased when he received a special cheer from the crowd on the Headingley balcony. His nickname does cause confusion: this summer both Salim Malik and Richie Richardson asked him why he was called 'Sexy'!

The West Indies had us in tatters in less than 10 overs before tea. England were 16 for 3 and once again Atherton, Hick and Lamb had failed. Then Ramps failed to get past the 20s again, and I left a ball from Walsh that came back and bowled me – a bad error of judgement. Half our side had gone for 84 before Robin Smith and Jack Russell stopped the rot. Smith did more than that on the Saturday, with a memorable undefeated innings of 148. Any hundred against the West Indies is special, but Smith's knock was something else. There had been criticism that he was coming in too low in the order at No.6, but we had decided to split up our experienced batters. I went in with Atherton, Lambie with Hick and Smith after Ramps. I'm sure Robin will make the England middle-order spot his own in years to come, but he has always done well at No.6, which is where he started out.

Robin's efforts at Lord's would have been wasted but for sterling work from the England tail. This was an important ingredient of our successes this summer. One of the West Indies' great strengths has been their ability to knock over the opposition tail in short order – the Australians had just discovered that in the Caribbean. And our tail had hardly covered itself in glory in Australia. But Robin received tremendous support from Jack Russell, Derek Pringle, Phillip DeFreitas and Steve Watkin on that Lord's Saturday. Jack's stand was worth 96 in $2\frac{1}{2}$ hours, Derek's 89 in 2 hours, Daffy's 47 in an hour and Steve's 37 in just under.

There was a great cheer when Derek took us past the follow-on target and when Devon was bowled by Ambrose, England trailed by only 65 runs. We had fought back well. That was important after Headingley – the Windies are a great side for bouncing straight back after a defeat, and we had managed to contain their counterattack. Unfortunately, the rain intervened and washed out the entire Sunday, leaving the TCCB to refund £400,000 in gate money. The final day was little better. We reduced the Windies to 12 for 2 at the start of the day, but only 4.5 overs were possible before the rains returned.

I was disappointed because it had looked a good morning for bowling and, even if we couldn't have forced a win, there was a chance to put the Windies on the defensive. Tony Lewis suggested during a BBC interview that the bad weather suited England. I resented that: it was a negative view. We had pulled ourselves right back into the second Test. Naturally, the possibility of winning introduces the chance of losing – but, if you can't accept that risk, there's no point in playing.

The rain did bring one bonus – a trip to Buckingham Palace. The Queen had been due to meet the teams at Lord's on Monday afternoon, but the weather put paid to that. Instead, we were invited to the Palace. That caused some dress problems, because the final day of a Test is not blazer and tie day. Players bring casual clothes because of the long drive home (they had been expecting to meet the Queen in cricket gear). Soon, we were all dipping into cases and hold-alls for reasonably clean shirts. I was driving my dad Alf home, so I asked the Queen's Private Secretary if there was a room he could wait in or if he might stay in the car. No way! Ten minutes later, Alf was chatting to Her Majesty, drinking tea and eating her Dundee cake. Well, not all of it. Half was wrapped in a napkin and taken home for Rose, my mum. Dad thoroughly enjoyed it, all the more because it was totally unexpected. Mind you, once the word got out at Chelmsford, he had to put up with a lot of mock bowing and scraping for a few weeks.

Third Test, Trent Bridge

Dad also came down with me to Devon for our opening NatWest game. I hadn't been there since I was a kid. The weather was still a problem and floods were predicted in Plymouth, so it looked like a two-day job. But the rain held off, and we won by 8 wickets. I've been on the wrong end of a giant-killing act (against Hertfordshire in 1976) and it's no fun. Hertfordshire got into the act again this year when they knocked out Derbyshire. That match was washed out and Herts won the stump shoot-out 2–1. Five bowlers from each side have two attempts to hit the stumps. Derbyshire's skipper Kim Barnett insisted afterwards; 'It's not cricket' – but anything's better than tossing a coin. Surrey nearly went out, too, but edged home 3–2 after Tony Murphy succeeded with the last two deliveries in the Oval indoor school against Oxford.

Our wicket at Exmouth was a wet pudding. These days professional cricketers have very little experience of wet wickets. There were arguments about whether it was better to bat first, but we put Devon in and there were no scares. My first cricket teacher, Leonard Hall from Cann Hall Junior School in Leytonstone, lives in Exmouth now. He's not too well, but he came to the match in a wheelchair with his wife.

The weather was hampering the chances of those knocking on the door of the Test team. Although some of the England batsmen hadn't found their form, nobody else was piling up enough runs to push their way in. Graeme Hick had made a troubled start to his Test career, but we believed it was best to give him a good run. When selectors have chopped and changed teams in the past they have been criticized; now we were coming under fire for sticking to the same squad. Ian Botham was still unfit, so Dermot Reeve and 'Syd' Lawrence were added to the Trent Bridge line-up for the Third Test, with Steve Watkin dropping out. Later, Hugh Morris was called up as cover for Mike Atherton, who was struggling with a stomach muscle strain.

I scored my third century of the season between the Tests at Lord's against Middlesex. But it was a gimme: Mike Gatting had agreed to chase 250 and the ball was being lobbed up for our declaration. Neil Foster then bowled us to victory, but we were helped by Gatt coming in at No. 8 because of a bad back. Three centuries so far this season, but I counted only one as genuine. That was scored against the best team, in England, the West Indies. The third had been against the weakest, Cambridge University.

Mike Atherton declared himself fit to play. Devon Malcolm and Dermot Reeve were left out, and Richard Illingworth made his Test debut after two appearances as 12th man. Devon was unlucky to miss out, but he'd been struggling. 'Syd' Lawrence had less control; but he was less experienced and deserved a second chance. His previous England appearance had been against Sri Lanka at Lord's in 1988.

Devon had done well for us over the previous 18 months, taking 60 wickets. He was a much improved bowler. When I said at Lord's that we were going to stick by him, that was taken as guaranteeing he would be in the next Test side. That wasn't the case; he still has days when he doesn't or can't get it right. But Devon is certainly part of the England set-up at the moment, even if he's out of the Test team. Accuracy is the key against the West Indies. Pace is still important, but they are less at home with sideways movement than with sheer speed.

Trent Bridge was a good toss to win. The wicket looked like it would be good for the first half of the match, so we batted and were well satisfied with an undefeated century opening stand on the first morning. I'd passed 2,000 runs in Tests against the Windies in the process, while Mike Atherton was back in the groove. Mike and I both went disappointingly early in the afternoon session, but the tea-time score of 175 for 3 was still respectable.

Then Curtly Ambrose, who had caused the damage after lunch, did the same after tea, removing Graeme Hick and Mark Ramprakash to start a slump which reduced us to 228 for 8. Robin Smith and Richard Illingworth ensured no further losses, adding 40 runs before the close, but we had blown our big chance. We finished up reaching 300, with Robin 64 not out and Ambrose taking 5 for 74. That wasn't a bad score, but it wasn't a good one either. I was disappointed for two reasons – first, because the pitch on the opening two days was as good as any in the series, and, second, because of our position of 106 for no wicket at lunch on the opening day. To get bowled out in less than three sessions after that was a poor performance. If we had batted for five good sessions, as we should have, our score would have been around 400 and that would have put them under pressure. As it was, a total of 300 had put us on the defensive.

By Friday's close, the tourists were 38 runs behind with five wickets left. They had been 45 for 3, but Richie Richardson, Viv Richards and Gus Logie batted them out of trouble. Richard Illingworth's two wickets included Simmons' with his first ball in Test cricket – only the 11th player in history to do this. Whatever happens in the future, that will be a moment for him to savour. Viv was his second victim, and the West Indies captain had the rare distinction of being given out by both umpires. It was a confusing dismissal, but I had a clear view from mid-wicket and was sure Viv was bowled. Some reckoned he'd been stumped off Jack Russell's pads. What wasn't in dispute was that Viv was out. He took a long time looking up for the umpire's decisions, but the fact that Merv Kitchen had moved across from square leg to point might not have helped. It certainly wasn't a case of dissent – there were a lot of confused people at Trent Bridge at the time.

The pitch was flooded by a thunderstorm on Saturday morning, but the groundstaff worked hard and only half an hour was lost. Despite two early breakthroughs (DeFreitas getting Logie first ball), Malcolm Marshall hit 67 to give the Windies a valuable lead of 97. And 'Maco' hadn't finished with us yet, Mike Atherton playing on to him as we started our reply. It went from bad to worse as Ambrose had Graeme Hick caught behind for a duck and then bowled me for 13. We were almost out of it, and finished the third day still 43 behind the tourists with seven wickets left. This was our only Test against the West Indies with a rest day. I went home on Saturday night and returned on Sunday. That 250-mile round trip might seem an unnecessary strain during a Test, but I grab whatever chances I can get to be with the family during the summer.

We needed a big innings from someone on Monday morning, but none came; and when our eighth wicket fell, our lead was only 18. The final two partnerships showed great determination in adding 96, and Phillip DeFreitas' and 'Syd' Lawrence's last-wicket stand of 58 really got the Trent Bridge crowd roaring. Daffy, after nearly five years with the England side, reached his first half-century; 'Syd' was really 'rocking and rumbling' – as he likes to describe it – hitting the ball cleanly and with some elegance for his 34. He was really fired up when the Windies began their second innings and had Simmons caught behind off his second ball. But the Windies needed only 115, and they completed the job by lunch on the final day without further loss to level the series.

We had been outplayed – no two ways about it. But after winning the toss we should have batted them out of the game on that track, and that's what annoyed me. We had surrendered the advantage gained at Headingley. It was going to be a hard fight to peg them back now.

Fourth Test, Edgbaston

The Test series took a holiday from the headlines for a few days after Trent Bridge when the International Cricket Council voted to re-admit South Africa to the fold. South Africa, then captained by the current supremo Dr Ali Bacher, had played their last official Tests against Australia in 1970, a series they won 4–0.

My name has been associated with South African cricket for nearly a decade. I went on an unoffical tour there in 1982 and received a three-year Test ban. Those connections led to the cancellation of England's tour to India in 1988/89 when I was captain. Instead, England's next Test was at Leeds against Australia and I'd lost the captaincy to David Gower.

What amazed me now was the speed of South Africa's return. Just 18 months earlier, the furore attending Mike Gatting's rebel tour suggested South Africa was more isolated than ever. For so long the cricketers there had no hope. But the dismantling of the apartheid laws, the amalgamation of the white and black cricket bodies, and the support of the African National Congress had changed all that. I never dreamed that they would be back in official cricket in my time. Now, I'll feel disappointed if I don't play in a Test match against them before I quit. I was pleased for the players and administrators in South Africa who have been working so hard for so long. I could well understand Ali Bacher's emotion at this final breakthrough. It's been a slow, painful process. I'm not an expert on the situation, but what has always puzzled me is why I was allowed to go to India for the 1987 World Cup, was banned the following year, and then admitted for the Nehru Cup in 1989. I had no contact with South Africa during that time, although I cancelled a contract to play for Western Province so that I could lead the aborted 1988/89 Indian tour.

My joy at South Africa's return to the international fold was dulled the next day by the news that South Africa would not be competing in the 1992 World Cup and that the five-year Test ban on Mike Gatting's rebels was to remain. I'm not suggesting any of them would have walked back into the England side, but England want all their best players available. I know Gatt is desperate to play again (I was surprised when he went on the rebel tour). John Emburey, Chris Broad, Neil Foster and Gatt are the four most obvious candidates for a return, and Matthew Maynard had a good end to the season. Fossie and Embers are two I've spoken to about the ban; both expected no favours and are prepared to serve their time. But I hope that they will be allowed back into the Test fold a year after South Africa.

Because of the Benson & Hedges Final, there's always an extra week between Tests in mid-summer. That gives the selectors a chance to judge candidates in first-class cricket outside the Tests. This time Micky, Ted and I picked the squad on the bench outside the physio's room at Southend. The announcement was delayed because of injuries to Mike Atherton and Robin Smith: Mike's stomach was still troubling him and Robin had been hit on the thumb by Ambrose in the tourists' match at Southampton before the Trent Bridge Test. Robin had further aggravated the injury when fielding and rated himself only 50–50 for Edgbaston. Chris Lewis was brought back after a good month with Leicestershire. Dermot Reeve was unlucky after he'd been brought in to give us an extra option at Trent Bridge; Devon Malcolm was omitted again: and Micky, after watching Ian Botham at Portsmouth, decided he wasn't fit enough yet for a five-day Test. Graeme Hick enjoyed the break to earn Denis Compton's Man of the Match award for his 88 in the B&H final that ended Worcestershire's duck; he then made 141 against Hampshire. Graeme wouldn't have lost his place without those runs, but we hoped his confidence had been boosted.

Essex reached the quarter-finals of the NatWest with a win over Sussex, Nasser Hussain and I both scoring 90s. Hove has been a good ground for me. Unfortuanately, I don't get there very often; Essex generally face Sussex at Horsham. Then I equalled Gordon Greenidge's Sunday League record of 11 centuries with 107 against Somerset. Peter Edwards, Essex's general manager, also told me that it was my third successive Sunday century at Southend, which was also the venue of my Sunday League record 176 against Glamorgan in 1983. A few days earlier Refuge had announced they were withdrawing from sponsoring the Sunday League; Refuge had been in favour of the two-division split that had been rejected by the counties earlier in the summer.

I had begun to feel unwell during my innings at Southend and was forced to cancel speaking at a David East Benefit Dinner on Monday evening. After a bad night, I went to see the doctor on the Tuesday before the Fourth Test, and he told me I'd caught tonsillitis off Brenda and the kids. It wasn't the best of 38th birthday presents; but although I missed practice and drove straight to the squad's Birmingham hotel, I was always confident of playing. The doctor had given me some heavy antibiotics; I had an early night and felt fit to play.

Sadly, Robin Smith didn't make it, and Hugh Morris, who had again been called up as cover, was in for his England debut. I had told Robin that if he was happy playing, we'd take that chance. If he said he was 80 per cent fit, then I would have gone along with that, just as we did with David Gower in Melbourne. I was prepared to go into the Test with him not fully fit, provided he was happy, because we needed him. Robin batted in the indoor nets on the morning of the match and he declared himself 'out'. That was a big blow: he produces the goods more often than not and you can't fault his contribution. We picked Hugh because he had been in tremendous form for most of the season; the press had been pushing him for about a year. Actually, he'd gone off the boil a bit and, worse still, had just picked up a pair, courtesy of Ambrose, in Glamorgan's game against the tourists.

Hugh didn't enjoy much better luck on his Test debut. Viv Richards put us in (I would in any case have chosen to bat). It was a poor-looking wicket and proved to be the worst of the series. Our Essex groundsman, Andy Atkinson, had moved to Edgbaston only recently. The pitch's lack of quality was nothing to do with him; all the work on it had already been done. The 1990 Test wicket, scene of our win over New Zealand, had been dug up, I don't know why – it had seemed a pretty good wicket to me. The pitch and conditions were similar to those for the Texaco match, so we plumped for tight attack and included Richard Illingworth at the expense of 'Syd' Lawrence. The start was delayed until 12.15.

Nobody can hide at Test level, and 45 minutes of the West Indies fast bowlers charging in at full throttle was going to be the ultimate baptism for Hugh Morris. He lasted just eight balls in what proved to be a torrid day for us. I should have gone second ball after flaying at a wide delivery from Ambrose, but Hooper dropped the catch at second slip. We finished up at 184 for 9.

Batting wasn't easy, but once again our first day's performance had put us in trouble. That was emphasized the following day as the Windies ended up at 253 for 4 in reply to our 188. Richie Richardson hit an undefeated century, and Derek Pringle summed up the achievement by saying it was worth a double hundred on that wicket. Richardson had not been a great success on his previous two tours of England, and there had been suggestions that he couldn't cope with conditions here, especially with late movement of the ball. His success in the Caribbean and Australia shows he likes to hit through the line of the ball, but he proved this year what a world-class performer he is. He works hard at his game and is a very nice guy.

The Windies should not, however, have scored so many runs on Friday on that wicket. Daffy and Pring bowled tightly, conceding little more than two runs an over, but Chris Lewis and Illy were hit for nearly five. Chris made full amends on Saturday morning. He started the session with figures of 1 for 95 and finished with 6 for 111 as they were bowled out for 292. Chris had got us right back into the game. A few weeks earlier his test future had been in doubt. Now he was showing what a cricketing talent he was.

The Windies lost their last six wickets for 39 runs. Unfortunately, we lost our first three for five runs and were all but finished. Patrick Patterson, back after injury, took the wickets of Hugh and Athers in his only over before lunch, so at 4 for 2 I didn't have much of an appetite. Graeme Hick followed soon after; Lambie, Ramps and I all got started but couldn't go on. But England, after losing the sixth wicket at 96, finished up at 156 for 8 to deny the Windies the three-day win that looked likely at one stage, with Derek Pringle and Chris Lewis holding the fort.

On Sunday, that small defending force threatened to overcome the attackers. Chris hit a 65 full of memorable attacking shots in a ninth-wicket stand of 92 with Pring, who made 45, leaving the West Indies needing 157 to make the series safe. Chris was out just before lunch; he was obviously furious with himself after over-hitting a defensive shot into cover's hands. It was a shame he didn't make it to the interval because that would have given the Windies time to dwell on the match situation.

Nonetheless Chris had given us a chance, and memories of Headingley 1981 were revived when Daffy took three wickets in seven balls to have the Windies tottering at 24 for 3. But the pitch went flat and the ball seemed to misbehave only when it was hard and new. Richards and Hooper saw the West Indies home with fourth-wicket stand of 133, and Viv finished things off with an immense straight six off Illy. He was chaired off by his players, who raced from the dressing-room. Viv had really wanted it. He played with great responsibility all summer, despite the odd rash moment. And yet I felt the West Indies' jubilation was mixed with more than a touch of relief.

Fifth Test, Oval

Although the West Indies now led 2–1 and so could not lose the series, the Fifth Test at the Oval, beginning in the second week of August, at least offered us the choice of finishing all-square. Their performances in July had shown why the West Indies had gone an astonishing 23 series without defeat. Once again, they had shown great resilience when fighting back; Viv's side must be given credit for that. They outplayed us in the Third and Fourth Tests; but those two defeats were due primarily to the failure of our batting. You need runs to be in the game. Even a weak bowling side can make things happen if they have runs on the board. The West Indies have the best bowlers, and you need runs against them most of all. If you score less than 200 you're under pressure, no matter who you're playing.

Our batting failures were the main topic of discussion when I met with Micky and Ted at Woodford Wells to select the team for the final Test. Allan Lamb, Mike Atherton and Graeme Hick had scored 233 runs in 23 innings in the series. I rate those three as quality batsmen and among England's best. Allan was having the worst summer of his career. Even when he hasn't been firing for the Test team in the past, Lambie's been a prolific run scorer with a batting average of around 50. Now he was struggling to get a decent score for Northants, never mind England. With six centuries to his credit against the fiercest bowling attack in the world, Lambie had been one of our batting bankers for this series. His failure was a big blow.

Mike Atherton's short Test career hadn't been smooth. It started badly at home against Australia in 1989, reached the heights against New Zealand and India in 1990, and finished well in Australia after a disastrous start. Moreover, he had been the batting star of the Texaco series against the Windies. Yet he had managed just 66 runs in four Tests.

But the biggest worry for English cricket had been Graeme Hick's failed entry into the Test scene. During his seven-year wait to qualify for England, Graeme had enjoyed success in every shape and form, becoming the youngest batsman to score 50 first-class hundreds. But in seven weeks his seven-year Test dream had become a nightmare as he struggled to cope with the West Indies' firepower. I'm convinced that he's going to be a successful Test batsman, but he's got problems with their sort of bowling. I was surprised someone of his ability struggled as badly as he did. He looked out of his depth, especially against short-pitched bowling, and his technique against bouncers was suspect. As a slip fielder, Graeme's got the safest pair of hands I've seen for a long time, and he also took some vital wickets with his off-spin. That his batting should let him down shows what a funny game cricket is and how nothing can be taken for granted.

I know what a struggle it's been for Graeme. I've told him that if he wants to discuss his game or any problems, I'm always available. That's part of my job as captain – but only if he *wants* help. Graeme must go to the person he has most confidence in, whoever that is, and get sorted out. I'm sure he'll get lots of conflicting advice as everyone shoves their oar in. That's no help: I've been down that road myself. Ultimately, Graeme has to find his own answers. I don't think that will be a major problem, but every individual takes his own route to the desired end. To take the example of what troubled Graeme this year, Robin Smith and I deal with fast, short-pitched bowling quite differently. He likes to duck and dive out of the way, while I try to play the ball. That can get me into trouble, and I would prefer to get out of the way like Robin, but I can't: I've tried it, and it doesn't work for me.

One option for England at the Oval was to play a wicket-keeper batsman. Alec Stewart had fulfilled that role for us in the final two Tests in Australia. Essex's NatWest quarter-final at the Oval gave me the opportunity of seeing Alec at first-hand. I met the Queen once again as she opened the Ken Barrington Indoor Centre at the Oval. That was the only highlight of what was a bad day for Essex as we lost our way again. Essex have the worst record of any county in the Gillette/NatWest 60-over game; for a talented and otherwise successful side, that's ridiculous. They say that catches win matches and Monte Lynch's effort to get rid of John Stephenson was one of the most unbelievable I've ever seen.

Alec, who was keeping only in one-day matches, looked in good form, so we decided to go into the final Test without our best keeper, Jack Russell. That was a gamble. Alec's chronic finger injury wasn't the only reason he wasn't keeping in championship games: he wanted to bat at No. 3 and he felt that and keeping imposed too much pressure. He'll be captain in 1992, so there will be even more pressure then. But for England desperate circumstances demanded desperate measures: we had to win the Oval Test.

I was rather uneasy about it at first. I had confidence in Alec behind the stumps and in his batting; he'd kept tidily for us in Adelaide and Perth and had taken his catches. Two things concerned me: going into a Test without our best wicket-keeper and the pressure that would impose on Alec. The keeper, in a way, is your only specialist fielder: everyone else is in the side for another reason. Alec would be on a hiding to nothing because we had also decided to go into this Test with the best attacking spinner in the country on a bouncy wicket. Jack Russell took the blow as you'd expect – with dignity. After Australia, it wasn't a total shock. We needed our No. 7 to get runs. Jack was coming up short in that department – although now he was also paying for others' failures.

Ian Botham was also brought back to strengthen our line-up. He celebrated in style, just as he had done at his Texaco selection. This time he produced his county-championship bowling best of 7 for 54 against the leaders, Warwickshire. With Robin Smith back, Alec in the top six, and Ian coming in at No. 7, two batters from Trent Bridge had to go. There were three, possibly four, candidates, but Graeme Hick and Lambie were the disappointed men. Hugh Morris hadn't made the best of starts, but it would bave been unfair to ditch him after one game. For the second time in a season I had some disappointing news for Lambie. He took it well, saying 'If you don't get runs, you can't expect to play.' That had happened to me and David Gower in 1981; the selectors had stuck with us, but we were dropped for the Oval Test after not producing the goods. It had been a close thing between Lambie and Athers. Philip Tufnell, like Alec, returned for his first Test since Perth. Tuffers had taken a lot of wickets, done all that was asked of him and deserved another chance. I'd always believed that he would play for England again, although he hadn't created a good impression in Australia. Richard Illingworth had done well in the Texaco series, but he had struggled in the Tests, causing the Windies batsmen little trouble.

It was rather a strange-looking wicket for the Oval. Normally, it's a straw-whitish colour with an even covering and very firm. But the square had been flooded by a thunderstorm the day after Essex's NatWest defeat against Surrey. It was greener than usual and more patchy. The 12th man spot was between 'Syd' Lawrence and Derek Pringle, but the decision was made for me when Pring went down with a virus. It would be easy now to say that Pring would have been left out; I'm not so sure – it would have been tough to drop one of our two most successful bowlers of the summer.

The West Indies gave us a right going over on the first day after I decided to bat. We saw more bouncers than in the rest of the series put together, yet we battled our way to 231 for 4. The ball that was just short of a length wasn't too difficult to deal with, but those that pitched half way down found extra bounce and often took off. It wasn't easy to get out of the way. Normally, those balls come off slowly. These didn't and more than once I had to get the tortoise on at the last minute.

Hugh batted well and bravely for his three-hour 44 and had his helmet smashed by Ambrose. The tall Antiguan bowled 11 overs in the afternoon session, taking 2 for 15 – that was all the runs that came from one end in a two-hour period, which shows how tough it was. There weren't many scoring balls about. We got about two bouncers an over; maybe the Windies were taking full advantage of their last opportunity before the ICC's one-bouncer-an-over rule came into Test cricket. I've no complaints about bouncers, as long as umpires are strong and apply the law.

After being 112 for no wicket, we were suddenly 120 for 3, and I had visions of Trent Bridge all over again. We'd made a great start, but you're never safe against these blokes. Hugh went when he fended off another ball to his body to short leg, Athers got a beauty from Walsh to continue his dismal run, and Ambrose trapped me lbw. Robin Smith and Ramps steadied the ship until Ramps fell in the tortuous 20s again. Robin went on to get another century – his sixth in his 50th Test innings and, with support from Ian Botham and Chris Lewis, helped England reach 400 for the first time in all my matches against the West Indies.

Robin's got the game for the Windies and I've nothing but admiration for his power. He thrives on the big occasion; I've seen others, just as talented, intimidated by nerves and the pressure. All it does to Robin is inspire him. Ian played the innings we needed, a hard-working two-hour 31, not the style of his early years. That had never brought him much success against the West Indies. He was out when he trampled on his wicket, just failing, as BBC Radio's new cricket correspondent Jonathan Agnew described it, 'to get his leg over,' which gave fellow commentator Brian Johnson a fit of the giggles. Chris hit an impressive undefeated 47 and had looked a class batsman in his last two innings.

The Windies finished the day at 90 for 1 – and I was 'gutted'. I dropped a sitter at slip off Ian Botham's fourth ball back in Test cricket. It spoilt my evening. Giving Desmond Haynes a life was bad enough; but I'd mucked up Ian's comeback script. Worse followed. On Saturday morning, Ladbroke's announced that I'd saved them about £150,000 – they had been offering the less-than-generous odds of 5/1 on Ian taking a wicket in his first over. Could it get worse? It could. Allan Lamb was on the phone complaining I'd cost him a 'monkey' after he'd backed his old mate to the tune of £100. I'll never hear the end of that.

My error appeared likely to have serious consequences on Saturday as Haynes was still there on 67 with the Windies at 158 for 3. At that stage, a useful first-innings lead was all I was after. But a combination of Phil Tufnell and some suicidal batting allowed me to be the first England captain in 22 years to enforce the follow-on against the West Indies. Debutant Clayton Lambert started the collapse when, after batting maturely for an enterprising 39, he slashed at Tuffers' first ball. That surprised me because he had played the Essex spinners, John Childs and Peter Such, so well as Chelmsford a few days earlier. But I know the problem – I've had it myself: a spinner comes on and you try to hit him over his head first ball just to show who's boss. Lambert's slash squirted into the covers for an easy catch by Ramprakash – and Tuffers danced for joy.

Richards, expected next, was struggling with a migraine, so Jeff Dujon came in at No.6, only to fall lbw almost at once to a 'Syd' express. He was followed by Malcolm Marshall, who attempted to cut Tufnell and was taken at slip by Botham. Richards could delay his entrance no longer, and a couple of minutes later lunch was taken with the West Indies 161 for 6.

Shortly after the interval Viv attempted to drive Tufnell and edged a sharpish catch to Alex Stewart. There was no attempt by the West Indies to dig in. Ambrose, trying to emulate Richards, snicked Tufnell and Botham bagged his second slip catch. Two balls later Tufnell took his third wicket of a momentous over when Courtney Walsh slogged a catch to me at mid-on. And in his next over, Patrick Patterson edged and Beefy, leaping like a (fairly) young salmon, took his third catch of the innings. Desmond Haynes, watching aghast as the mayhem unfolded at the other end of the wicket, carried his bat for a fine 75.

Tufnell's astonishing return to Test cricket had yielded him 6 for 25, his last 33 balls bringing him all his wickets at the cost of four runs and turning the Oval into a cauldron of noise. The Windies collapse was astonishing. To avert the follow-on – and so give themselves a pretty good chance of saving the match and winning the series – they needed only 64 runs from their last seven wickets. They carelessly threw the chance away.

Still, I was delighted for Tuffers, who brought the good spinner's armoury to bear – variation, flight, aggression and cunning. Before the side was picked for this Test, I had talked to John Emburey, who was convinced that Phil was the best spinner in England. I was also pleased with Alec Stewart's performance behind the stumps. His catching of Richards was critically important. Though not terribly difficult, there would have been an outcry from those critical of his selection if he had missed it.

I didn't need to think twice before enforcing the follow-on. There was so long to go and the Windies were 243 behind. If the pitch had looked as if it might later take a lot of turn and become uneven, I might have considered going in again. As it was I decided to keep chipping away, although I knew bowling them out for a second time wouldn't be as easy.

They had reduced the deficit by 158 runs for the loss of three wickets by the close of Saturday. Ian Botham took two of them, Chris Lewis starting the ball rolling with a brilliant catch in the gully to dismiss Simmons.

The Windies went on the attack on Sunday, 50 runs coming in the first half hour. Hooper was particularly severe on Tufnell, hitting him for two sixes, and also smashing 'Syd' into the Bedser Stand. As in the first innings, they were determined not to let Tuffers dominate; this time they succeeded up to a point. But Tuffers eventually got his man when Hooper drove the ball to me at cover.

Viv Richards came out for his last Test innings to a prolonged standing ovation. It occurred to me that it would suit us fine if he emulated Bradman's final Test knock at the Oval in 1948: a second-ball duck (when the great Don required only four runs to make sure his career Test average would be 100!). Viv was clearly in no mood to accommodate me, playing his typical discouraging mixture of caution and confidence. At the other end Richardson, who had let Hooper dominate their stand of 83, was now beginning to play his shots. He and his captain shared a stand of 97 before Viv failed to middle a drive to Lawrence's inswinger and was caught by Hugh Morris at mid-on. He walked slowly back to the pavilion, to yet another standing ovation.

Jeff Dujon lasted only a few minutes. He was distracted by a pigeon, which had wandered around the square for a few minutes, then took up residence at short mid-wicket. When play resumed, Jeff immediately edged a lifter from 'Syd' to the keeper. Richardson now took control. He was especially severe on 'Syd', most memorably when thrashing him for six over the square-leg boundary and reached his century just before tea. But shortly after the interval Richie and Malcolm Marshall unsurprisingly accepted a 'bad light' offer, leaving the West Indies 356 for 6 – just 113 runs ahead with the final day to come.

On the Monday morning in our dressing-room the lads were really keyed up and they needed no pep talk from me. All I said was: 'Sunday was their day: this is ours. Let's go out and win it.'

England were certainly in the driving seat but the West Indies are especially dangerous when they have their backs to the wall. I saw our immediate target as getting the Windies out for 150 or thereabouts, preferably before lunch. If they made another 30 on top of that, or if they managed to survive for an hour or so after lunch, they could take a hell of a lot of beating. Remember – they needed only a draw to win the series.

Dramatically, the match was decided in the first few deliveries. Phil DeFreitas's first ball rapped Malcolm Marshall on the front pad and there was a loud appeal. It was turned down, but next ball Daffy settled the argument as Malcolm's middle stump went cartwheeling away. Two balls later, Ambrose was trapped leg before. Courtney Walsh, who had already proved his nuisance value as an inelegant but useful contributor of late runs, hung around for 47 infuriating minutes before 'Syd', our runaway train, trapped him leg before. Soon after, Richie, hitting out for runs, gave me a high catch at mid-wicket. This prize gave 'Syd' his first five-wicket haul in Test cricket. He fully deserved it. He would never dream of giving less than 100 per cent. You should have seen him in the dressing-room afterwards: he had given his all and was totally wiped out – but happy with it.

We'd reached my immediate target: we had got the Windies out well before lunch and left ourselves with a target of 143, with plenty of time to get them and the weather set fair. The Oval had been half full at the start of play, but it started to fill during the morning session and by lunchtime it was bursting at the seams as we went for that memorable finale to the series.

We knew the West Indies well enough by now to know they wouldn't be taking any prisoners and that, if we allowed them any kind of a start, they were quite capable of blowing us away. Sure enough, in the second over, Patrick Patterson uncorked a real brute of a ball for Hugh Morris who gloved it to the wicket-keeper. The following morning most of the papers showed Hugh going into orbit, head snapped sideways, trying to evade the missile, which brushed his gloves and was taken high above his head by Jeff Dujon. The score was 3 for 1.

Enter Mike Atherton, who after being the Texaco batting star had suffered a real nightmare in the test series: 66 runs in eight innings. I told him this was his day and he responded, as I knew he would, and we jogged along, picking up the odd single here and there, intent on weathering the pre-lunch barrage. As so often happens when a batsman is out of form, Mike's one false stroke cost him his wicket, when he edged a very quick one from Patterson to Carl Hooper in the slips. We took a pretty thoughtful lunch with the score at 40 for 2. The Windies had bowled with great ferocity and had made the breakthrough. Now, after a rest, they would be at full throttle on the resumption.

To my surprise and relief, they bowled poorly after lunch, and Robin Smith and I doubled the score in the space of seven overs, Robin smashing anything that was not absolutely straight. And then, quite suddenly, we had both gone. I was leg before to a pretty good inswinger from Marshall, and the following over Robin mistimed a pull from Walsh, spooning the ball to Patterson at mid-on. 80 for 4: crisis time!

Another wicket then might really have put the skids under us. England had just lost their two most experienced batsmen – both new-comers were on nought. As it was, Mark Ramprakash and Alec Stewart shouldered their responsibilities like veterans. The runs slowed to a trickle while they concentrated totally on survival. But eventually Alec, in particular, began to play his shots and soon he was dealing severely with anything loose. Slowly but surely they took us out of danger – until, with the stand worth 62, one run was required for victory.

The finale was pure theatre. Viv Richards asked Clayton Lambert to bowl the last over. Ramprakash attempted to pull the third of Lambert's innocuous medium-pacers – and was given out leg before. So out strode English cricket's greatest hero to administer the last rites. Cheered all the way to the wicket, Beefy pulled his first ball to the long leg boundary – and a memorable series was over.

Players and umpires made a grab for stumps as the crowd raced on to the field. Ian threw his arms skywards at the fairy-tale finish – and who could blame him? For all his astonishing feats on the cricket field down the years, he had had to wait until he was 35 years old and in his 98th Test before being on the winning side against the West Indies. But it was a special moment for all of us. Chris Lewis, Philip Tufnell, 'Syd' Lawrence and Hugh Morris shared Ian's delight at a first victory over the world's best side; for Alec Stewart, Phillip DeFreitas, Mike Atherton and Mark Ramprakash it was their second triumph. And for Robin Smith and me, it marked a hat-trick of wins in the space of 18 months.

Afterwards, Ray Illingworth named Robin as Man of the Match. Micky Stewart named Curtly Ambrose as the tourist Man of the Series, just ahead of Richie; while the Windies manager, Lance Gibbs, nominated me as England's Man of the Series. But over and above any awards, the thing that gave me the greatest satisfaction was that England's Test team had regained its self-respect and had gone some way towards erasing memories of the disastrous Ashes tour of the previous winter.

Sri Lanka Test, Lord's

I was named captain for the winter tour to New Zealand and the World Cup there and in Australia a few days after our victory in the Fifth Test. The Oval side, plus Jack Russell and minus Mike Atherton (who was having a back operation), then went to Lord's and beat Sri Lanka. There was danger of a feeling of anti-climax after the West Indies series, and we started sluggishly at Lord's. But Alec Stewart rescued England with his maiden Test century and then Daffy continued his top form with a Test-best 7 for 70.

In the second innings I hit 174 – overtaking Sir Len Hutton and Sir Don Bradman in the all-time total Test runs list and becoming the 13th batsman in history to reach 7,000 Test runs. It was century No.88 in my first-class career. The Sri Lankans took some shifting, but Philip Tufnell spun us to victory with his third five-wicket haul of the year.

It was important that we finished the summer on a high note. I want a team that gives nothing away, whatever the circumstances or occasion. If we can develop that killer instinct, England will give every other Test country in the world a hard time. And that's my prime concern as England captain.

Being Essex skipper has its rewards too. Six weeks before the end of the season, we were 51 points behind Warwickshire, but we took the title by winning six of our last seven matches. After finishing third in 1988 and runners-up in the previous two seasons, I had begun to fear we were fated. We nearly clinched the title at Leicester, but Warwicks won a thriller against Northants to keep their hopes and the title race alive. But we demolished the 1990 champions Middlesex in the final round of matches when we bowled them out for just 51 on the first morning. I then scored the highest score of the season – 259 – as we reached 566–6 declared and went on to win by an innings and 208 runs. Fittingly, Neil Foster claimed the final wicket, his 97th of the season, in figures of 6/104. It was our fifth title in 13 seasons and I was pleased the lads efforts were rewarded with the Britannic trophy after recent disappointments.

Conclusion

By the end of August 1991 England had played 21 Tests in an 18-month spell – that's a pretty frantic schedule by anyone's standards. It was made up of two series against the West Indies, one in Australia, series at home against New Zealand and India and a Test at the end of the 1991 summer against Sri Lanka. Not surprisingly, there was no England ever-present over that period. Robin Smith comes closest; his damaged finger kept him out of the Trent Bridge Test against the West Indies. I missed three Tests – two in the Caribbean, the other in Australia – with hand injuries.

The international schedule of Tests and one-dayers is hectic enough; but for nearly six months in the middle of the year county calls fill up most of the remaining time. I've been a loyal supporter of Essex and the county game all my career, but I've come to the conclusion that certain changes are long overdue. Sometimes we play 28 days on the trot, with back to back matches. That's of no benefit to a professional sportsman. You need time off to deal with injuries, to work on your game, sorting out technical problems, and to enjoy something of a home life.

It's time cricketers were given two regular days off a week for recovery and rest. I played in the Currie Cup in South Africa with that sort of set-up. It made a great difference; the breaks allowed you to look forward to your cricket as something special. As for four-day matches, I'm in favour of it purely from a cricket point of view, especially with pitches as they are at the moment and the attitude of some county captains. It would enable us to have a championship with every county playing the others once.

The biggest difference in Test matches this summer has been the extra day of preparation. Unfortunately, that has meant doing away with the rest day – and that was very tough on our bowlers at the Oval when the West Indies followed on. But getting the Test team together on Tuesdays has been a tremendous advantage: it obviously helps team spirit, but the main bonus is the fact that we enjoy the luxury of two days without cricket. You're practising, of course, but it's still a rest from playing – an opportunity to recharge the batteries. England look for high-quality performances in Test matches. For that, the players have to be fresh, well-prepared and in the right frame of mind. That's what the extra day gives us. If I had to choose between that and the rest day, I'd sacrifice the rest day. Hopefully, one day, if the fixtures can be worked out to everyone's satisfaction, we will have both.

England sides are much better prepared when they go abroad these days, too. I've captained two hours. The one that was relatively successful came after the squad had been together at home for several weeks; the other, when we had little time to work together before we left, went downhill fast. Now that winter contracts have been introduced, England touring parties will be ready and toned up before they set off. The way we went about things in Australia was appalling, and consequently our standard of play wasn't good enough. Even when we had the Aussies struggling, we couldn't force home our advantage and made silly mistakes.

Our future winter tours got a boost at the end of the 1991 season when it was announced that Whittingdale, an Investment Trust firm in the city, were putting in £1m over the next four years to sponsor all our coaching. I'd met Patrick Whittingdale in Perth at the end of the Ashes tour – he'd put on a special photographic exhibition, the Ashes Flashes, displaying the best action from our series against Australia – and we had discussed ways of how Whittingdale might make a useful contribution to English cricket and the Test team. This sponsorship will certainly do that; it allows the top England players to get the best specialist coaching we need, as well as benefitting the side as a whole.

Part of the problem was going on tour at the end of our summer, with very little break. The ideal time to tour, as far as I'm concerned, is between the New Year and the start of the new

English season. Even though that means you're straight into the new season when you come home, you will have had three months off at the end of the previous summer. That will have enabled you to wind down, have a holiday, and generally feel as if you've had a real rest before you set off on tour.

I've also changed my views on the presence of wives and girlfriends on tour. I've been converted to Allan Border's way of thinking. I wouldn't issue a ban, but I've come to believe they tend to be disruptive of the team spirit. The problem is one of divided loyalties: you are working, they're on holiday. Moreover, players with the families go their separate ways on the social front, so that the team spends less time together. This needs tactful controlling. I have to say that managers of England parties have gone out of their way to make wives and girlfriends welcome; there's nothing worse for everyone if the womenfolk are made to feel unwanted.

It's not an easy problem to solve. Different destinations bring different problems. We never recaptured the team spirit of the Caribbean in Australia. Because there were more things to see and do, we didn't see as much of each other in the evening; whereas in the West Indies, most of the players seemed to finish up in the same restaurant. It's important, too, that none of the players feels neglected by the captain or, at the opposite pole, that he's watching their every move. The captain must be rather aloof by the very nature of his job, yet he must always be approachable.

I've been helped in my time as captain by the fact that I've been playing some of the best cricket of my career. The sheer volume of runs in my 'Indian summer' of 1990 showed that. I hadn't been totally happy at the start of the year in the Caribbean, but I got into gear with my double hundred against Jamaica when, for the first time in a long while I felt totally at ease. While I've always succeeded against very fast bowling, I've had problems with medium pacers. I like the ball coming onto the bat. David Gower is the same, and so are Lambie and Robin Smith. The nub of my problem against Terry Alderman in 1989 was footwork. When I feel comfortable, my shots are technically better. I've always tended to hit the ball through mid-wicket, hopefully with a straight bat rather than pulling across the line.

When batting against the West Indies you need lots of confidence and a definite plan. There's always plenty of short-pitched bowling apart from the bouncers, and you spend a lot of time on the back foot. I've learnt to work the ball off my body. I don't cut unless the ball is short and wide, wheras Gower, Lamb and Smith cut balls off a fuller length and nearer the stumps. With the Windies bowling, not too much time is spent on the front foot. Patterson and Marshall bowl a fuller length, but there's little of that from Ambrose and Walsh. You must learn to duck and weave and watch the ball all the way. Graeme Hick's problems came from being too static and from taking his eyes off the ball (he was often hit). No matter how talented a player you are, being used as target practice by the Windies quartet will affect your confidence.

Batting against the West Indies is about making decisions in advance – for instance, whether to hook or not. Some days I just won't hook anything; other days, you look at the wicket, who's bowling and how much bounce there is. The Windies tie you down, but like anyone else, if you get on top of them, they don't bowl so well. They're not used to being dominated by batsmen. On the other hand, you can bat well against them for a session – and find yourself with only 15 runs on the board.

Experience counts for a lot against all the Test-playing counties, not just the West Indies. Once I'm in, I try to eliminate mistakes. That doesn't mean I block, but I don't step outside the bounds of my normal rhythm of play. There's a difference between making a century and scoring one; I'm talking not about being slow, but about being patient, prepared to graft for your runs, and not making mistakes. It's about taking control of the game. Once players like Geoff Boycott and John Edrich had dug themselves in, they were desperately difficult to get out. David Gower and Viv Richards are brilliant, able to destroy any attack in the world and look marvellous while they're doing it. But they make mistakes – so the bowlers always have a chance.

The hardest thing for any cricketer to work out is what his game is all about. You've got to have a method. You can't play the same way every time. It's imperative to work out the shots you can and can't play. You must evaluate wickets and bowlers and the best way for you to play them. Most youngsters play shots. I've used a method since 1985 which I evolved. Before then, I was a much more forceful and attacking player. Now I'm more consistent and conservative, less flamboyant. I'm still able to dominate, but I don't destroy the bowling any more. I believe I'm a better player these days and more effective. It's not how you get them, but 'if'. At my age, the natural skills are beginning to deteriorate and you have to compensate by using your head.

John Morris, Graeme Hick, Alec Stewart and Neil Fairbrother are four young England batsmen who have all had problems adapting to Test cricket. Alec works very hard and has a great attitude. But he has a technical weakness with certain shots. Alec's had nearly 30 innings for England and in more than half has got himself out in the slip-to-gully area. He realizes his problems and is trying to eliminate them. You can rarely eliminate or cure that sort of problem, it's more a case of keeping it in check.

John Morris has no deficiencies in the way Alec has. He fits neatly into the 'scores runs' category, he doesn't make them. He's a super player, but he gives it away. His biggest weakness is that he can get to 80, never really look secure, and then get out.

Neil Fairbrother's problem at Test level is that he's not sure how to play. I believe that he has to play the way in which he is happiest, most natural and comfortable. That's easier said than done. But it's his Lancashire performances that got him recognized and he wasn't picked by England to play a different game. 'If you get in, make it count' was the best piece of advice Kenny Barrington gave me; after all, next time you might get an unplayable delivery first ball. Neil plays very aggressively for Lancs, and he worries that he'll be castigated if he gets out playing an irresponsible shot for England. It's the classic dilemma. His thrilling century against the Windies at Lord's in the Texaco should have gone some way to solving the problem, but he'll still have that decision to make the next time he has a Test chance. He'll have to work that out for himself. We gave him three Tests in 1990 – and he knew he was in for the series – but even that security didn't help. John Morris was given three Tests later that summer. Three Tests is a fair crack.

Graeme Hick got four in 1991, but struggled. No other successful batsman has ever had to wait so long for a Test chance. It came against the best attack in the world – and he was found wanting. Maybe county cricket had become too easy for him and he'd got into bad habits. Graeme couldn't get out of the way of short-pitch bowling; not only was he getting hit, he was getting out – six times in seven knocks to Ambrose. But he's a conscientious player and will work a way round the problem. And once he's overcome it, the experience will make him a better player.

Graeme's been helped, as everyone has, by our team manager Micky Stewart. I've got only praise for the help he's given me in my spell as captain. He's always enthusiastic and encouraging. Maybe he's a bit of a sergeant-major, but I don't mind that. His heart's in the right place and he works tirelessly to help. You can't blame the team's failures on him. He's also become the link between players and the media. Micky takes the brunt of their attacks. I prefer that. I want to get on with playing the game. His job is not to dictate the style of play – it's to take some of the load off the captain and advise and organize matters before, during and after the match. I'm sure I wouldn't have enjoyed the success I have if he hadn't been around.

GRAHAM Alan GOOCH

Born Leytonstone, 23 July, 1953
Essex debut 1973, cap 1975
Test debut v Australia (Edgbaston, July 1975)
Test career: 91 Tests, 7,028 runs @ 43.92, 94 catches, 17 wickets @ 47.05.
Test captaincy: debut v West Indies (Oval, August 1988)
Captaincy record: 20 Tests, seven wins, five defeats, eight draws.

GRAHAM GOOCH IN 1990 & 1991

	M	I	NO	Runs	HS	Avge	100	50
First-class matches								
Tests v West Indies 90	2	4	1	128	84	42.66	—	1
Tests v New Zealand	3	5	0	306	154	61.20	1	1
Tests v India	3	6	0	752	333	125.33	3	2
Tests v Australia	4	8	0	426	117	53.25	1	4
Tests v West Indies 91	5	9	1	480	154*	60.00	1	2
Test v Sri Lanka	1	2	0	212	174	106.00	1	—
Other WI tour 90	4	7	0	488	229	69.71	1	3
Britannic 90	11	18	2	1586	215	99.12	7	5
Other Aust tour 90/91	4	6	1	197	93	39.40	—	1
Britannic 91	11	16	1	996	259	66.40	3	3
Other	4	5	3	325	102*	162.50	2	1
Total	52	86	9	5904	333	76.67	20	27

GRAHAM GOOCH CENTURIES 1990 & 1991

239 – England XI v Jamaica, 1st ins, Sabina Park, 19–2–90
137 – Essex v Middx, 1st ins, Lord's, 27/8–4–90
215 – Essex v Leics, 1st ins, Chelmsford, 4/5–5–90
121 – Essex v Worcs, 1st ins, Worcester, 19–5–90
215 – Essex v Middx, 2nd ins, Ilford, 4/5–6–90
102* – Essex v NZ, Chelmsford, 1–7–90
154 – England v NZ, 3rd Test, Edgbaston, 5/6–7–90
177 – Essex v Lancashire, 2nd ins, Colchester, 24–7–90
333 – England v India, 1st Test, Lord's, 26/7–7–90
123 – England v India, 1st Test, Lord's 30–7–90
116 – England v India, 2nd Test, 1st ins, Old Trafford, 9–8–90
174 – Essex v Northants, Northampton, 29–8–90
126 – Essex v Northants, Northampton, 31–8–90
117 – England v Aust, 4th Test, 2nd ins, Adelaide, 29–1–91
101* – Essex v Cambridge U, 1st ins, Fenners, 19–4–91
154* – England v WI, 1st Test, 2nd ins, Headingley, 8/9–6–91
106 – Essex v Middlesex, 2nd ins, Lord's, 30–6/1–7–91
173 – Essex v Northants, 1st ins, Colchester, 16–8–91
174 – England v Sri Lanka, 2nd ins, Lord's, 24/26–8–91
259 – Essex Middlesex, 1st ins, Chelmsford, 17/8–9–91

TESTS

FIRST INNINGS		SECOND INNINGS	
West Indies, 1st Test, Jamaica, February/March 1990			
		1c	
1. c Dujon b Patterson	18	1. c Greenidge b Bishop	8
West Indies, 3rd Test, Trinidad, March 1990			
		1c	
1. c Dujon b Bishop	84	1. retired hurt	18
New Zealand, 1st Test, Trent Bridge, June 1990			
2c			
1. lbw b Hadlee	0		
New Zealand, 2nd Test, Lord's, June 1990			
1. c & b Bracewell	85	1. b Hadlee	37
13–7–25–0			
New Zealand, 3rd Test, Edgbaston, July 1990			
1. c Hadlee b Morrison	154	1. b Snedden	30
		1c	
India, 1st Test, Lord's, July 1990			
1. b Prabhakar	333	1. c Azharuddin b Sharma	123
6–3–26–1 1c		1c	
India, 2nd Test, Old Trafford, August 1990			
1. c More b Prabhakar	116	1. c More b Prabhakar	7
2c			
India, 3rd Test, Oval, August 1990			
12–1–44–0			
1. c Shastri b Hirwani	85	2. c Vengsarkar b Hirwani	88
Australia, 2nd Test, Melbourne, December 1990			
1. lbw b Alderman	20	1. c Alderman b Reid	58
Australia, 3rd Test, Sydney, January 1991			
14–3–46–1		2c	
1. c Healy b Reid	59	1. c Border b Matthews	54
Australia, 4th Test, Adelaide, January 1991			
9–2–23–1 1c		2c	
1. c Healy b Reid	87	1. c Marsh b Reid	117
Australia, 5th Test, Perth, February 1991			
1. c Healy b McDermott	13	1. c Alderman b Hughes	18
1c			
West Indies, 1st Test, Headingley, June 1991			
1. c Dujon b Marshall	34	1. not out	154
1c		2c	

West Indies, 2nd Test, Lord's, June 1991
2–0–3–0
1. b Walsh 37

West Indies, 3rd Test, Trent Bridge, July 1991
1. lbw b Marshall 68 1. b Ambrose 13

West Indies, 4th Test, Edgbaston, July 1991
1. b Marshall 45 1. b Patterson 40
6–1–11–0

West Indies, 5th Test, Oval, August 1991
1. lbw b Ambrose 60 1. lbw b Marshall 29
1c 2c

Sri Lanka, Lord's, August 1991
1. c & b Ratnayake 38 1. b Anurasiri 174

BATTING

	M	I	NO	Runs	HS	Avge	100	50	Ct
WI 90	2	4	1	128	84	42.66	—	1	2
NZ 90	3	5	0	306	154	61.20	1	1	3
Ind 90	3	6	0	752	333	125.33	3	2	4
Aus 90/91	4	8	0	426	117	53.25	1	4	6
WI 91	5	9	1	480	154*	60.00	1	2	6
SL 91	1	2	0	212	174	106.00	1	—	—
Total	18	34	2	2304	333	72.00	7	10	21

BOWLING

	Ov	Mdns	Runs	W	Avge	Best	5w	10w
NZ 90	13	7	25	0	—	—	—	—
Ind 90	18	4	70	1	70.00	1–26	—	—
Aus 90/91	23	5	69	2	34.50	1–23	—	—
WI 91	8	1	14	0	—	—	—	—
Total	62	17	178	3	59.33	1–23	—	—

ONE-DAY INTERNATIONALS

West Indies, Trinidad, February 14, 1990
8–0–26–1 1c 1. not out 13

West Indies, Trinidad, February 17, 1990 (match abandoned after 5.5 overs)

West Indies, Jamaica, March 3, 1990
1. b Bishop 2 2–0–15–0 1c

West Indies, Guyana, March 7, 1990
1. b Moseley 33

West Indies, Guyana, March 15, 1990
1. b Hooper 42 5–1–22–0

New Zealand, Headingley, May 23, 1990
1. c Millmow b C Pringle 55 4–0–23–2

New Zealand, Oval, May 25, 1990
1. not out 112

India, Headingley, July 18, 1990
1. c & b Shastri 45

India, Trent Bridge, July 20, 1990
1. b Prabhakar 7

World Series: New Zealand, Sydney, December 13, 1990
1. c Young b Petrie 3

World Series: New Zealand, Brisbane, December 15, 1990
1. b Harris 48 1c

World Series: Australia, Brisbane, December 16, 1990
1. b Matthews 41 1c

World Series: Australia, Sydney, January 1, 1991
1. b O'Donnell 37

World Series: Australia, Melbourne, January 10, 1991
10–0–39–1 1. c Healy b M Waugh 37

New Zealand, Christchurch, February 9, 1991
1. b C Pringle 17 10–0–31–0 1c

New Zealand, Wellington, February 13, 1991
10–2–33–0 1. c Wright b Cairns 41

New Zealand, Auckland, February 16, 1991
10–0–40–1 1. b Larsen 47

West Indies, Edgbaston, May 23, 24, 1991
1. b Ambrose 0

West Indies, Old Trafford, May 25, 1991
1. b Hooper 54 11–1–51–1

West Indies, Lord's, May 27, 1991
2–0–9–1 1c 1. run out 11

BATTING

	M	I	NO	Runs	HS	Avge	100	50	Ct
WI 90	5	4	1	90	42	30.00	—	—	2
NZ 90	2	2	1	167	112*	167.00	1	1	—
Ind 90	2	2	0	52	45	26.00	—	—	—
Aus 90/91	5	5	0	166	48	33.20	—	—	2

	M	I	NO	Runs	HS	Avge	100	50	Ct
NZ 91	3	3	0	105	47	35.00	—	—	1
WI 91	3	3	0	65	54	21.66	—	1	1
Total	20	19	2	645	112*	37.94	1	2	6

BOWLING

	Ov	Mdns	Runs	W	Avge	Best	5w
WI 90	15	1	63	1	63.00	1–26	—
NZ 90	4	0	23	2	11.50	2–23	—
Aus 90/91	10	0	39	1	39.00	1–39	—
NZ 91	30	2	104	1	104.00	1–40	—
WI 91	13	1	60	2	30.00	1–9	—
Total	72	4	289	7	41.28	1–9	—

ENGLAND'S TESTS

West Indies v England 1990

1st Test, Sabina Park, Kingston, Jamaica, February 24–March 1 (February 28, washed out)

West Indies	164	(Fraser 5–28)
	240	(Best 64)
England	364	(Lamb 132, Smith 57; Walsh 5–68)
	41–1	

England won by 9 wickets

2nd Test, Bourda, Georgetown, Guyana, March 9–14

Test match abandoned without a ball being bowled

3rd Test, Queens Park, Port of Spain, Trinidad, March 23–28

West Indies	199	(Logie 98)
	239	(Malcolm 6–77)
England	288	(Gooch 84, Larkins 54)
	120–5	

Draw

†4th Test, Kensington Oval, Bridgetown, Barbados, April 5–10

West Indies	446	(Best 164, Richards 70)
	267–8 dec	(Haynes 109)
England	358	(Lamb 119, Smith 62)
	191	(Russell 55; Ambrose 8–45)

West Indies won by 164 runs

†5th Test, Recreation Ground, St John's, Antigua, April 12–16

England	260	(Bishop 5–84)
	154	

West Indies 446 (Haynes 167, Greenidge 149)
West Indies won by Innings & 32 runs

† Gooch injured, replaced by Allan Lamb as captain

England v New Zealand 1990

1st Test, Trent Bridge, June 7, 8, 9, 11, 12

New Zealand 208 (Crowe 59; DeFreitas 5–53)
36–2
England 345–9 dec (Atherton 151, Smith 55)
Draw

2nd Test, Lord's, June 22, 23, 24, 26, 27

England 334 (Gooch 85, Smith 64, Stewart 54)
272–4 dec (Lamb 84*, Atherton 54)
New Zealand 462–9 dec (Franklin 101, Wright 98, Hadlee 86; Malcolm 5–94)
Draw

3rd Test, Edgbaston, July 5, 6, 7, 9, 10

England 435 (Gooch 154, Atherton 82)
158 (Atherton 70; Hadlee 5–53)
New Zealand 249 (Franklin 66; Hemmings 6–58)
230 (Malcolm 5–46)
England won by 114 runs

England v India 1990

1st Test, Lord's, July 26, 27, 28, 30, 31

England 653–4 dec (Gooch 333, Lamb 139, Smith 100*)
272–4 dec (Gooch 123, Atherton 72)
India 454 (Azharuddin 121, Shastri 100, Kapil Dev 77*; Fraser 5–104)
224
England won by 247 runs

2nd Test, Old Trafford, August 9, 10, 11, 13, 14

England 519 (Atherton 131, Smith 121*, Gooch 116)
320–4 dec (Lamb 109, Atherton 74, Smith 61*)
India 432 (Azharuddin 179, Manjrekar 93, Tendulkar 68; Fraser 5–124)
343–6 (Tendulkar 119*, Prabhakar 67*, Manjrekar 50)
Draw

3rd Test, Oval, August 23, 24, 25, 27, 28

India 606–9 dec (Shastri 187, Kapil Dev 110, Azharuddin 78, More 61*)
England 340 (Gooch 85, Smith 57, Hemmings 51)
477–4 dec (Gower 157*, Gooch 88, Atherton 86, Lamb 52)
Draw

Australia v England 1990–91

†1st Test, The Gabba, Brisbane, November 23–25

England	194	Gower 61)
	114	(Alderman 6–47)
Australia	152	
	157–0	(Marsh 72*, Taylor 67*)

Australia won by 10 wickets

† Gooch injured, replaced by Allan Lamb as captain

2nd Test, Melbourne Cricket Ground, December 26–30

England	352	(Gower 100, Stewart 79, Larkins 64; Reid 6–97)
	150	(Gooch 58, Larkins 54; Reid 7–51)
Australia	306	(Border 62, Taylor 61; Fraser 6–82)
	197–2	(Boon 94*, Marsh 79*)

Australia won by 8 wickets

3rd Test, Sydney Cricket Ground, January 4–8

Australia	518	(Matthews 128, Boon 97, Border 78, Jones 60)
	205	(Healy 69; Tufnell 5–61)
England	469–8 dec	(Gower 123, Atherton 105, Stewart 91, Gooch 59)
	113–4	(Gooch 54)

Draw

4th Test, Adelaide Oval, January 25–29

Australia	386	(M Waugh 138, Matthews 65)
	314–6 dec	(Boon 121, Border 83*)
England	229	(Gooch 87, Smith 53; McDermott 5–97)
	335–5	(Gooch 117, Atherton 87, Lamb 53)

Draw

5th Test, WACA, Perth, February 1, 2, 3, 5

England	244	(Lamb 91, Smith 58; McDermott 8–97)
	182	
Australia	307	(Boon 64, Matthews 60*)
	120–1	(Marsh 63*)

Australia won by 9 wickets

England v West Indies 1991

1st Test, Headingley, June 6–10

England	198	(Smith 54)
	252	(Gooch 154*; Ambrose 6–52)
West Indies	173	(Richards 73)
	162	(Richardson 68)

England won by 115 runs

2nd Test, Lord's, June 20–24

West Indies	419	(Hooper 111, Richards 63, Haynes 60, Richardson 57; Pringle 5–100)
	12–2	
England	354	(Smith 143*)

Draw

3rd Test, Trent Bridge, July 4, 5, 6, 8, 9

England	300 (Gooch 68, Smith 64*; Ambrose 5–74)
	211 (DeFreitas 55*)
West Indies	397 (Richards 80, Logie 78, Marshall 67)
	115–1 (Haynes 57*, Richardson 52*)

West Indies won by 9 wickets

4th Test, Edgbaston, July 25–28

England	188
	255 (Lewis 65; Patterson 5–81)
West Indies	292 (Richardson 104; Lewis 6–111)
	157–3 (Richards 73*, Hooper 55*)

West Indies won by 7 wickets

5th Test, Oval, August 8–12

England	419 (Smith 109, Gooch 60)
	146–5
West Indies	176 (Haynes 75*, Tufnell 6–25)
	385 (Richardson 121, Richards 60, Hooper 54; Lawrence 5–106) WI followed on

England won by 5 wickets

England v Sri Lanka 1991

Lord's, August 22, 23, 24, 26, 27

England	282 (Stewart 113*; Ratnayake 5–69)
	364–3 dec (Gooch 174, Smith 63*)
Sri Lanka	224 (Hathurusinghe 66, Ratnayake 52; DeFreitas 7–70)
	285 (Jayasuriya 66; Tufnell 5–94)

England won by 137 runs

ENGLAND'S ONE-DAY INTERNATIONALS

West Indies v England 1990

Trinidad, February 14

West Indies	208–8 (50 overs) Richardson 51
England	26–1 (13 overs)

No result

Trinidad, February 17

West Indies	13–0 (5.5 overs)

No result

Jamaica, March 3

England	214–8 (50 overs) Lamb 66; Bishop 4–28
West Indies	216–7 (50 overs) Richardson 108*

West Indies won by 3 wickets. Man of the Match: Richardson

Guyana, March 7

England	188–8 (48 overs)
West Indies	191–4 (45.2 overs) Best 100, Haynes 50

West Indies won by 6 wickets. Man of the Match: Best

Guyana, March 15
England 166–9 (49 overs) Ambrose 4–18
West Indies 167–3 (40.2 overs) Greenidge 77
West Indies won by 7 wickets. Man of the Match: Greenidge

Barbados, April 3
†England 214–3 (38 overs) Smith 69, Lamb 55*
West Indies 217–6 (37.3 overs) Richardson 80, Best 51
West Indies won by 4 wickets. Man of the Match: Richardson

England v New Zealand
Headingley, May 23
England 295–6 (55 overs) Smith 128, Gooch 55
New Zealand 298–6 (54.5 overs) Greatbatch 102*, Wright 52, Jones 51
New Zealand won by 4 wickets. Man of the Match: Greatbatch

Oval, May 25
New Zealand 212–6 (55 overs) Greatbatch 111
England 213–4 (49.3 overs) Gooch 112*
England won by 6 wickets. Man of the Match: Malcolm
England took the Texaco Trophy on faster scoring rate
Men of the Series: Gooch/Greatbatch

England v India
Headingley, July 18
England 229 (54.3 overs) Lamb 56, Gower 50
India 233–4 (53 overs) Manjrekar 82, Azharuddin 55*
India won by 6 wickets. Man of the Match: Kumble

Trent Bridge, July 20
England 281 (55 overs) Smith 103, Atherton 59, Russell 50
India 282–5 (53 overs) Azharuddin 63*, Manjrekar 59, Vengsarkar 54
India won by 5 wickets. Man of the Match: Smith
Men of the Series: Russell/Azharuddin

World Series, Australia
Adelaide, December 1, 1990
New Zealand 199–6 (40 overs) Wright 67, Rutherford 50
†England 192–9 (40 overs) J Morris 63*
New Zealand won by 7 runs. Man of the Match: Wright

Perth, December 7
New Zealand 158 (49.2 overs)
†England 161–6 (43.5 overs)
England won by 4 wickets. Man of the Match: Stewart

Perth, December 9

†England	192–9 (50 overs) O'Donnell 4–45
Australia	193–4 (41 overs) Jones 63*

Australia won by 6 wickets. Man of the Match: O'Donnell

Sydney, December 13

England	194 (46.4 overs) Lamb 72; C Pringle 4–35
New Zealand	161 (48.1 overs) M Crowe 76; Lewis 4–35

England won by 33 runs. Man of the Match: Lamb

Brisbane, December 15

England	203–6 (50 overs)
New Zealand	204–2 (44.3 overs) M Crowe 78, Wright 54

New Zealand won by 8 wickets. Man of the Match: Crowe

Brisbane, December 16

Australia	283–5 (50 overs) Jones 145, Marsh 82
England	246–7 (50 overs)

Australia won by 37 runs. Man of the Match: Jones

Sydney, January 1, 1991

Australia	221–7 (50 overs) O'Donnell 71*, M Waugh 62
England	153 (45.5 overs)

Australia won by 68 runs. Man of the Match: P Taylor

Melbourne, January 10

Australia	222–6 (50 overs) S Waugh 65*, Healy 50*
England	219–9 (50 overs) Stewart 55; M Waugh 4–37

Australia won by 3 runs. Man of the Match: Healy

	P	W	L	Pts	Rate
Australia	8	7	1	14	4.77
New Zealand	8	3	5	6	4.06
England	8	2	6	4	4.06

Australia beat New Zealand 2–0 in the best of three final.

Christchurch, February 9

England	230–7 (50 overs) Smith 65, Lamb 61
New Zealand	216–8 (50 overs) Rutherford 77, Harris 56

England won by 14 runs. Man of the Match: Rutherford

Wellington, February 13

New Zealand	196–8 (49 overs) Jones 64
England	187 (48 overs)

New Zealand won by 9 runs. Man of the Match: Jones

Auckland, February 16

New Zealand	224–7 (50 overs) Jones 64, Smith 51*
England	217 (49.5 overs) Cairns 4–55

New Zealand won by 7 runs. Man of the Match: Harris

England v West Indies
Edgbaston, May 23, 24

West Indies	173—8	(55 overs) Botham 4–55
England	175—9	(49.4 overs) Atherton 69*

England won by 1 wicket. Man of the Match: Atherton

Old Trafford, May 25

England	270—4	(55 overs) Atherton 74, Lamb 62, Gooch 54
West Indies	261—8	(55 overs) Richards 78

England won by 9 runs. Man of the Match: Lamb

Lord's, May 27

West Indies	264—9	(55 overs) Logie 82; Lawrence 4–67
England	265—3	(46.1 overs) Fairbrother 113, Hick 86*

England won by 7 wickets. Man of the Match: Fairbrother
Men of the Series: Atherton/Richards

† Gooch injured, replaced by Allan Lamb as captain

MICHAEL Andrew ATHERTON

Born Manchester, 23 March, 1968
Lancashire debut 1987, cap 1989
Test debut v Australia (Trent Bridge, August 1989)
Test career: 18 Tests, 1166 runs @ 35.33, 15 catches, 1 wicket @ 282.

FIRST INNINGS		SECOND INNINGS	
New Zealand, 1st Test, Trent Bridge, June 1990			
2. c Snedden b Priest	151		
New Zealand, 2nd Test, Lord's, June 1990			
2. b Morrison	0	2. c Bracewell b Jones	54
1–1–0–0			
New Zealand, 3rd Test, Edgbaston, July 1990			
2. lbw b Snedden	82	2. c Rutherford b Bracewell	70
9–5–17–0 1c		2c	
India, 1st Test, Lord's, July 1990			
2. b Kapil Dev	8	2. c Vengsarkar b Sharma	72
		1–0–11–0 1c	
India, 2nd Test, Old Trafford, August 1990			
2. c More b Hirwani	131	2. lbw b Kapil Dev	74
16–3–68–0 1c		4–0–22–0	
India, 3rd Test, Oval, August 1990			
7–0–60–1 1c			
2. c More b Prabhakar	7	2. lbw b Kapil Dev	86
Australia, 1st Test, Brisbane, November 1990			
1. lbw b Reid	13	1. b Alderman	15
2c		2–0–16–0	

FIRST INNINGS | SECOND INNINGS

Australia, 2nd Test, Melbourne, December 1991
2. c Boon b Reid 0 | 2. c Healy b Reid 4
2–1–3–0 | 3–0–14–0 2c

Australia, 3rd Test, Sydney, January 1991
5–0–28–0 1c | 3–1–9–0
2. c Boon b Matthews 105 | 6. not out 3

Australia, 4th Test, Adelaide, January 1991
2. lbw b McDermott 0 | 2. c M Waugh b Reid 87

Australia, 5th Test, Perth, February 1991
2. c Healy b McDermott 27 | 2. c Boon b Hughes 25

West Indies, 1st Test, Headingley, June 1991
2. b Patterson 2 | 2. c Dujon b Ambrose 6
1c

West Indies, 2nd Test, Lord's, June 1991
2. b Ambrose 5
1c

West Indies, 3rd Test, Trent Bridge, July 1991
2. lbw b Ambrose 32 | 2. b Ambrose 4

West Indies, 4th Test, Edgbaston, July 1991
3. lbw b Walsh 16 | 3. c Hooper b Patterson 1
1c

West Indies, 5th Test, Oval, August 1991
3. c Hooper b Walsh 0 | 3. c Hooper b Patterson 13

BATTING

	M	I	NO	Runs	HS	Avge	100	50	Ct
NZ 90	3	5	0	357	151	71.40	1	3	3
Ind 90	3	6	0	378	131	63.00	1	3	3
Aus 90/91	5	10	1	279	105	31.00	1	1	5
WI 91	5	9	0	79	32	8.77	—	—	3
Total	16	30	1	1093	151	37.68	3	7	14

BOWLING

	Ov	Mdns	Runs	W	Avge	Best	5w	10w
NZ 90	10	6	17	0	—	—	—	—
Ind 90	28	3	161	1	161.00	1–60	—	—
Aus 90/91	15	2	70	0	—	—	—	—
Total	53	11	248	1	248.00	1–60	—	—

ROBERT John BAILEY

Born Biddulph, Stoke-on-Trent, 28 October, 1963
Northants debut 1982, cap 1985
Test debut v West Indies (Oval, August 1988)
Test career: 4 Tests, 119 runs @ 14.87.

FIRST INNINGS		SECOND INNINGS	
West Indies, 3rd Test, Trinidad, March 1990			
6. c Logie b Moseley	0	6. b Walsh	0
West Indies, 4th Test, Barbados, April 1990			
3. b Bishop	17	3. c Dujon b Ambrose	6
West Indies, 5th Test, Antigua, April 1990			
3. c Dujon b Bishop	42	4. c Dujon b Bishop	8

BATTING

	M	I	NO	Runs	HS	Avge	100	50	Ct
WI 90	3	6	0	73	42	12.16	—	—	—
Total	3	6	0	73	42	12.16	—	—	—

IAN Terence BOTHAM

Born Heswall, Cheshire, 24 November, 1955
Somerset debut 1974, cap 1976; Worcs debut 1987, cap 1987
Test debut v Australia (Trent Bridge, July 1977)
Test career: 99 Tests, 5176 runs @ 34.27, 117 catches, 380 wickets @ 28.26.

FIRST INNINGS		SECOND INNINGS	
West Indies, 5th Test, Oval, August 1991			
7. hit wicket b Ambrose	31	7. not out	4
11–4–27–1 3c		16–4–40–2	
Sri Lanka, Lord's, August 1991			
6. c Mahanama b Ramanayake	22		
10–3–36–1		6–2–15–0 2c	

BATTING

	M	I	NO	Runs	HS	Avge	100	50	Ct
WI 90	1	2	1	35	31	35.00	—	—	3
SL 91	1	1	0	22	22	22.00	—	—	2
Total	2	3	1	57	31	28.50	—	—	5

BOWLING

	Ov	Mdns	Runs	W	Avge	Best	5w	10w
WI 91	27	8	67	3	22.33	2–40	—	—
SL 91	16	5	51	1	51.00	1–36	—	—
Total	43	13	118	3	29.50	2–40	—	—

DAVID John CAPEL

Born Northampton, 6 February, 1963
Northants debut 1981, cap 1986
Test career: 15 Tests, 374 runs @ 15.58, 6 catches, 21 wickets @ 50.66.

FIRST INNINGS		SECOND INNINGS	
West Indies, 1st Test, Jamaica, February/March 1990			
13–4–31–2 1c		15–1–50–0	
7. c Richardson b Walsh	5		
West Indies, 3rd Test, Trinidad, March 1990			
15–2–53–1		13–3–30–0	
7. c Moseley b Ambrose	40	7. not out	17
West Indies, 4th Test, Barbados, April 1990			
24–5–88–3	2	16–1–66–1 1c	
7. c Greenidge b Marshall		9. lbw b Ambrose	6
West Indies, 5th Test, Antigua, April 1990			
7. c Haynes b Bishop	10	8. run out	1
28–1–118–2			

BATTING

	M	I	NO	Runs	HS	Avge	100	50	Ct
WI 90	4	7	1	81	40	13.50	—	—	2
Total	4	7	1	81	40	13.50	—	—	2

BOWLING

	Ov	Mdns	Runs	W	Avge	Best	5w	10w
WI 90	124	17	436	9	48.44	3–88	—	—
Total	124	17	436	9	48.44	3–88	—	—

PHILLIP Anthony Jason DeFREITAS

Born Dominica, 18 February, 1966
Leicestershire debut 1985, cap 1986; Lancashire debut 1989, cap 1989
Test debut v Australia (Brisbane, November 1986)
Test career: 26 Tests, 513 runs @ 13.86, 6 catches, 78 wickets @ 33.37.

FIRST INNINGS		SECOND INNINGS	
West Indies, 4th Test, Barbados, April 1990			
29.5–5–99–2		22–2–69–3	
9. c & b Ambrose	24	10. lbw b Ambrose	0
West Indies, 5th Test, Barbados, April 1990			
9. lbw b Bishop	21	10. c Greenidge b Ambrose	0
27–4–74–1 1c			

FIRST INNINGS		SECOND INNINGS	
New Zealand, 1st Test, Trent Bridge, June 1990			
22–6–53–5		2–2–0–1	
8. lbw b Bracewell	14		
New Zealand, 2nd Test, Lord's, June 1990			
8. c Franklin b Morrison	38		
35.4–1–122–0			
Australia, 2nd Test, Melbourne, December 1990			
8. c Healy b Reid	3	8. lbw b Reid	0
25–5–69–2		16–3–46–0	
Australia, 4th Test, Adelaide, January 1991			
26.2–6–56–4		23–6–61–1	
7. c Matthews b McDermott	45	7. not out	19
Australia, 5th Test, Perth, February 1991			
7. c Marsh b McDermott	5	7. c Healy b Alderman	5
16.5–2–57–2		6.2–0–29–1	
West Indies, 1st Test, Headingley, June 1991			
9. c Simmons b Ambrose	15	9. lbw b Walsh	3
17.1–5–34–4		21–4–59–4	
West Indies, 2nd Test, Lord's, June 1991			
31–6–93–2 1c		3–2–1–1	
9. c Dujon b Marshall	29		
West Indies, 3rd Test, Trent Bridge, July 1991			
9. b Walsh	8	9. not out	55
31.1–9–67–3		11–3–29–0	
West Indies, 4th Test, Edgbaston, July 1991			
9. c Richardson b Marshall	10	9. b Patterson	7
25.3–9–40–2		13–2–54–3	
West Indies, 5th Test, Oval, August 1991			
9. c Dujon b Walsh	7		
13–6–38–1		20–9–42–2	
Sri Lanka, Lord's, August 1991			
9. b Ratnayake	1		
26–8–70–7		22–8–45–1	

BATTING

	M	I	NO	Runs	HS	Avge	100	50	Ct
WI 90	2	4	0	45	24	11.25	—	—	1
NZ 90	2	2	0	52	38	26.00	—	—	—
Aus 90/91	3	6	1	77	45	15.40	—	—	—
WI 91	5	8	1	134	55*	19.14	—	1	1
SL 91	1	1	0	1	1	1.00	—	—	—
Total	13	21	2	309	55*	16.26	—	1	1

BOWLING

	Ov	Mdns	Runs	W	Avge	Best	5w	10w
WI 90	78.5	11	242	6	40.33	3–69	—	—
NZ 90	59.4	9	175	6	29.16	5–53	1	—
Aus 90/91	113.3	22	318	10	31.80	4–56	—	—
WI 91	185.5	55	457	22	20.77	4–34	—	—
SL 91	48	16	115	8	14.37	7–70	1	—
Total	485.5	113	1307	52	25.13	7–70	2	—

NEIL Harvey FAIRBROTHER

Born Warrington, 9 September, 1963
Lancashire debut 1982, cap 1985
Test debut v Pakistan (Old Trafford, June 1987)
Test career: 7 Tests, 64 runs @ 8.00, 4 catches.

FIRST INNINGS SECOND INNINGS

New Zealand, 1st Test, Trent Bridge, June 1990
6. c Franklin b Snedden 19

New Zealand, 2nd Test, Lord's, June 1990
6. c Morrison b Bracewell 2 6. not out 33
1c

New Zealand, 3rd Test, Edgbaston, July 1990
6. lbw b Snedden 2 6. lbw b Bracewell 3

BATTING

	M	I	NO	Runs	HS	Avge	100	50	Ct
NZ 90	3	5	1	32*	59	14.75	—	—	1
Total	3	5	1	32*	59	14.75	—	—	1

ANGUS Robert Charles FRASER

Born Billinge, Lancashire, 8 August, 1965
Middlesex debut 1984, cap 1988
Test debut v Australia (Edgbaston, July/August 1989)
Test career: 11 Tests, 88 runs @ 6.76, 1 catch, 47 wickets @ 26.70.

FIRST INNINGS SECOND INNINGS

West Indies, 1st Test, Jamaica, February/March 1990
20–8–28–5 14–4–31–1
10. not out 2

West Indies, 3rd Test, Trinidad, March 1990
13.1–2–41–3 24–4–61–2
10. c Hooper b Ambrose 11

FIRST INNINGS		SECOND INNINGS	
India, 1st Test, Lord's, July 1990			
39.1–9–104–5		22–7–39–3	
India, 2nd Test, Old Trafford, August 1990			
10. c Tendulkar b Kumble	1		
35–5–124–5		21–3–81–1	
India, 3rd Test, Oval, August 1990			
42–17–112–2			
10. c More b Prabhakar	0		
Australia, 1st Test, Brisbane, November 1990			
10. c Healy b Alderman	1	10. c sub b Alderman	0
21–6–33–3		14–2–49–0	
Australia, 2nd Test, Melbourne, December 1990			
9. c Jones b Alderman	24	10. c Taylor b Reid	0
39–10–82–6		20–4–33–1	
Australia, 4th Test, Adelaide, January 1991			
23–6–48–0 1c		26–3–66–1	
9. c Healy b Reid	2		

BATTING

	M	I	NO	Runs	HS	Avge	100	50	Ct
WI 90	2	2	1	13	11	13.00	—	—	—
Ind 90	3	2	0	1	1	0.50	—	—	—
Aus 90/91	3	5	0	27	24	5.40	—	—	1
Total	8	9	1	41	24	5.12	—	—	1

BOWLING

	Ov	Mdns	Runs	W	Avge	Best	5w	10w
WI 90	71.1	18	161	11	14.63	5–28	1	—
Ind 90	159.1	41	460	16	28.75	5–104	2	—
Aus 90/91	143	31	311	11	28.27	6–82	1	—
Total	373.2	90	932	38	24.52	6–82	4	—

DAVID Ivon GOWER

Born Tunbridge Wells, 1 April, 1957
Leics debut 1975, cap 1977; Hampshire debut 1990
Test debut v Pakistan (Edgbaston, June 1978)
Test career: 114 Tests, 8,081 runs @ 44.15, 18 centuries, 73 catches, 1 wicket @ 20.

FIRST INNINGS		SECOND INNINGS	
India, 1st Test, Lord's, July 1990			
3. c Manjrekar b Hirwani	40	3. not out	32

FIRST INNINGS		SECOND INNINGS	
India, 2nd Test, Old Trafford, August 1990			
3. c Tendulkar b Kapil Dev	38	3. b Hirwani	16
India, 3rd Test, Oval, August 1990			
4. lbw b Wassan	8	3. not out	157
Australia, 1st Test, Brisbane, November 1990			
3. c Healy b Reid	61	3. b Hughes	27
Australia, 2nd Test, Melbourne, December 1990			
5. c & b Reid	100	5. c Border b Matthews	0
Australia, 3rd Test, Sydney, January 1991			
5. c Marsh b Reid	123	2. c Taylor b Matthews 1c	36
Australia, 4th Test, Adelaide, January 1991			
5. c Hughes b McDermott	11	4. lbw b Hughes	16
Australia, 5th Test, Perth, February 1991			
5. not out	28	5. c Taylor b Alderman	5

BATTING

	M	I	NO	Runs	HS	Avge	100	50	Ct
Ind 90	3	6	2	291	157*	72.75	1	—	—
Aus 90/91	5	10	1	407	123	45.22	2	1	1
Total	8	16	3	698	157*	53.69	3	1	1

Edward 'EDDIE' Ernest HEMMINGS

Born Leamington Spa, 20 February, 1949
Warwicks debut 1966, cap 1974; Notts debut 1979, cap 1980
Test debut v Pakistan (Edgbaston, July/August 1982)
Test career: 16 Tests, 383 runs @ 22.52, 5 catches, 43 wickets @ 42.44.

FIRST INNINGS		SECOND INNINGS	
New Zealand, 1st Test, Trent Bridge, June 1990			
19–6–47–1		2–2–0–0	
10. not out	13		
New Zealand, 2nd Test, Lord's, June 1990			
10. b Hadlee	0		
30–13–67–2			
New Zealand, 3rd Test, Edgbaston, July 1990			
10. c Parore b Hadlee	20	10. b Hadlee	0
27.3–10–58–6		29–13–43–1	
India, 1st Test, Lord's, July 1990			
20–3–109–2		21–2–79–2	

FIRST INNINGS | SECOND INNINGS

India, 2nd Test, Old Trafford, August 1990
9. lbw b Hirwani 19
29.2–8–74–2 | 31–10–75–3

India, 3rd Test, Oval, August 1990
36–3–117–2
9. c Vengsakar b Prabhakar 51

Australia, 3rd Test, Sydney, January 1991
32–7–105–3 1c | 41–9–94–3
9. b Alderman 0

BATTING

	M	I	NO	Runs	HS	Avge	100	50	Ct
NZ 90	3	4	1	33	20	11.00	—	—	—
Ind 90	3	2	0	70	51	35.00	—	1	—
Aus 90/91	1	1	0	0	0	0.00	—	—	1
Total	7	7	1	103	51	17.16	—	1	1

BOWLING

	Ov	Mdns	Runs	W	Avge	Best	5w	10w
NZ 90	107.3	44	215	10	21.5	6–58	1	—
Ind 90	137.2	26	454	11	41.27	3–75	—	—
Aus 90/91	73	16	199	6	33.16	3–94	—	—
Total	317.5	86	868	27	32.14	6–58	1	—

GRAEME Ashley HICK

Born Salisbury, Rhodesia (Zimbabwe), 23 May, 1966
Worcestershire debut 1984, cap 1986
Test debut v West Indies (Headingley, June 1991)
Test career: 4 Tests, 75 runs @ 10.71, 8 catches, 2 wickets @ 47.50.

FIRST INNINGS | SECOND INNINGS

West Indies, 1st Test, Headingley, June 1991
3. c Dujon b Walsh 6 | 3. b Ambrose 6
2c

West Indies, 2nd Test, Lord's, June 1991
3. c Richardson b Ambrose 0
18–4–77–2 | 1c

West Indies, 3rd Test, Trent Bridge, July 1991
3. c Dujon b Ambrose 43 | 3. c Dujon b Ambrose 0
5–0–18–0 1c

West Indies, 4th Test, Edgbaston, July 1991
4. c Richards b Ambrose 19 | 4. b Ambrose 1
1–1–0–0 2c | 2c

BATTING

	M	I	NO	Runs	HS	Avge	100	50	Ct
WI 91	4	7	0	75	43	10.71	—	—	8
Total	4	7	0	75	43	10.71	—	—	8

BOWLING

	Ov	Mdns	Runs	W	Avge	Best	5w	10w
WI 91	24	5	95	2	47.50	2–77	—	—
Total	24	5	95	2	47.50	2–77	—	—

NASSER HUSSAIN

Born Madras, India, 28 March, 1968
Essex debut 1987, cap 1989
Test debut v West Indies (Jamaica, February/March 1990)
Test career: 3 Tests, 100 runs @ 20.00, 1 catch.

FIRST INNINGS		SECOND INNINGS	
West Indies, 1st Test, Jamaica, February/March 1990			
6. c Dujon b Bishop	13		
		1c	
West Indies, 4th Test, Barbados, April 1990			
6. lbw b Marshall	18	8. lbw b Ambrose	0
West Indies, 5th Test, Antigua, April 1990			
6. c Dujon b Bishop	35	7. c Dujon b Bishop	34

BATTING

	M	I	NO	Runs	HS	Avge	100	50	Ct
WI 90	3	5	0	100	35	20.00	—	—	1
Total	3	5	0	100	35	20.00	—	—	1

RICHARD Keith ILLINGWORTH

Born Bradford, 23 August, 1963
Worcestershire debut 1982, cap 1986
Test debut v West Indies (Trent Bridge, July 1991)
Test career: 2 Tests, 31 runs @ 15.50, 1 catch, 4 wickets @ 53.25.

FIRST INNINGS		SECOND INNINGS	
West Indies, 3rd Test, Trent Bridge, July 1991			
10. c Hooper b Ambrose	13	10. c Simmons b Walsh	13
33–8–110–3 1c		2–0–5–0	
West Indies, 4th Test, Edgbaston, July 1991			
11. not out	0	11. not out	5
17–2–75–1		4.4–0–23–0	

BATTING

	M	I	NO	Runs	HS	Avge	100	50	Ct
WI 91	2	4	2	31	13	15.50	—	—	1
Total	2	4	2	31	13	15.50	—	—	1

BOWLING

	Ov	Mdns	Runs	W	Avge	Best	5w	10w
WI 91	56.4	10	213	4	53.25	3–110	—	—
Total	56.4	10	213	4	53.25	3–110	—	—

ALLAN Joseph LAMB

Born Langebannweg, Cape Province, South Africa, 20 June, 1954
Northants debut 1978, cap 1978
Test debut v India (Lord's, June 1982)
Test career: 74 Tests, 4264 runs @ 35.23, 13 centuries, 73 catches, 1 wicket @ 23.

FIRST INNINGS		SECOND INNINGS	
West Indies, 1st Test, Jamaica, February/March 1990			
4. c Hooper b Walsh	132		
West Indies, 3rd Test, Trinidad, March 1990			
4. b Bishop	32	4. lbw b Bishop	25
3c		2c	
West Indies, 4th Test, Barbados, April 1990			
†4. lbw b Ambrose	119	*6. c Dujon b Moseley	10
1c			
West Indies, 5th Test, Antigua, April 1990			
†4. c Richards b Ambrose	37	*5. b Baptiste	35
1c			
New Zealand, 1st Test, Trent Bridge, June 1990			
4. lbw b Hadlee	0		
New Zealand, 2nd Test, Lord's, June 1990			
4. lbw b Snedden	39	4. not out	84
New Zealand, 3rd Test, Edgbaston, July 1990			
4. c Parore b Hadlee	2	4. st Parore b Bracewell	4
		2c	
India, 1st Test, Lord's, July 1990			
4. c Manjrekar b Sharma	139	4. c Tendulkar b Hirwani	19
India, 2nd Test, Old Trafford, August 1990			
4. c Manjrekar b Kumble	38	4. b Kapil Dev	109

FIRST INNINGS		SECOND INNINGS	
India, 3rd Test, Oval, August 1990			
6. b Kapil Dev	7	5. c Shastri b Kapil Dev	52
2c			
Australia, 1st Test, Brisbane, November 1990			
†4. c Hughes b Matthews	32	*4. lbw b Alderman	14
Australia, 4th Test, Adelaide, January 1991			
3. c Healy b McDermott	0	3. b McDermott	53
1c			
Australia, 5th Test, Perth, February 1991			
3. c Border b McDermott	91	3. lbw b McDermott	5
1c			
West Indies, 1st Test, Headingley, June 1991			
4. c Hooper b Marshall	11	4. c Hooper b Ambrose	0
2c		2c	
West Indies, 2nd Test, Lord's, June 1991			
4. c Haynes b Marshall	1		
3c			
West Indies, 3rd Test, Trent Bridge, July 1991			
4. lbw b Ambrose	13	4. lbw b Marshall	29
West Indies, 4th Test, Edgbaston, July 1991			
5. lbw b Marshall	9	5. c Dujon b Walsh	25

† Captain

BATTING

	M	I	NO	Runs	HS	Avge	100	50	Ct
WI 90	4	7	0	390	132	55.71	2	—	7
NZ 90	3	5	1	129	84*	32.25	—	1	2
Ind 90	3	6	0	378	131	63.00	2	1	2
Aus 90/91	3	6	0	195	91	32.50	—	2	2
WI 91	4	7	0	88	29	12.57	—	—	7
Total	17	31	1	1180	132	39.33	4	4	20

WAYNE 'NED' LARKINS

Born Roxton, Beds, 22 November, 1953
Northants debut 1972, cap 1976
Test debut v Australia (Melbourne, February 1980)
Test career: 13 Tests, 493 runs @ 20.54, 8 catches.

FIRST INNINGS		SECOND INNINGS	
West Indies, 1st Test, Jamaica, February/March 1990			
2. lbw b Walsh	46	2. not out	29
1c		2c	

FIRST INNINGS SECOND INNINGS

West Indies, 3rd Test, Trinidad, March 1990

2. c Dujon b Ambrose 54 2. c Dujon b Moseley 7
1c

West Indies, 4th Test, Barbados, April 1990

2. c Richardson b Bishop 0 2. c Dujon b Bishop 0

West Indies, 5th Test, Antigua, April 1990

2. c Hooper b Ambrose 30 2. b Ambrose 10

Australia, 1st Test, Brisbane, November 1990

2. c Healy b Hughes 12 2. lbw b Reid 0

Australia, 2nd Test, Melbourne, December 1990

3. c Healy b Reid 64 3. c Healy b Reid 54

Australia, 3rd Test, Sydney, January 1991

3. run out 11 3. lbw b Border 0
1c

BATTING

	M	I	NO	Runs	HS	Avge	100	50	Ct
WI 90	4	8	1	176	54	25.14	—	1	4
Aus 90/91	3	6	0	141	64	23.50	—	2	1
Total	7	14	1	317	64	24.38	—	3	5

David Keith 'SYD' LAWRENCE

Born Gloucester, 28 January, 1964
Gloucestershire debut 1981, cap 1985
Test debut v Sri Lanka (Lord's, August 1988)
Test career: 4 Tests, 54 runs @ 10.80, 17 wickets @ 35.58.

FIRST INNINGS SECOND INNINGS

West Indies, 3rd Test, Trent Bridge, July 1991

11. c Allen b Marshall 4 11. c Hooper b Allen 34
24–2–116–2 12.2–0–61–1

West Indies, 5th Test, Oval, August 1991

10. c Richards b Walsh 9
16–1–67–2 25.5–4–106–5

Sri Lanka, Lord's, August 1991

10. c & b Ratnayake 3
15.1–3–61–2 23–7–83–2

BATTING

	M	I	NO	Runs	HS	Avge	100	50	Ct
WI 91	2	3	0	47	34	15.66	—	—	—
SL 91	1	1	0	3	3	3.00	—	—	—
Total	3	4	0	50	34	12.50	—	—	—

BOWLING

	Ov	Mdns	Runs	W	Avge	Best	5w	10w
WI 91	78.1	7	350	10	35.00	5–106	1	—
SL 91	38.1	10	144	4	36.00	2–61	—	—
Total	116.2	17	494	14	35.28	5–106	1	—

CHRISTOPHER Clairmonte LEWIS

Born Georgetown, Guyana, 14 February, 1968
Leicestershire debut 1987, cap 1990
Test debut v New Zealand (Edgbaston, July 1990)
Test record: 7 Tests, 206 runs @ 25.75, 9 catches, 20 wickets @ 36.35.

FIRST INNINGS		SECOND INNINGS	
New Zealand, 3rd Test, Edgbaston, July 1990			
8. c Rutherford b Bracewell	32	8. c Parore b Hadlee	1
19–5–51–1		22–3–76–3	
India, 1st Test, Lord's, July 1990			
24–3–108–1 1c		8–1–26–2 1c	
India, 2nd Test, Old Trafford, August 1990			
8. b Hirwani	3		
13–1–61–1 1c		20–3–86–1 1c	
Australia, 1st Test, Brisbane, November 1990			
8. c Border b Hughes	20	8. lbw b Alderman	14
9–0–29–3 1c		6–0–29–0	
West Indies, 4th Test, Edgbaston, July 1991			
10. lbw b Marshall	13	10. c sub b Ambrose	65
35–10–111–6 2c		16–7–45–0	
West Indies, 5th Test, Oval, August 1991			
8. not out	47		
3–1–10–0		25–12–35–0 1c	
Sri Lanka, Lord's, August 1991			
7. c De Silva b Anurasiri	11		
10–5–29–0 1c		18–4–31–2	

BATTING

	M	I	NO	Runs	HS	Avge	100	50	Ct
NZ 90	1	2	0	33	32	16.50	—	—	—
Ind 90	2	1	0	3	3	3.00	—	—	4
Aus 90/91	1	2	0	34	20	17.00	—	—	1
WI 91	2	3	1	125	65	62.50	—	1	3
SL 91	1	1	0	11	11	11.00	—	—	1
Total	7	9	1	206	65	27.75	—	1	9

BOWLING

	Ov	Mdns	Runs	W	Avge	Best	5w	10w
NZ 90	41	8	127	4	31.75	3–76	—	—
Ind 90	65	8	281	5	56.20	2–26	—	—
Aus 90/91	15	0	58	3	19.33	3–29	—	—
WI 91	79	30	201	6	33.50	6–111	1	—
SL 91	28	9	60	2	30.00	2–31	—	—
Total	228	55	727	20	36.35	6–111	1	—

DEVON Eugene MALCOLM

Born Kingston, Jamaica, 22 February, 1963
Derbyshire debut 1984, cap 1989
Test debut v Australia (Trent Bridge, August 1989)
Test career: 18 Tests, 99 runs @ 6.18, 2 catches, 61 wickets @ 37.59.

FIRST INNINGS		SECOND INNINGS	
West Indies, 1st Test, Jamaica, February/March 1990			
16–4–49–1		21.3–2–77–4	
11. lbw b Walsh	0		
West Indies, 3rd Test, Trinidad, March 1990			
20–2–60–4		26.2–4–77–6	
11. not out	0		
West Indies, 4th Test, Barbados, April 1990			
33–6–142–0		10–0–46–0 1c	
11. b Bishop	12	11. lbw b Ambrose	4
		1c	
West Indies, 5th Test, Antigua, April 1990			
11. not out	0	11. not out	1
34.5–3–126–4			
New Zealand, 1st Test, Trent Bridge, June 1990			
19–7–48–2		7–2–22–0	
11. not out	4		
New Zealand, 2nd Test, Lord's, June 1990			
11. not out	0		
43–14–94–5			
New Zealand, 3rd Test, Edgbaston, July 1990			
11. b Hadlee	0	11. lbw b Hadlee	0
25–7–59–3		24.4–8–46–5	
India, 1st Test, Lord's, July 1990			
25–1–106–1		10–0–65–2	

FIRST INNINGS		SECOND INNINGS	
India, 2nd Test, Old Trafford, August 1990			
11. b Shastri	13		
26–3–96–1		14–5–59–1	
India, 3rd Test, Oval, August 1990			
35–7–110–2			
11. not out	15		
Australia, 1st Test, Brisbane, November 1990			
11. c S Waugh b Hughes	5	11. not out	0
17–2–45–1		9–5–22–0	
Australia, 2nd Test, Melbourne, December 1990			
10. c Taylor b Reid	6	10. lbw b Matthews	1
25.5–4–74–2		23–7–52–1	
Australia, 3rd Test, Sydney, January 1991			
45–12–128–4		6–1–19–2	
Australia, 4th Test, Adelaide, January 1991			
38–7–104–2		21–0–87–1	
10. c Healy b Reid	2		
Australia, 5th Test, Perth, February 1991			
11. c Marsh b McDermott	7	11. c Jones b McDermott	6
30–4–94–3		9–0–40–0	
West Indies, 1st Test, Headingley, June 1991			
11. not out	5	11. b Marshall	4
14–0–69–0		6.4–0–26–1	
West Indies, 2nd Test, Lord's, June 1991			
19–3–76–1 1c		2.5–0–9–1	
11. b Ambrose	0		

BATTING

	M	I	NO	Runs	HS	Avge	100	50	Ct
WI 90	4	6	3	17	12	5.66	—	—	1
NZ 90	3	4	2	4	4*	2.00	—	—	—
Ind 90	3	2	1	28	15*	28.00	—	—	—
Aus 90/91	5	7	1	27	7	4.50	—	—	—
WI 91	2	3	1	9	5*	4.50	—	—	1
Total	17	22	8	85	15*	6.07	—	—	2

BOWLING

	Ov	Mdns	Runs	W	Avge	Best	5w	10w
WI 90	161.4	21	577	19	30.36	6–77	1	1
NZ 90	118.4	38	269	15	17.93	5–46	2	—
Ind 90	110	16	436	7	62.28	2–65	—	—

BOWLING

	Ov	Mdns	Runs	W	Avge	Best	5w	10w
Aus 90/91	223.5	42	665	16	41.56	4–128	—	—
WI 91	42.3	3	180	3	60.00	1–9	—	—
Total	656.4	120	2127	60	35.45	6–77	3	1

HUGH MORRIS

Born Cardiff, 5 October, 1963
Glamorgan debut 1981, cap 1986
Test debut v West Indies (Edgbaston, July 1991)
Test career: 3 Tests, 115 runs @ 19.16, 3 catches.

FIRST INNINGS		SECOND INNINGS	
West Indies, 4th Test, Edgbaston, July 1991			
2. c Dujon b Patterson	3	2. lbw b Patterson	1
West Indies, 5th Test, Oval, August 1991			
2. c Lambert b Ambrose	44	2. c Dujon b Patterson	2
		1c	
Sri Lanka, Lord's, August 1991			
2. lbw b Ramanayake	42	2. c Mahanama b Anurasiri	23
1c		1c	

BATTING

	M	I	NO	Runs	HS	Avge	100	50	Ct
WI 91	2	4	0	50	44	12.50	—	—	1
SL 91	1	2	0	65	42	32.50	—	—	2
Total	3	6	0	115	44	19.16	—	—	3

JOHN Edward MORRIS

Born Crewe, 1 April, 1964
Derbyshire debut 1982, cap 1986
Test debut v India (Lord's, July 1990)
Test career: 3 Tests, 71 runs @ 23.66, 3 catches.

FIRST INNINGS		SECOND INNINGS	
India, 1st Test, Lord's, July 1990			
6. not out	4		
2c		1c	
India, 2nd Test, Old Trafford, August 1990			
7. b Kumble	13	6. retired hurt	15
India, 3rd Test, Oval, August 1990			
5. c More b Wassan	7	4. c More b Wassan	32

BATTING

	M	I	NO	Runs	HS	Avge	100	50	Ct
Ind 90	3	5	2	71	32	23.66	—	—	3
Total	3	5	2	71	32	23.66	—	—	3

PHILIP John NEWPORT

Born High Wycombe, 11 October, 1962
Worcestershire debut 1982, cap 1986
Test debut v Sri Lanka (Lord's, August 1988)
Test career: 3 Tests, 110 runs @ 27.50, 1 catch, 10 wickets @ 41.70.

FIRST INNINGS		SECOND INNINGS	
Australia, 5th Test, Perth, February 1991			
8. c Healy b McDermott	0	8. not out	40
14–0–56–1		6–0–22–0	

BATTING

	M	I	NO	Runs	HS	Avge	100	50	Ct
Aus 90/91	1	2	1	40	40*	40.00	—	—	—
Total	1	2	1	40	40*	40.00	—	—	—

BOWLING

	Ov	Mdns	Runs	W	Avge	Best	5w	10w
Aus 90/91	20	0	78	1	78.00	1–56	—	—
Total	20	0	78	1	78.00	1–56	—	—

DEREK Raymond PRINGLE

Born Nairobi, 18 September, 1958
Essex debut 1978, cap 1982
Test debut v India (Lord's, June 1982)
Test career: 25 Tests, 640 runs @ 16.00, 8 catches, 60 wickets @ 35.48.

FIRST INNINGS		SECOND INNINGS	
West Indies, 1st Test, Headingley, June 1991			
8. c Logie b Patterson	16	8. c Dujon b Marshall	27
9–3–14–2		22–6–38–2 1c	
West Indies, 2nd Test, Lord's, June 1991			
35.1–6–100–5			
8. c Simmons b Allen	35		
West Indies, 3rd Test, Trent Bridge, July 1991			
8. c sub b Allen	0	8. c Simmons b Walsh	3
26–6–71–2		7–2–20–0	

FIRST INNINGS		SECOND INNINGS	
West Indies, 4th Test, Edgbaston, July 1991			
8. b Ambrose	2	8. c Logie b Marshall	45
23–9–48–1		7–1–31–0	

BATTING

	M	I	NO	Runs	HS	Avge	100	50	Ct
WI 91	4	7	0	128	45	18.28	—	—	1
Total	4	7	0	128	45	18.28	—	—	1

BOWLING

	Ov	Mdns	Runs	W	Avge	Best	5w	10w
WI 91	128.1	33	322	12	26.83	5–100	1	—
Total	128.1	33	322	12	26.83	5–100	1	—

MARK Ravin RAMPRAKASH

Born Bushey, Hertfordshire, 5 September, 1969
Middlesex debut 1987, cap 1990
England debut v West Indies (Headingley, June 1991)
Test career: 6 Tests, 210 runs @ 21.00, 4 catches.

FIRST INNINGS		SECOND INNINGS	
West Indies, 1st Test, Headingley, June 1991			
5. c Hooper b Marshall	27	5. c Dujon b Ambrose	27
2c			
West Indies, 2nd Test, Lord's, June 1991			
5. c Richards b Allen	24		
West Indies, 3rd Test, Trent Bridge, July 1991			
5. b Ambrose	13	5. c Dujon b Ambrose	21
1c			
West Indies, 4th Test, Edgbaston, July 1991			
5. c Logie b Walsh	29	5. c Dujon b Marshall	25
West Indies, 5th Test, Oval, August 1991			
5. c Lambert b Hooper	25	5. lbw b Lambert	19
1c			
Sri Lanka, Lord's, August 1991			
5. c Mahanama b Hathurusinghe	0		

BATTING

	M	I	NO	Runs	HS	Avge	100	50	Ct
WI 91	5	9	0	210	29	23.33	—	—	4
SL 91	1	1	0	0	0	0.00	—	—	—
Total	6	10	0	210	29	21.00	—	—	4

Robert Charles 'JACK' RUSSELL

Born Stroud, 15 August, 1963
Gloucestershire debut 1981, cap 1985
Test debut v Sri Lanka (Lord's, August 1988)
Test career: 25 Tests, 869 runs @ 26.33, 66 catches/6 stumpings.

FIRST INNINGS			SECOND INNINGS		
West Indies, 1st Test, Jamaica, February/March 1990					
8.	c Patterson b Walsh	26			
1c					
West Indies, 3rd Test, Trinidad, March 1990					
4c			1c		
8.	c Best b Walsh	15	8.	not out	5
West Indies, 4th Test, Barbados, April 1990					
5c					
8.	lbw b Bishop	7	5.	b Ambrose	55
West Indies, 5th Test, Antigua, April 1990					
8.	c Dujon b Bishop	7	9.	c Richardson b Ambrose	24
3c					
New Zealand, 1st Test, Trent Bridge, June 1990					
1c			2c		
7.	c Snedden b Morrison	28			
New Zealand, 2nd Test, Lord's, June 1990					
7.	b Hadlee	13			
2c					
New Zealand, 3rd Test, Edgbaston, July 1990					
7.	b Snedden	43	7.	c sub b Hadlee	0
2c					
India, 1st Test, Lord's, July 1990					
3c			3c		
India, 2nd Test, Old Trafford, August 1990					
5.	c More b Hirwani	8	7.	not out	16
2c					
India, 3rd Test, Oval, August 1990					
3c/1st					
8.	run out	35			
Australia, 1st Test, Brisbane, November 1990					
7.	c & b Alderman	16	5.	lbw b S Waugh	15
1c					
Australia, 2nd Test, Melbourne, December 1990					
7.	c Healy b Hughes	15	7.	c Jones b Matthews	1
6c					

FIRST INNINGS SECOND INNINGS

Australia, 3rd Test, Sydney, January 1991
1c 1st 1c
7. not out 30

West Indies, 1st Test, Headingley, June 1991
7. lbw b Patterson 5 7. c Dujon b Ambrose 4
1c

West Indies, 2nd Test, Lord's, June 1991
7. c Dujon b Hooper 46
1c

West Indies, 3rd Test, Trent Bridge, July 1991
7. c Logie b Allen 3 7. b Walsh 3
1c 1c

West Indies, 4th Test, Edgbaston, July 1991
7. c Richardson b Ambrose 12 7. c Dujon b Patterson 0
1c

Sri Lanka, Lord's, August 1991
8. b Anurasiri 17 5. not out 12
1c 2c

BATTING

	M	I	NO	Runs	HS	Avge	100	50	Ct/st
WI 90	4	7	1	139	55	23.16	—	1	14/—
NZ 90	3	4	0	84	43	21.00	—	—	7/—
Ind 90	3	3	1	59	35	29.50	—	—	11/1
Aus 90/91	3	5	1	77	30*	19.25	—	—	9/1
WI 91	4	7	0	73	46	10.42	—	—	5/—
SL 91	1	2	1	29	17	29.00	—	—	3/—
Total	18	28	4	461	55	19.20	—	—	49/2

GLADSTONE Cleophas SMALL

Born St George, Barbados, 18 October, 1961
Warwickshire debut 1980, cap 1982
Test debut v New Zealand (Trent Bridge, August 1986)
Test career: 17 Tests, 263 runs @ 15.47, 9 catches, 55 wickets @ 34.01.

FIRST INNINGS SECOND INNINGS

West Indies, 1st Test, Jamaica, February/March 1990
15–6–44–1 2c 22–6–58–4
9. lbw b Marshall 4

West Indies, 3rd Test, Trinidad, March 1990
17–4–41–2 21–8–56–1
9. lbw b Bishop 0

FIRST INNINGS		SECOND INNINGS	
West Indies, 4th Test, Barbados, April 1990			
35–5–109–4		20–1–74–4 1c	
10. not out	1	4. lbw b Ambrose	0
West Indies, 5th Test, Antigua, April 1990			
10. lbw b Walsh	8	3. b Ambrose	4
31–3–123–1			
New Zealand, 1st Test, Trent Bridge, June 1990			
29–9–49–2		6–2–14–1	
9. c Crowe b Hadlee	26		
New Zealand, 2nd Test, Lord's, June 1990			
9. b Morrison	3		
35–4–127–1 1c			
New Zealand, 3rd Test, Edgbaston, July 1990			
9. not out	44	9. not out	11
18–7–44–0		16–5–56–1	
Australia, 1st Test, Brisbane, November 1990			
9. not out	12	9. c Alderman b Hughes	15
16–4–34–3 2c		15–2–36–0	
Australia, 3rd Test, Sydney, January 1991			
31–5–103–1 1c		2–1–6–0	
8. lbw b Alderman	10		
Australia, 4th Test, Adelaide, January 1991			
34–10–92–2		18–3–64–1	
8. b McDermott	1		
Australia, 5th Test, Perth, February 1991			
9. c Boon b Hughes	0	9. c Taylor b Hughes	4
23–3–65–2 1c		10–5–24–0	

BATTING

	M	I	NO	Runs	HS	Avge	100	50	Ct
WI 90	4	6	1	17	8	3.40	—	—	3
NZ 90	3	4	2	84	44*	42.00	—	—	1
Aus 90/91	4	6	1	42	15	8.40	—	—	4
Total	11	16	4	143	44*	11.91	—	—	5

BOWLING

	Ov	Mdns	Runs	W	Avge	Best	5w	10w
WI 90	161	33	505	17	29.70	4–58	—	—
NZ 90	104	27	290	5	58.00	2–49	—	—
Aus 90/91	149	33	424	9	47.11	3–34	—	—
Total	414	93	1219	31	39.32	4–58	—	—

ROBIN Arnold SMITH

Born Durban, South Africa, 13 September, 1963
Hampshire debut 1982, cap 1985
England debut v West Indies (Headingley, July 1988)
Test career: 28 Tests, 2118 runs @ 52.95, 6 centuries, 14 catches.

FIRST INNINGS			SECOND INNINGS		
West Indies, 1st Test, Jamaica, February/March 1990					
5.	c Best b Bishop	57			
West Indies, 3rd Test, Trinidad, March 1990					
5.	c Dujon b Moseley	5	5.	lbw b Walsh	2
West Indies, 4th Test, Barbados, April 1990					
5.	b Moseley	62	7.	not out	40
1c					
West Indies, 5th Test, Antigua, April 1990					
5.	lbw b Walsh	12	6.	retired hurt	8
1c					
New Zealand, 1st Test, Trent Bridge, June 1990					
5.	c Smith b Bracewell	55			
New Zealand, 2nd Test, Lord's, June 1990					
5.	c Bracewell b Morrison	64	5.	hit wicket b Bracewell	0
New Zealand, 3rd Test, Edgbaston, July 1990					
5.	c Jones b Bracewell	19	5.	c & b Hadlee	14
1c			1c		
India, 1st Test, Lord's, July 1990					
5.	not out	100	5.	b Prabhakar	15
India, 2nd Test, Old Trafford, August 1990					
6.	not out	121	5.	not out	61
1c					
India, 3rd Test, Oval, August 1990					
7.	c Manjrekar b Shastri	57	6.	not out	7
Australia, 1st Test, Brisbane, November 1990					
5.	b Reid	7	6.	c Taylor b Alderman	1
1c					
Australia, 2nd Test, Melbourne, December 1990					
4.	c Healy b Hughes	30	4.	c Taylor b Reid	8
Australia, 3rd Test, Sydney, January 1991					
4.	c Healy b Reid	18	5.	not out	10
1c			1c		

FIRST INNINGS		SECOND INNINGS	
Australia, 4th Test, Adelaide, January 1991			
4. c & b Hughes	53	5. not out	10
Australia, 5th Test, Perth, February 1991			
4. c Taylor b McDermott	58	4. lbw b Alderman	43
West Indies, 1st Test, Headingley, June 1991			
6. run out	54	6. lbw b Ambrose	0
		1c	
West Indies, 2nd Test, Lord's, June 1991			
6. not out	143		
West Indies, 3rd Test, Trent Bridge, July 1991			
6. not out	64	6. c Richards b Walsh	15
1c			
West Indies, 5th Test, Oval, August 1991			
4. lbw b Marshall	109	4. c Patterson b Walsh	26
Sri Lanka, Lord's, August 1991			
4. c Tillekeratne b Ratnayake	4	4. not out	63
1c			

BATTING

	M	I	NO	Runs	HS	Avge	100	50	Ct
WI 90	4	7	2	186	62	37.20	—	2	2
NZ 90	3	5	0	152	64	30.40	—	2	2
Ind 90	3	6	4	361	121*	180.50	2	2	1
Aus 90/91	5	10	2	238	58	29.75	—	2	3
WI 91	4	7	2	416	143*	83.20	2	2	2
SL 91	1	2	1	68	64*	68.00	—	1	1
Total	20	37	11	1421	143*	54.65	4	11	11

ALEC STEWART

Born Merton, Surrey, April 8, 1963
Surrey debut 1981, cap 1985
Test debut v West Indies (Jamaica, February/March. 1990)
Test career: 14 Tests, 766 runs @ 31.91, 1 century, 19 catches (10 as wicket-keeper)

FIRST INNINGS		SECOND INNINGS	
West Indies, 1st Test, Jamaica, February/March 1990			
3. c Best b Bishop	13	3. not out	0
West Indies, 3rd Test, Trinidad, March 1990			
3. c Dujon b Ambrose	9	3. c Bishop b Walsh	31
1c			

FIRST INNINGS		SECOND INNINGS	
*West Indies, 4th Test, **Barbados**, April 1990*			
1. c Richards b Moseley	45	1. c Richards b Ambrose	37
1c			
*West Indies, 5th Test, **Antigua**, April 1990*			
1. c Richards b Walsh	27	1. c Richardson b Bishop	8
*New Zealand, 1st Test, **Trent Bridge**, June 1990*			
3. c Smith b Hadlee	27		
2c			
*New Zealand, 2nd Test, **Lord's**, June 1990*			
3. lbw b Hadlee	54	3. c sub b Bracewell	42
2c			
*New Zealand, 3rd Test, **Edgbaston**, July 1990*			
3. c Parore b Morrison	9	3. lbw b Bracewell	15
1c			
*Australia, 1st Test, **Brisbane**, November 1990*			
6. lbw b Reid	4	7. c sub b Alderman	6
*Australia, 2nd Test, **Melbourne**, December 1990*			
6. c Healy b Reid	79	6. c Marsh b Reid	8
*Australia, 3rd Test, **Sydney**, January 1991*			
6. lbw b Alderman	91	4. run out	7
1c		1c	
*Australia, 4th Test, **Adelaide**, January 1991*			
2c*			
6. c Healy b Reid	11	6. c Hughes b McDermott	9
*Australia, 5th Test, **Perth**, February 1991*			
6. lbw b McDermott	2	6. c Healy b McDermott	7
3c*		1c*	
*West Indies, 5th Test, **Oval**, August 1991*			
6. c Richardson b Patterson	31	6. not out	38
3c*		1c*	
*Sri Lanka, **Lord's**, August 1991*			
3. not out	113	3. c De Silva b Anurasiri	43

BATTING

	M	I	NO	Runs	HS	Avge	100	50	Ct
WI 90	4	8	1	170	45	24.28	—	—	2
NZ 90	3	5	0	147	54	29.40	—	1	5
Aus 90/91	5	10	0	224	91	22.40	—	2	8*a

BATTING

	M	I	NO	Runs	HS	Avge	100	50	Ct
WI 91	1	2	1	69	38*	69.00	—	—	4*b
SL 91	1	2	1	156	113*	156.00	1	—	—
Total	14	27	3	766	113*	31.91	1	3	19*c

*a – 6 as wicket-keeper; *b all as wicket-keeper *c – 10 as wicket-keeper

PHILIP Clive Roderick TUFNELL

Born Hadley Wood, Hertfordshire, 29 April, 1966
Middlesex debut 1986, cap 1990
Test debut v Australia (Melbourne, December 1990)
Test career: 6 Tests, 15 runs @ 3.76, 2 catches, 21 wickets @ 30.33.

FIRST INNINGS		SECOND INNINGS	
Australia, 2nd Test, Melbourne, December 1990			
11. not out	0	11. not out	0
21–5–62–0		24–12–36–0	
Australia, 3rd Test, Sydney, January 1991			
30–6–95–1		37–18–61–5 1c	
10. not out	5		
Australia, 4th Test, Adelaide, January 1991			
5–0–38–0		16–3–28–1	
11. not out	0		
Australia, 5th Test, Perth, February 1991			
10. c Healy b Hughes	0	10. c Healy b Hughes	8
7–1–25–2			
West Indies, 5th Test, Oval, August 1991			
11. c Haynes b Patterson	2		
14.3–3–25–6		46–6–150–1	
Sri Lanka, Lord's, August 1991			
11. lbw b Ratnayake	0		
7–2–23–0 1c		34.3–14–94–5	

BATTING

	M	I	NO	Runs	HS	Avge	100	50	Ct
Aus 90/91	4	6	4	13	8	6.50	—	—	1
WI 91	1	1	0	2	2	2.00	—	—	—
SL 91	1	1	0	0	0	0.00	—	—	1
Total	6	8	4	15	8	3.75	—	—	2

BOWLING

	Ov	Mdns	Runs	W	Avge	Best	5w	10w
Aus 90/91	140	45	345	9	38.33	5–61	1	—
WI 91	60.3	9	175	7	25.00	6–25	1	—
SL 91	41	16	117	5	23.40	5–94	1	—
Total	241.3	70	637	21	30.33	6–25	3	—

STEVEN Llewellyn WATKIN

Born Maesteg, 15 September, 1964
Glamorgan debut 1986, cap 1989
Test debut v West Indies (Headingley, June 1991)
Test career: 2 Tests, 8 runs @ 2.66, 5 wickets @ 30.60.

FIRST INNINGS		SECOND INNINGS	
West Indies, 1st Test, Headingley, June 1991			
10. b Ambrose	2	10. c Hooper b Marshall	0
14–2–55–2		7–0–38–3	
West Indies, 2nd Test, Lord's, June 1991			
15–2–60–0			
10. b Ambrose	6		

BATTING

	M	I	NO	Runs	HS	Avge	100	50	Ct
WI 91	2	3	0	8	6	2.66	—	—	—
Total	2	3	0	8	6	2.66	—	—	—

BOWLING

	Ov	Mdns	Runs	W	Avge	Best	5w	10w
WI 91	36	4	153	5	30.60	3–38	—	—
Total	36	4	153	5	30.60	3–38	—	—

NEIL FitzGerald WILLIAMS

Born Hope Well, St Vincent, 2 July, 1962
Middlesex debut 1982, cap 1984
Test debut v India (Oval, August 1990)
Test career: 1 Test, 38 runs @ 38.00, 2 wickets @ 74.00.

FIRST INNINGS		SECOND INNINGS
India, 3rd Test, Oval, August 1990		
41–5–148–2		
3. lbw b Prabhakar	38	

BATTING

	M	I	NO	Runs	HS	Avge	100	50	Ct
Ind 90	1	1	0	38	38	38.00	—	—	—
Total	1	1	0	38	38	38.00	—	—	—

BOWLING

	Ov	Mdns	Runs	W	Avge	Best	5w	10w
Ind 90	41	5	148	2	74.00	2–148	—	—
Total	41	5	148	2	74.00	2–148	—	—